PARACUELLOS

CARLOS GIMÉNEZ

PARACUELLOS

CHILDREN OF THE DEFEATED
IN FRANCO'S FASCIST SPAIN

EURO COMICS
ENGLISH EDITION   GRAPHIC NOVELS

An imprint of IDW PUBLISHING

Edited and Designed by Dean Mullaney

Translation Sonya Jones

Cover coloring and hand-lettering William Stout

Art Director Lorraine Turner

Consulting editor Bruce Canwell

Digital lettering font created from hand-lettering by Carlos Giménez.

EuroComics.us

EuroComics is an imprint of
IDW Publishing
a Division of Idea and Design Works, LLC
2765 Truxtun Road
San Diego, CA 92106
www.idwpublishing.com

Distributed by Diamond Book Distributors
1-410-560-7100

ISBN: 978-1-63140-468-9
First Printing, March 2016

IDW Publishing
Ted Adams, Chief Executive Officer/Publisher
Greg Goldstein, Chief Operating Officer/President
Robbie Robbins, EVP/Sr. Graphic Artist
Chris Ryall, Chief Creative Officer/Editor-in-Chief
Matthew Ruzicka, CPA, Chief Financial Officer
Dirk Wood, VP of Marketing
Lorelei Bunjes, VP of Digital Services
Jeff Webber, VP of Licensing, Digital and Subsidiary Rights
Jerry Bennington, VP of New Product Development

Library of Congress Cataloging-in-Publication Data

Names: Giménez, Carlos, 1941- author, illustrator. | Mullaney, Dean, 1954- editor,
book designer. | Jones, Sonya, translator. | Stout, William, 1949- illustrator.
Title: Paracuellos / by Carlos Gimenez ; preface by Will Eisner ; edited and designed by Dean
Mullaney ; translation, Sonya Jones ; cover coloring and hand-lettering, William Stout.
Description: San Diego, CA : EuroComics/IDW Publishing, [2016]
Identifiers: LCCN 2015048812 | ISBN 9781631404689 (pbk.)
Subjects: LCSH: Giménez, Carlos, 1941---Comic books, strips, etc. |
Spain--History--1939-1975--Comic books, strips, etc. | Graphic novels. |
GSAFD: Comic books, strips, etc.
Classification: LCC PN6777.G54 P3713 2016 | DDC 741.5/946--dc23
LC record available at http://lccn.loc.gov/2015048812

FOREWORD

I have for a long time now paid special attention to the work of
Carlos Giménez. Not only have I been attracted by the warm human
personality of his draftsmanship, but I greatly admire his story-telling
ability. Surrounded as he is by the stunning and bravura art of the
European scene his work has nevertheless established a special place
for itself. He speaks with humor and sensitivity to the human condition.
His work is international. Not an easy thing for humor. I believe an
American audience awaits him.

—Will Eisner, 1991

Carlos Giménez during his internment in one of the Social Aid "homes," dressed in his Sunday best for the benefit of visitors.

EDITOR'S NOTE

BY Dean Mullaney

Carlos Giménez entered the Social Aid system when he was about six years old and spent the next eight years being shuffled through five of the different Social Aid "Homes."

The stories related in this book occurred in several of these institutions, among them Bibona, General Mola, Battle of Jarama, Battle of Brunete, Generalissimo Franco, and Joaquin Garcia Morata. Some of the anecdotes are from Giménez's personal recollection; others from the memories of children he knew. In preparation for creating these stories in the 1970s and '80s, the survivors would meet in threes and fours to recall their experiences, recording their remembrances on cassette and sharing photographs and letters.

There was no "Home" actually called "Paracuellos." It was the name the children gave to the Battle of Jarama "Home" because that important battle of the Spanish Civil War occurred at the small town of Paracuellos del Jarama on the outskirts of Madrid. Only a few of these stories actually took place at the Battle of Jarama "Home."

While the events depicted are taken from direct memory, Giménez has changed the names of children, guardians, and teachers. For example, while there was an actual instructor named Antonio in one of the "Homes," the character in the stories is a construct made up of many instructors in the Social Aid system.

• • • • •

The first episode of what became known as "Paracuellos" was published in the premiere issue of *Muchas Gracias* six months after the death, on November 20, 1975, of Spain's dictator, Francisco Franco. Some readers hailed the stories for breaking the taboo against criticism of the Franco regime; others denounced the cartoonist for not adhering to the spirit of reconciliation in the "new" democratic Spain (i.e., continuing to sweep the past under the rug).

At the time Giménez had no plans for the vignettes to be a series. As he published more installments, readers began referring to the collective stories by the name "Paracuellos." When in 1977 a publisher asked the cartoonist for a title to an omnibus edition, the choice, Giménez recalled, was obvious and the name stuck. He eventually published a second book, *Paracuellos 2,* in 1982 and four more volumes from 1997 to 2003.

This book, comprised of *Paracuellos* and *Paracuellos 2,* is the first English translation of Carlos Giménez's seminal work of recovered memory.

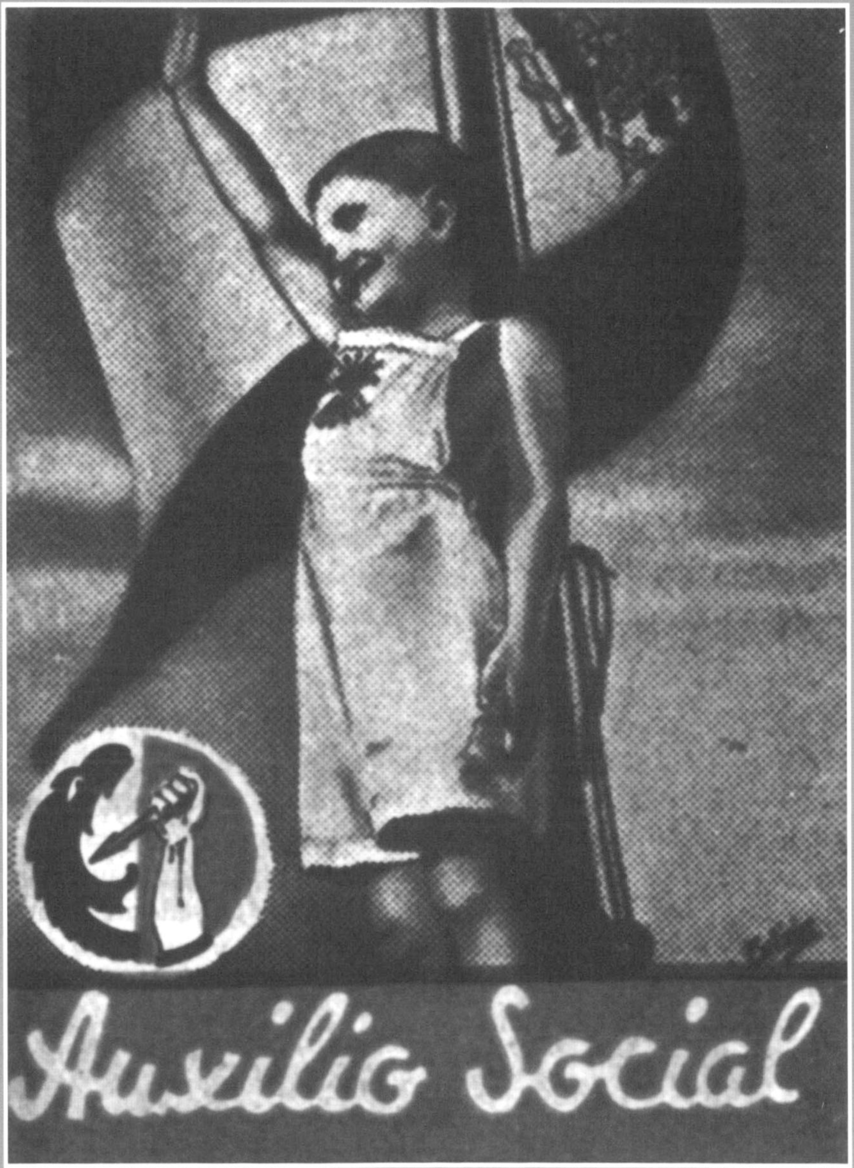
Auxilio Social

Social Aid poster, c. late 1930s.

BY Antonio Martin

THE NATIONAL WORKS OF SOCIAL AID

They were dark days. Days in which the summer turned into night and the nights into a lament. And then the thunderbolt descended...

It was 1936, and Civil War flared in Spain. A war of ideas, a political war, a social war, a class war. The Army rose up against the Nation, the rich against the poor, the *petit bourgeois* against the proletariat, the monarchists against the republicans.... How can one forget a collective tragedy that marks an entire people for generations?

The seeds of death and destruction were sown in 1931, when a new constitution abolished the monarchy and established the democratic Second Spanish Republic. The election of a leftist Popular Front government in 1936 engendered an insurrection by four army generals, including Francisco Franco, who eventually became its leader and assumed control of the nationalist *Falange* and other conservative movements. Accepting aid from Hitler and Mussolini, Franco's Nationalists defeated the Republicans in 1939 and established a totalitarian regime that lasted until his death in 1975.

That period—from 1936 to 1939—was a bloody three years. Executions on the shoulders of the highways, against cemetery walls, in corrals and pigsties, next to the factory walls and in the trenches. Executions at night and in broad daylight, with an audience watching the spectacle. All of the victims, dying on both sides while shouting, "Long live Spain!"

The rawness of the *Falangist* and military repression created "an extraordinary number of poor and recently orphaned children," according to Dionisio Ridruejo, a member of the *Falangist* hierarchy. "The orphans of death in the rear guard."

The *Auxilio de Invierno* (Winter Aid) organization was created in 1936, it was claimed, to provide for the orphans and widows. It was a literal transposition of the Nazis' *Das Winterhilfswerk des Deutschen Volkes* (Winter Relief for The German People), from which it assumed its name, its logo, and a good part of its initial philosophy. It was eventually renamed *Obra Nacional de Auxilio Social* (National Works of Social Aid). By the time the war was over, it had turned into a venal bureaucracy.

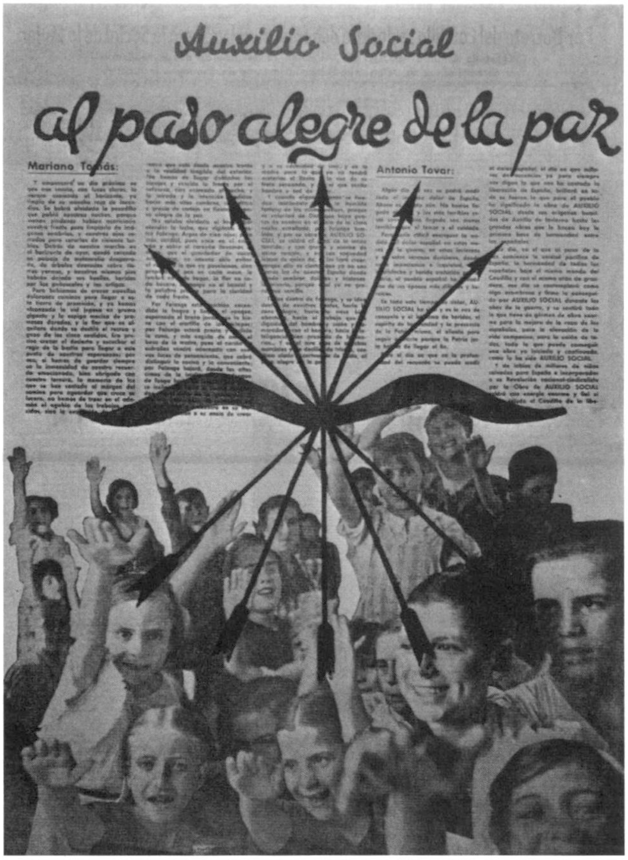
Auxilio Social
al paso alegre de la paz
Mariano Tomás:
Antonio Tovar:

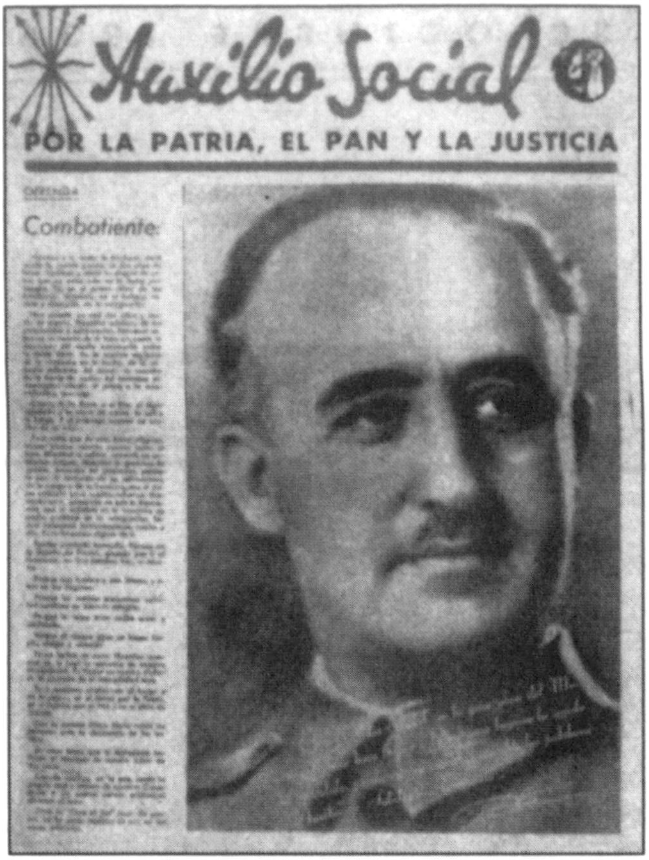
Auxilio Social
POR LA PATRIA, EL PAN Y LA JUSTICIA
Combatiente

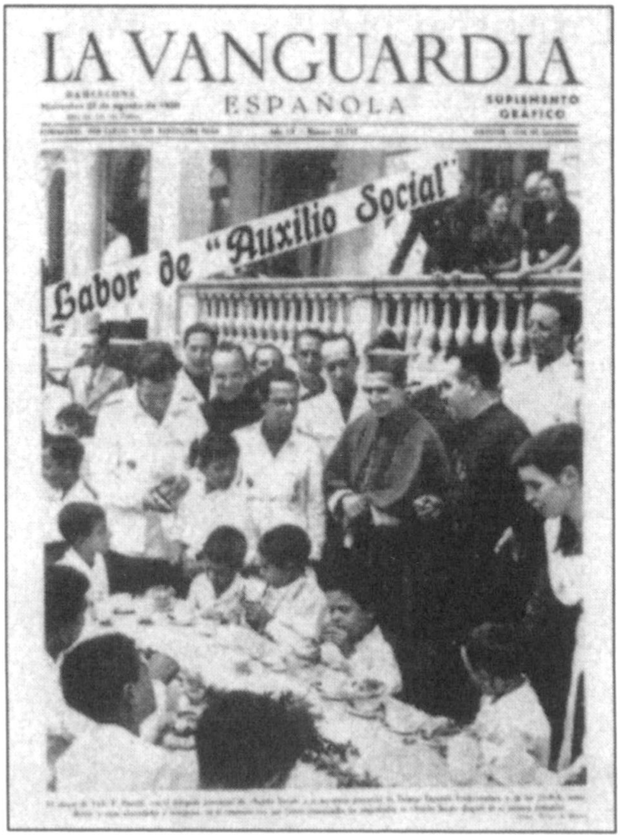
LA VANGUARDIA
ESPAÑOLA
SUPLEMENTO GRÁFICO
Labor de "Auxilio Social"

Examples of the pervasive propaganda carried out by the regime.

The war's images were made up of a thousand symbols: fists and hands raised high, red stars and provisional ones, blue shirts and maroon bandanas, hammers and sickles, crosses, tricolored flags and solid red pennants, songs and hymns and religious talismans. Its sounds were the endless cacophony of battle: Mausers and rifles, army-issued pistols and ladies' handguns, hand grenades, mortar shells, cannons, planes, tanks. Battalions and regiments on the move, marking time in a monotonous and repetitive backdrop that had the rhythm of death.

Until, suddenly, a great silence.

The war ended and the silence spread over a nation leveled to the ground, an incarcerated country, a beaten country. From among the ruins emerged women, children, old people, skeletal men…lice-ridden, malnourished, filthy, sick.

Waiting for them were the monks, friars, nuns, acolytes, and priests of the asylums, poorhouses, colonies, and workshops, the judges of the Juvenile Ward Tribunals. The Youth Front instructors, the comrades from the Women's Division. The nurses, chaperones, and matrons from Social Aid, all of whom gathered their harvest day by day, to make "good little Spaniards" of them all, these "men" of the Spain that was beginning to dawn…

In 1941 the *Falangist* policeman Carlos Groocke, Chief of Information and Investigations, referred to the children lodged in Social Aid Homes as he said to a sympathetic witness, "You understand…these children aren't responsible. And they represent the Spain of the future. We want them to say one day: '*Falangist* Spain certainly executed our parents, but it was because they deserved it. In exchange, Spain has enveloped our childhood with comforts and care.' The ones that, in spite of everything, still hate us when they're twenty will be the ones who aren't worth anything. The trash."

How can one forget twenty, thirty…fifty years later?

Easily, it turns out. Franco's brutal authoritarian regime immediately set out to control all means of communication and education. To speak against the state was simply not tolerated. To teach tenets that did not accord with government policy could be cause for prison—or worse. The Franco regime wanted to hide, erase, and refute all prior history, creating an enormous void in those of us who were children. The victors submit their invoice; the losers shut up and pay… with their lives and many times, with their deaths.

While on the surface it appeared that the 1940s was a decade of songs, of folklore, of bread and soccer and other florid topics, the Forties were also about the concentration camps: Albateras, Almendros, San Javier, Portaceli, Burgo de Osma, San Marcos, and many others. And the jails—Porlier, Yeserías, Vallecas, San Antón, Alcalá, La Modelo, Ventas, and so many more, jails where opponents of the government were tortured and beaten, confessions torn from their flesh, where one was sent to tribunals and from there to the final destination—death by firing squad, strangulation, or the living death of perpetual confinement.

There is no consensus among historians on the exact number of casualties—it has been written on the left, quoting anonymous figures from the Ministry of Justice, that nearly 200,000 people were executed or died while imprisoned between the years 1939 and 1944. Others on the right state that "only" 25,000 or so were executed. Whether on the high or the low end, the figures reveal the dimensions of the organized violence by the state.

A country silenced and terrified was a nation that was safe for the victors.

* * * * *

It is worth remembering the adage that those who forget the past are condemned to repeat it. Carlos Giménez didn't want to forget. No one could publish this work while Franco was alive; when he submitted the first installments for print, a frightened publisher asked the cartoonist to edit his script. That initial publication precipitated constant death threats from right-wing groups.

Yet Giménez prevailed because this work is something in his blood, an integral part of him that shapes his being. This book is proof of that passion. In it Carlos Giménez conveys the rage, frustration, and small tragedy—small because it was personal—that the children in the first Social Aid Homes experienced, those orphans of the "reds" shot by the same individuals who handed them hunks of bread and a plate of stew. He conveys the rage, frustration, and tragedy of children who ended up in those Homes because their parents were in Franco's jails or because they belonged to the families of the defeated, the ones who dragged along, day by day, in their collective and frightening misery. Just as tragic is the experience of the Spanish children who had to be "aided" in the Fifties because their fathers had died or because there was no bread to eat, because their mothers were sick or because the number of siblings at home condemned them to hunger.

Carlos Giménez teaches his audience that the history he lived through is part of our collective history, and as such is common patrimony for us all. Because the Franco regime suppressed knowledge of these events, Spaniards had to learn all over again who we were and where we came from, starting by giving life again to that which the regime wanted to remain dead. It has been an arduous path to rejuvenate our marks of identity because of fear, the fear we lived with for forty years, fear that had penetrated the depths of our souls. We must continue to fight in order to keep power out of the hands of those who would be our masters.

Carlos Giménez refuses to forget, and with these stories reminds us that we too must never forget.

Antonio Martin was born in 1939, three months after the end of the civil war. He is a venerated comics editor and Spain's foremost comics historian. His books include the seminal Historia del Comic Español: 1875-1939 (History of Spanish Comics, 1875-1939) *and he curated the museum exhibit,* The Civil War in Comics: Children and Propaganda, 1936-1939. *This essay is adapted and expanded from his introduction to the 1982 first edition of* Paracuellos 2.

PARACUELLOS
Auxilio
Auxilio Social
CARLOS
GIMÉNEZ

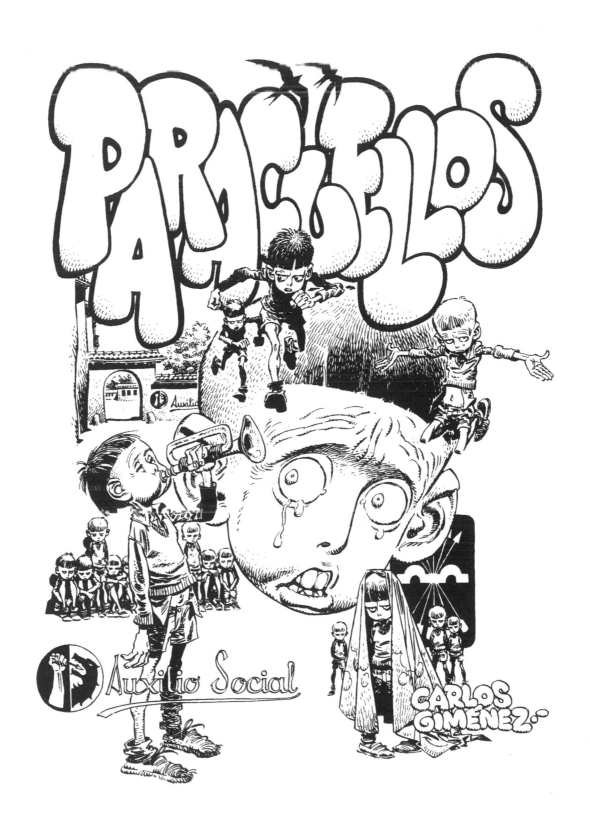

Cover to the first edition of **Paracuellos**,
published by Ediciones Amaika in July 1977.

PARACUELLOS
1

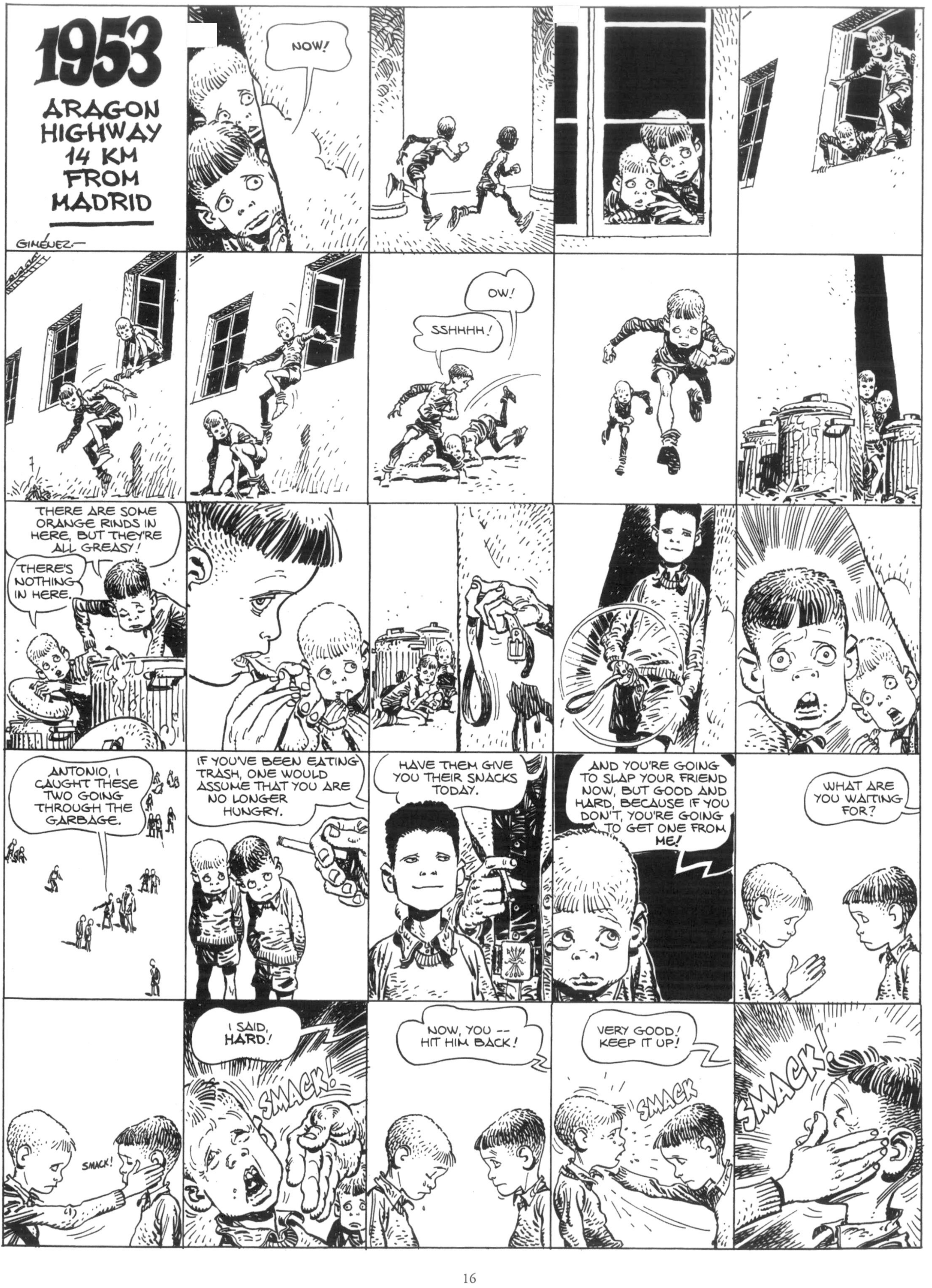
1953
ARAGON HIGHWAY 14 KM FROM MADRID
GIMÉNEZ
NOW!
OW!
SSHHHH!
THERE ARE SOME ORANGE RINDS IN HERE, BUT THEY'RE ALL GREASY!
THERE'S NOTHING IN HERE.
ANTONIO, I CAUGHT THESE TWO GOING THROUGH THE GARBAGE.
IF YOU'VE BEEN EATING TRASH, ONE WOULD ASSUME THAT YOU ARE NO LONGER HUNGRY.
HAVE THEM GIVE YOU THEIR SNACKS TODAY.
AND YOU'RE GOING TO SLAP YOUR FRIEND NOW, BUT GOOD AND HARD, BECAUSE IF YOU DON'T, YOU'RE GOING TO GET ONE FROM ME!
WHAT ARE YOU WAITING FOR?
SMACK!
I SAID, HARD!
SMACK!
NOW, YOU -- HIT HIM BACK!
VERY GOOD! KEEP IT UP!
SMACK
SMACK!

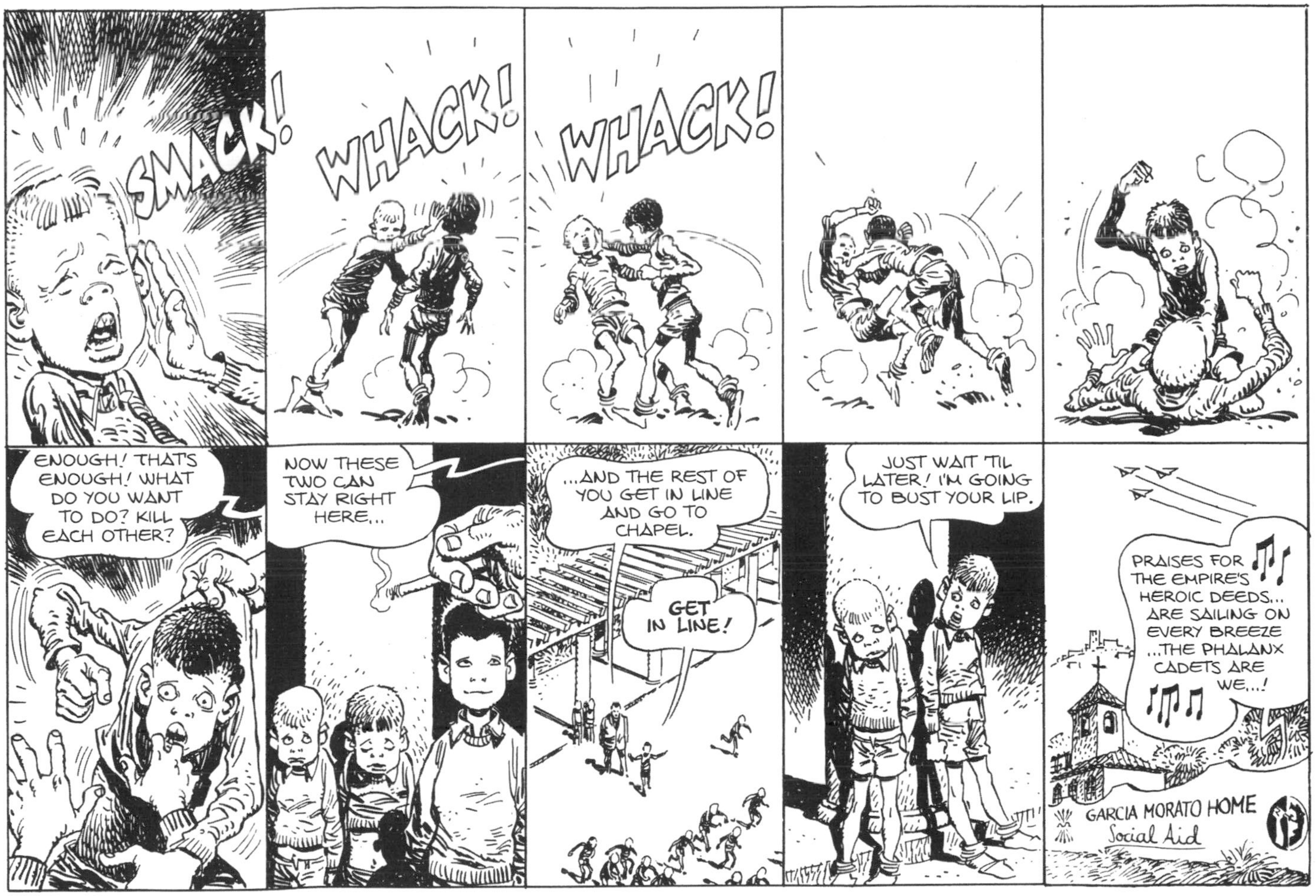
SMACK!
WHACK!
WHACK!
ENOUGH! THAT'S ENOUGH! WHAT DO YOU WANT TO DO? KILL EACH OTHER?
NOW THESE TWO CAN STAY RIGHT HERE...
...AND THE REST OF YOU GET IN LINE AND GO TO CHAPEL.
GET IN LINE!
JUST WAIT 'TIL LATER! I'M GOING TO BUST YOUR LIP.
PRAISES FOR THE EMPIRE'S HEROIC DEEDS... ARE SAILING ON EVERY BREEZE ...THE PHALANX CADETS ARE WE...!
GARCIA MORATO HOME
Social Aid

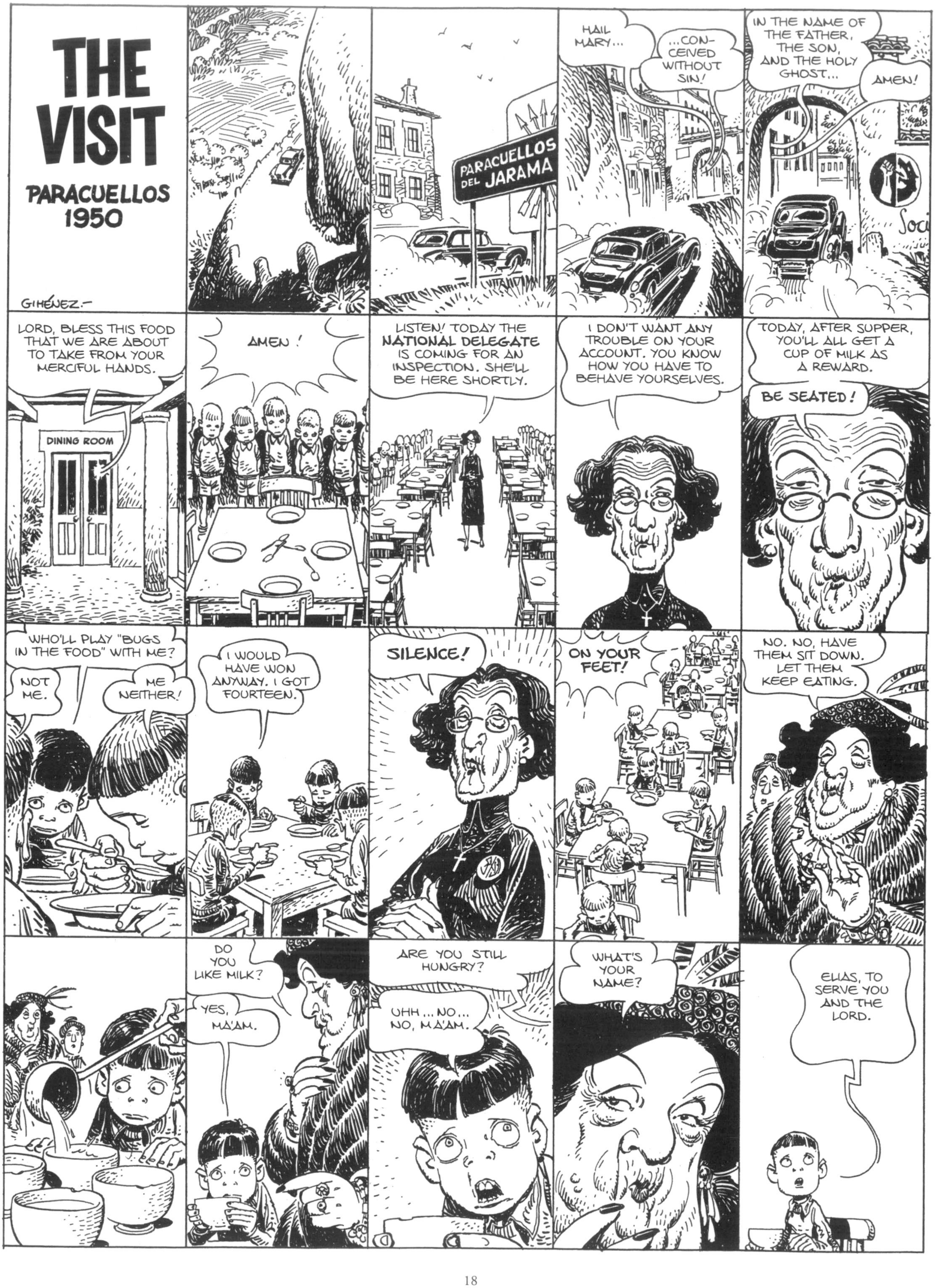
THE VISIT
PARACUELLOS 1950
GIMÉNEZ.-
PARACUELLOS DEL JARAMA
HAIL MARY...
...CONCEIVED WITHOUT SIN!
IN THE NAME OF THE FATHER, THE SON, AND THE HOLY GHOST...
AMEN!
LORD, BLESS THIS FOOD THAT WE ARE ABOUT TO TAKE FROM YOUR MERCIFUL HANDS.
DINING ROOM
AMEN!
LISTEN! TODAY THE NATIONAL DELEGATE IS COMING FOR AN INSPECTION. SHE'LL BE HERE SHORTLY.
I DON'T WANT ANY TROUBLE ON YOUR ACCOUNT. YOU KNOW HOW YOU HAVE TO BEHAVE YOURSELVES.
TODAY, AFTER SUPPER, YOU'LL ALL GET A CUP OF MILK AS A REWARD.
BE SEATED!
WHO'LL PLAY "BUGS IN THE FOOD" WITH ME?
NOT ME.
ME NEITHER!
I WOULD HAVE WON ANYWAY. I GOT FOURTEEN.
SILENCE!
ON YOUR FEET!
NO. NO, HAVE THEM SIT DOWN. LET THEM KEEP EATING.
DO YOU LIKE MILK?
YES, MA'AM.
ARE YOU STILL HUNGRY?
UHH... NO... NO, MA'AM.
WHAT'S YOUR NAME?
ELIAS, TO SERVE YOU AND THE LORD.

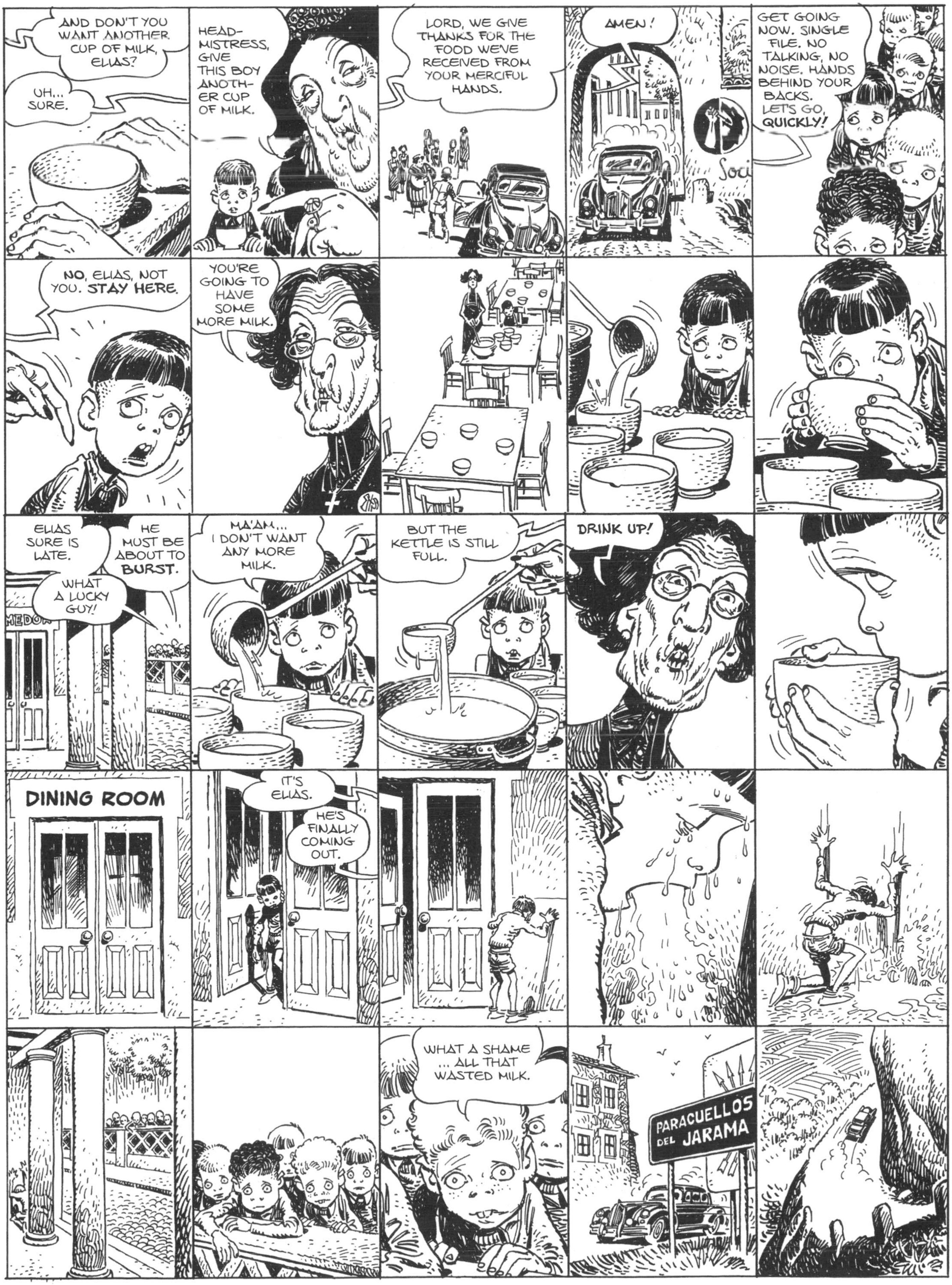
AND DON'T YOU WANT ANOTHER CUP OF MILK, ELIAS?
UH... SURE.
HEAD-MISTRESS, GIVE THIS BOY ANOTH-ER CUP OF MILK.
LORD, WE GIVE THANKS FOR THE FOOD WE'VE RECEIVED FROM YOUR MERCIFUL HANDS.
AMEN!
GET GOING NOW. SINGLE FILE. NO TALKING, NO NOISE. HANDS BEHIND YOUR BACKS. LET'S GO, QUICKLY!
NO, ELIAS, NOT YOU. STAY HERE.
YOU'RE GOING TO HAVE SOME MORE MILK.
ELIAS SURE IS LATE.
WHAT A LUCKY GUY!
HE MUST BE ABOUT TO BURST.
MA'AM... I DON'T WANT ANY MORE MILK.
BUT THE KETTLE IS STILL FULL.
DRINK UP!
DINING ROOM
IT'S ELIAS.
HE'S FINALLY COMING OUT.
WHAT A SHAME ... ALL THAT WASTED MILK.
PARACUELLOS DEL JARAMA

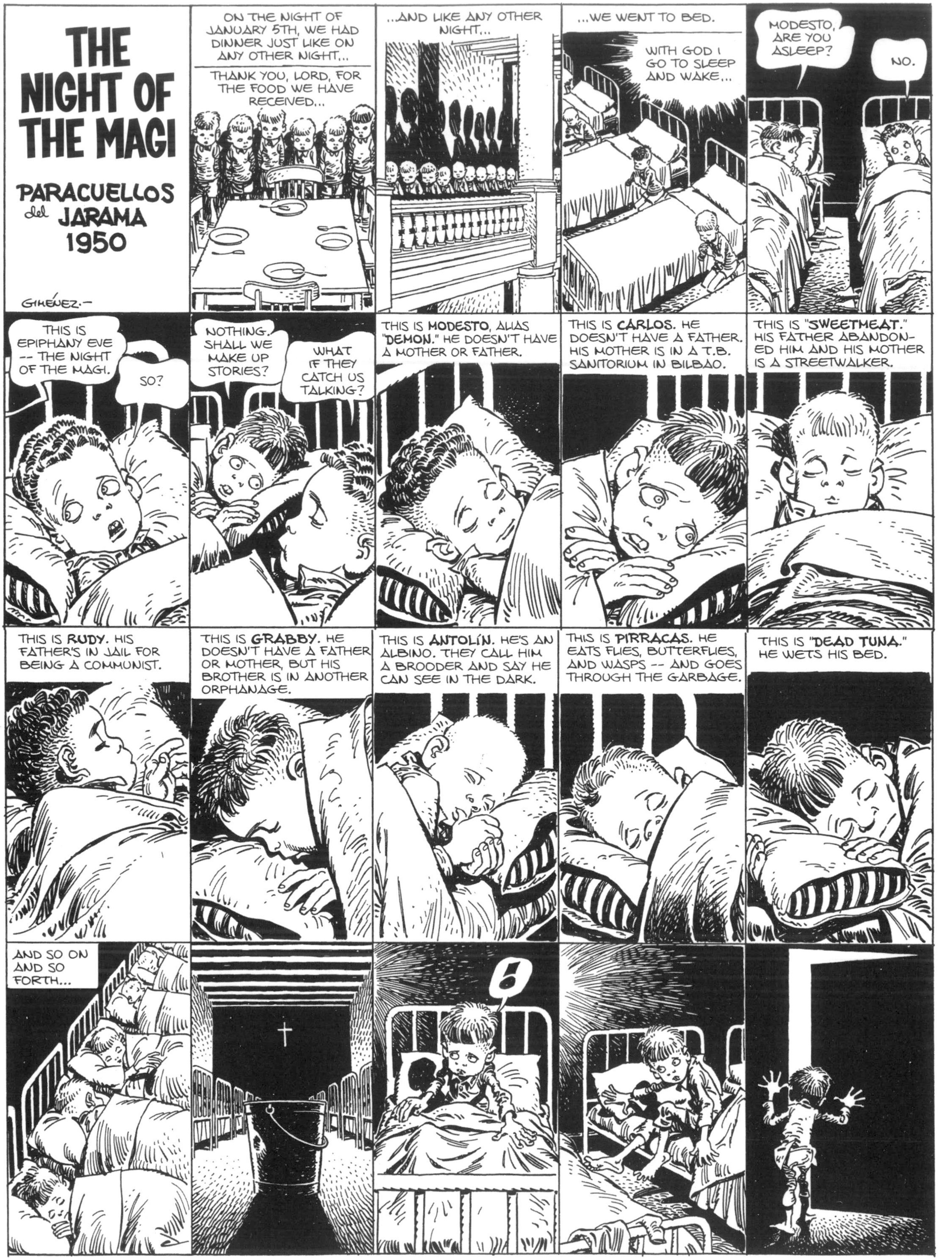
THE NIGHT OF THE MAGI
PARACUELLOS del JARAMA 1950
GIMÉNEZ.-
ON THE NIGHT OF JANUARY 5TH, WE HAD DINNER JUST LIKE ON ANY OTHER NIGHT...
THANK YOU, LORD, FOR THE FOOD WE HAVE RECEIVED...
...AND LIKE ANY OTHER NIGHT...
...WE WENT TO BED.
WITH GOD I GO TO SLEEP AND WAKE...
MODESTO, ARE YOU ASLEEP?
NO.
THIS IS EPIPHANY EVE -- THE NIGHT OF THE MAGI.
SO?
NOTHING. SHALL WE MAKE UP STORIES?
WHAT IF THEY CATCH US TALKING?
THIS IS MODESTO, ALIAS "DEMON." HE DOESN'T HAVE A MOTHER OR FATHER.
THIS IS CARLOS. HE DOESN'T HAVE A FATHER. HIS MOTHER IS IN A T.B. SANITORIUM IN BILBAO.
THIS IS "SWEETMEAT." HIS FATHER ABANDONED HIM AND HIS MOTHER IS A STREETWALKER.
THIS IS RUDY. HIS FATHER'S IN JAIL FOR BEING A COMMUNIST.
THIS IS GRABBY. HE DOESN'T HAVE A FATHER OR MOTHER, BUT HIS BROTHER IS IN ANOTHER ORPHANAGE.
THIS IS ANTOLÍN. HE'S AN ALBINO. THEY CALL HIM A BROODER AND SAY HE CAN SEE IN THE DARK.
THIS IS PIRRACAS. HE EATS FLIES, BUTTERFLIES, AND WASPS -- AND GOES THROUGH THE GARBAGE.
THIS IS "DEAD TUNA." HE WETS HIS BED.
AND SO ON AND SO FORTH...
¡

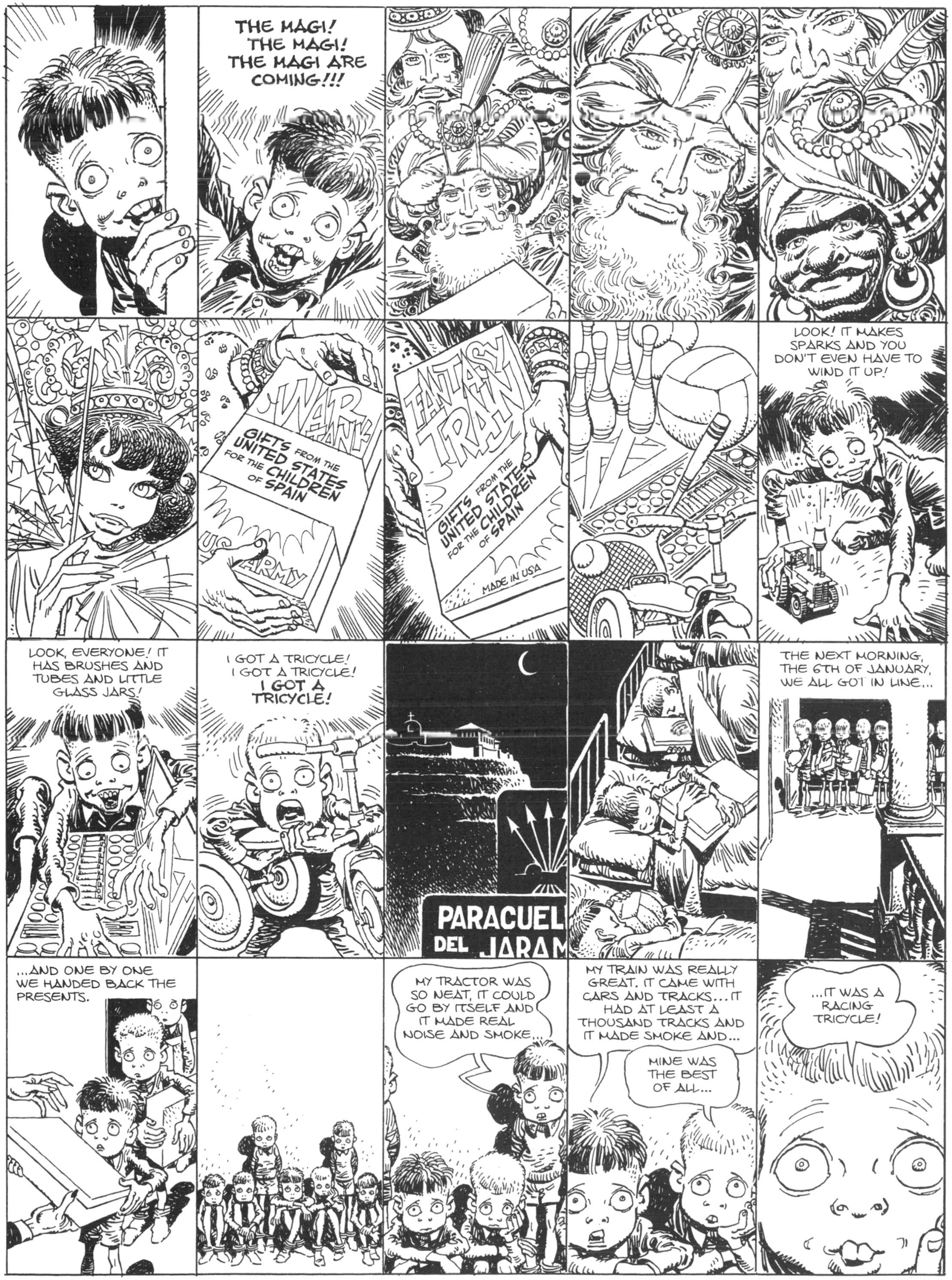
THE MAGI! THE MAGI! THE MAGI ARE COMING!!!
WAR
GIFTS FROM THE UNITED STATES FOR THE CHILDREN OF SPAIN
US ARMY
FANTASY TRAIN
GIFTS FROM THE UNITED STATES FOR THE CHILDREN OF SPAIN
MADE IN USA
LOOK! IT MAKES SPARKS AND YOU DON'T EVEN HAVE TO WIND IT UP!
LOOK, EVERYONE! IT HAS BRUSHES AND TUBES AND LITTLE GLASS JARS!
I GOT A TRICYCLE! I GOT A TRICYCLE! I GOT A TRICYCLE!
PARACUEL
DEL JARAM
THE NEXT MORNING, THE 6TH OF JANUARY, WE ALL GOT IN LINE...
...AND ONE BY ONE WE HANDED BACK THE PRESENTS.
MY TRACTOR WAS SO NEAT, IT COULD GO BY ITSELF AND IT MADE REAL NOISE AND SMOKE...
MY TRAIN WAS REALLY GREAT. IT CAME WITH CARS AND TRACKS... IT HAD AT LEAST A THOUSAND TRACKS AND IT MADE SMOKE AND...
MINE WAS THE BEST OF ALL...
...IT WAS A RACING TRICYCLE!

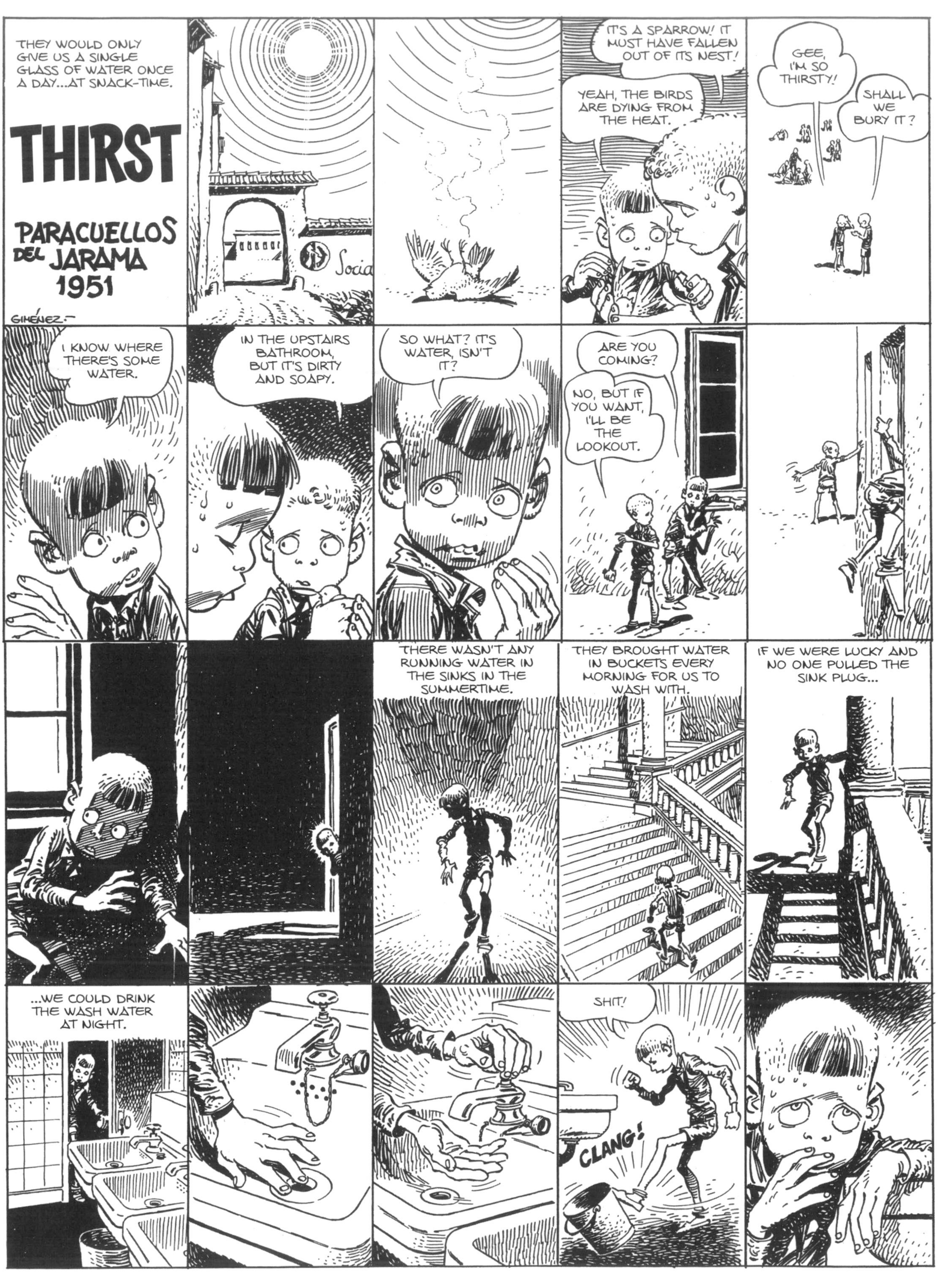
THEY WOULD ONLY GIVE US A SINGLE GLASS OF WATER ONCE A DAY...AT SNACK-TIME.
THIRST
PARACUELLOS DEL JARAMA 1951
GIMÉNEZ
Socia
IT'S A SPARROW! IT MUST HAVE FALLEN OUT OF ITS NEST!
YEAH, THE BIRDS ARE DYING FROM THE HEAT.
GEE, I'M SO THIRSTY!
SHALL WE BURY IT?
I KNOW WHERE THERE'S SOME WATER.
IN THE UPSTAIRS BATHROOM, BUT IT'S DIRTY AND SOAPY.
SO WHAT? IT'S WATER, ISN'T IT?
ARE YOU COMING?
NO, BUT IF YOU WANT, I'LL BE THE LOOKOUT.
THERE WASN'T ANY RUNNING WATER IN THE SINKS IN THE SUMMERTIME.
THEY BROUGHT WATER IN BUCKETS EVERY MORNING FOR US TO WASH WITH.
IF WE WERE LUCKY AND NO ONE PULLED THE SINK PLUG...
...WE COULD DRINK THE WASH WATER AT NIGHT.
SHIT!
CLANG!

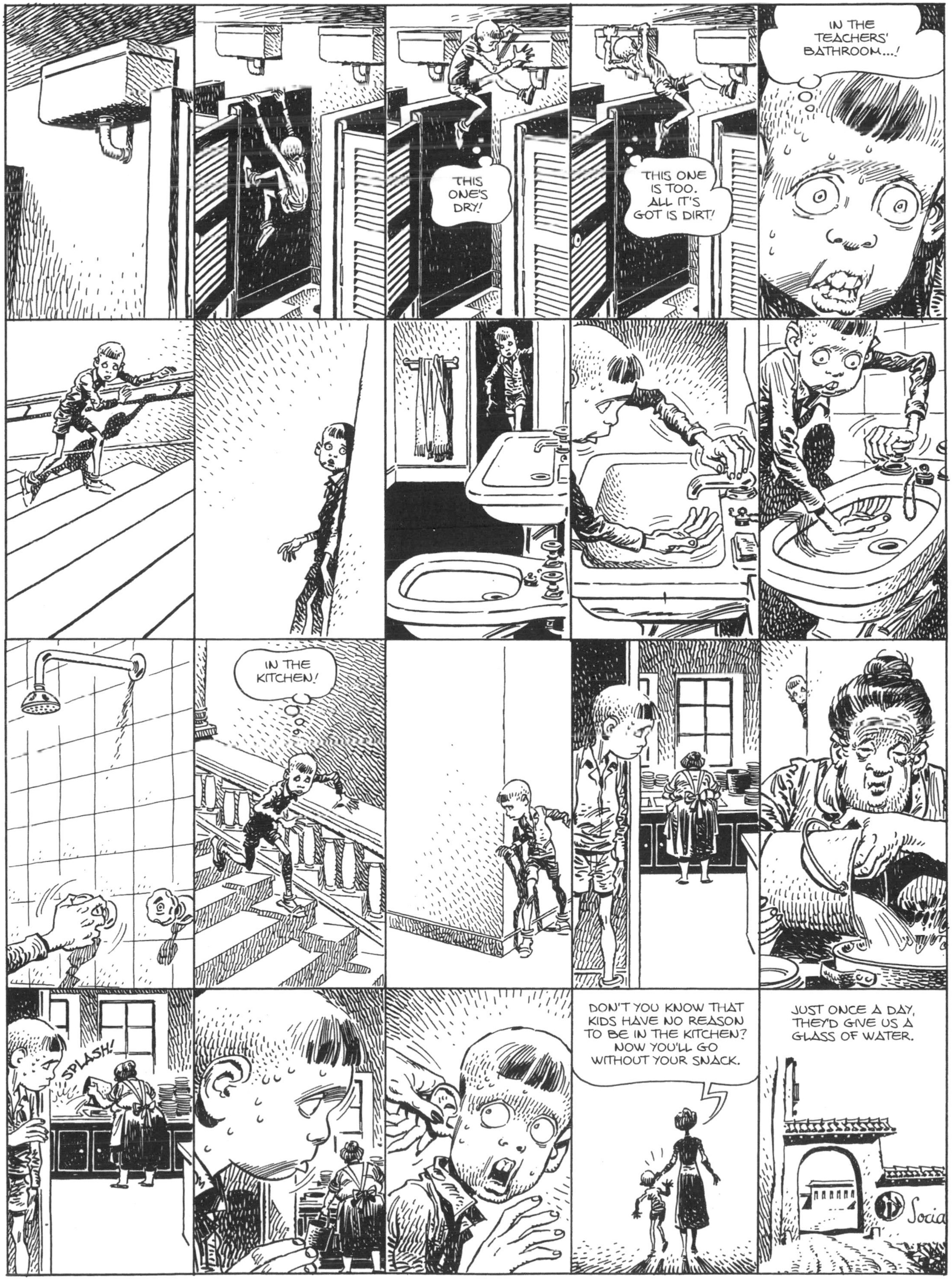
THIS ONE'S DRY!
THIS ONE IS TOO. ALL IT'S GOT IS DIRT!
IN THE TEACHERS' BATHROOM...!
IN THE KITCHEN!
SPLASH!
DON'T YOU KNOW THAT KIDS HAVE NO REASON TO BE IN THE KITCHEN? NOW YOU'LL GO WITHOUT YOUR SNACK.
JUST ONCE A DAY, THEY'D GIVE US A GLASS OF WATER.

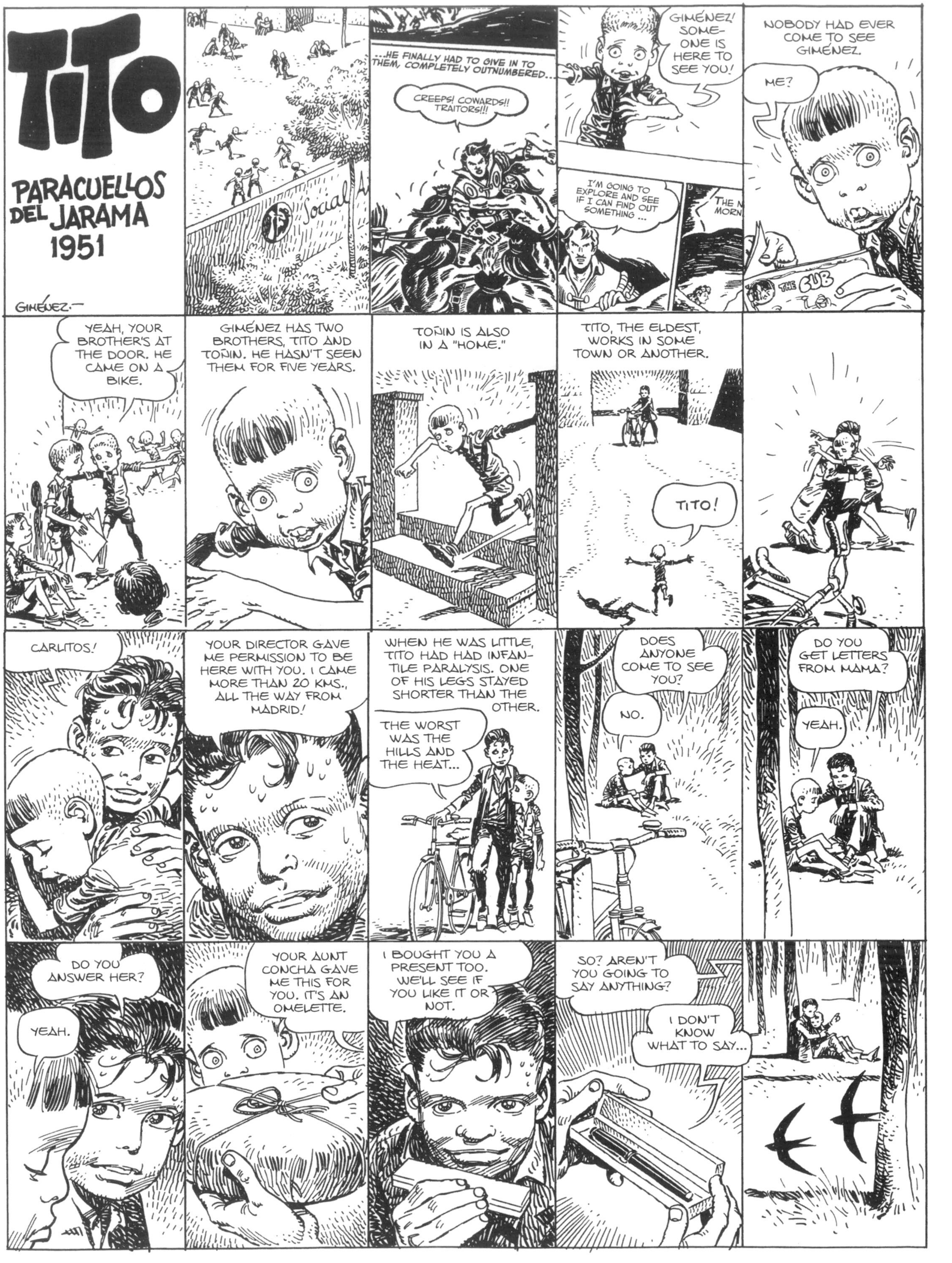
TITO
PARACUELLOS DEL JARAMA 1951
GIMÉNEZ
...HE FINALLY HAD TO GIVE IN TO THEM, COMPLETELY OUTNUMBERED...
CREEPS! COWARDS!! TRAITORS!!!
GIMÉNEZ! SOME-ONE IS HERE TO SEE YOU!
I'M GOING TO EXPLORE AND SEE IF I CAN FIND OUT SOMETHING ...
NOBODY HAD EVER COME TO SEE GIMÉNEZ.
ME?
THE CUB
YEAH, YOUR BROTHER'S AT THE DOOR. HE CAME ON A BIKE.
GIMÉNEZ HAS TWO BROTHERS, TITO AND TOÑIN. HE HASN'T SEEN THEM FOR FIVE YEARS.
TOÑIN IS ALSO IN A "HOME."
TITO, THE ELDEST, WORKS IN SOME TOWN OR ANOTHER.
TITO!
CARLITOS!
YOUR DIRECTOR GAVE ME PERMISSION TO BE HERE WITH YOU. I CAME MORE THAN 20 KMS., ALL THE WAY FROM MADRID!
WHEN HE WAS LITTLE, TITO HAD HAD INFAN-TILE PARALYSIS. ONE OF HIS LEGS STAYED SHORTER THAN THE OTHER.
THE WORST WAS THE HILLS AND THE HEAT...
DOES ANYONE COME TO SEE YOU?
NO.
DO YOU GET LETTERS FROM MAMA?
YEAH.
DO YOU ANSWER HER?
YEAH.
YOUR AUNT CONCHA GAVE ME THIS FOR YOU. IT'S AN OMELETTE.
I BOUGHT YOU A PRESENT TOO. WE'LL SEE IF YOU LIKE IT OR NOT.
SO? AREN'T YOU GOING TO SAY ANYTHING?
I DON'T KNOW WHAT TO SAY...

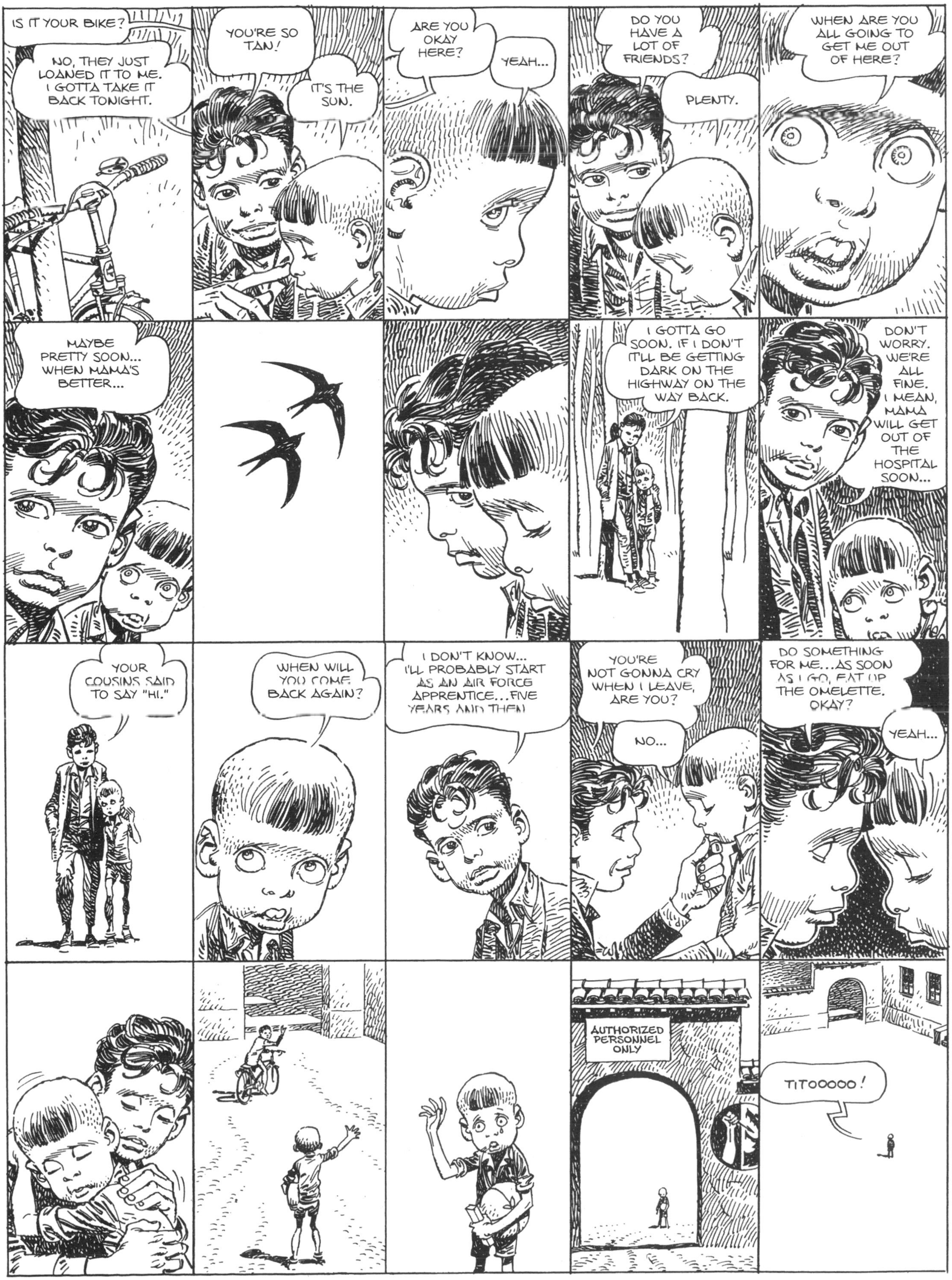
IS IT YOUR BIKE?
NO, THEY JUST LOANED IT TO ME. I GOTTA TAKE IT BACK TONIGHT.
YOU'RE SO TAN!
IT'S THE SUN.
ARE YOU OKAY HERE?
YEAH...
DO YOU HAVE A LOT OF FRIENDS?
PLENTY.
WHEN ARE YOU ALL GOING TO GET ME OUT OF HERE?
MAYBE PRETTY SOON... WHEN MAMA'S BETTER...
I GOTTA GO SOON. IF I DON'T IT'LL BE GETTING DARK ON THE HIGHWAY ON THE WAY BACK.
DON'T WORRY. WE'RE ALL FINE. I MEAN, MAMA WILL GET OUT OF THE HOSPITAL SOON...
YOUR COUSINS SAID TO SAY "HI."
WHEN WILL YOU COME BACK AGAIN?
I DON'T KNOW... I'LL PROBABLY START AS AN AIR FORCE APPRENTICE...FIVE YEARS AND THEN
YOU'RE NOT GONNA CRY WHEN I LEAVE, ARE YOU?
NO...
DO SOMETHING FOR ME...AS SOON AS I GO, EAT UP THE OMELETTE. OKAY?
YEAH...
AUTHORIZED PERSONNEL ONLY
TITOOOOO!

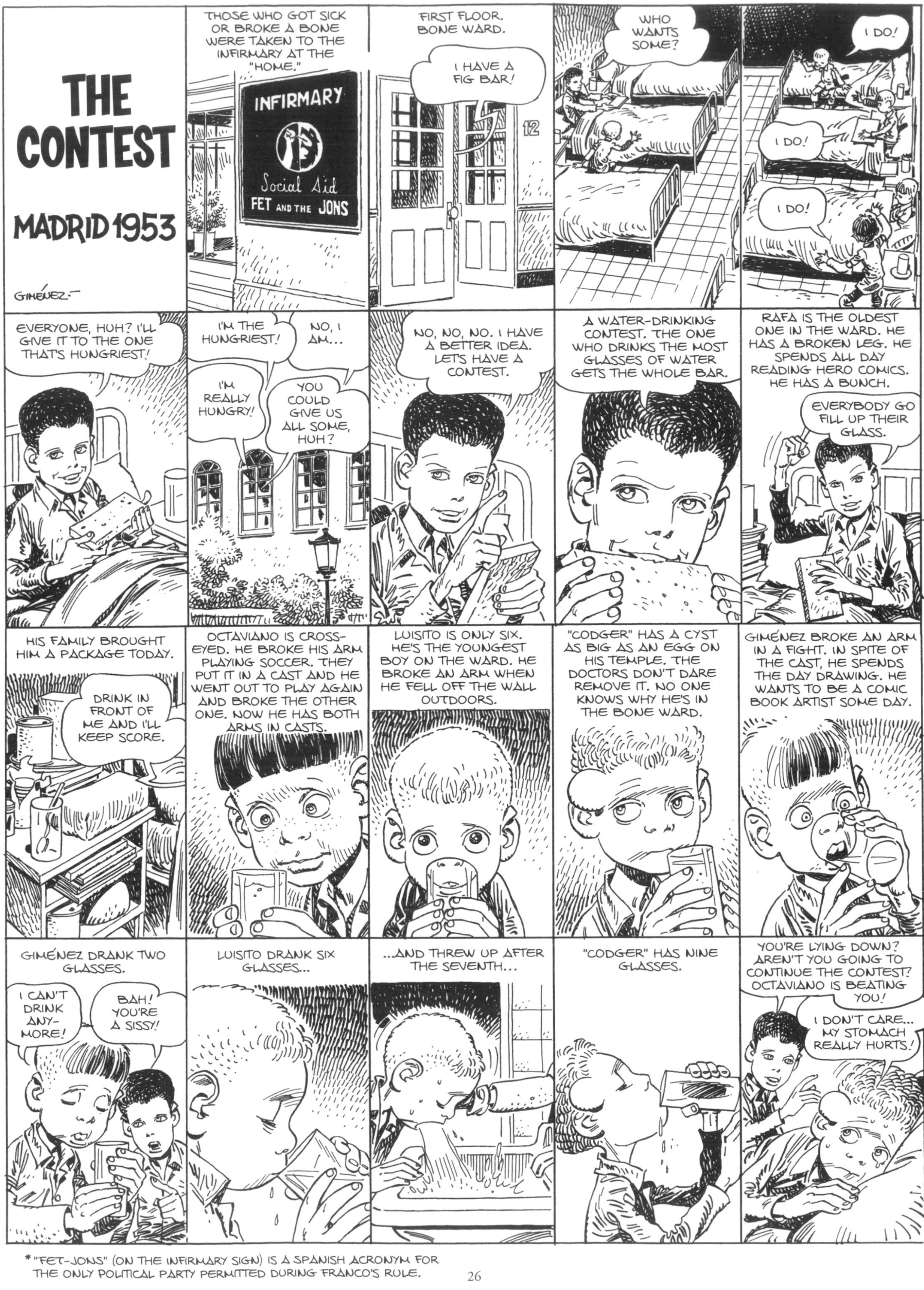
THE CONTEST
MADRID 1953
GIMÉNEZ
THOSE WHO GOT SICK OR BROKE A BONE WERE TAKEN TO THE INFIRMARY AT THE "HOME."
INFIRMARY
Social Aid
FET AND THE JONS
FIRST FLOOR. BONE WARD.
I HAVE A FIG BAR!
12
WHO WANTS SOME?
I DO!
I DO!
I DO!
EVERYONE, HUH? I'LL GIVE IT TO THE ONE THAT'S HUNGRIEST!
I'M THE HUNGRIEST!
NO, I AM...
I'M REALLY HUNGRY!
YOU COULD GIVE US ALL SOME, HUH?
NO, NO, NO. I HAVE A BETTER IDEA. LET'S HAVE A CONTEST.
A WATER-DRINKING CONTEST. THE ONE WHO DRINKS THE MOST GLASSES OF WATER GETS THE WHOLE BAR.
RAFA IS THE OLDEST ONE IN THE WARD. HE HAS A BROKEN LEG. HE SPENDS ALL DAY READING HERO COMICS. HE HAS A BUNCH.
EVERYBODY GO FILL UP THEIR GLASS.
HIS FAMILY BROUGHT HIM A PACKAGE TODAY.
DRINK IN FRONT OF ME AND I'LL KEEP SCORE.
OCTAVIANO IS CROSS-EYED. HE BROKE HIS ARM PLAYING SOCCER. THEY PUT IT IN A CAST AND HE WENT OUT TO PLAY AGAIN AND BROKE THE OTHER ONE. NOW HE HAS BOTH ARMS IN CASTS.
LUISITO IS ONLY SIX. HE'S THE YOUNGEST BOY ON THE WARD. HE BROKE AN ARM WHEN HE FELL OFF THE WALL OUTDOORS.
"CODGER" HAS A CYST AS BIG AS AN EGG ON HIS TEMPLE. THE DOCTORS DON'T DARE REMOVE IT. NO ONE KNOWS WHY HE'S IN THE BONE WARD.
GIMÉNEZ BROKE AN ARM IN A FIGHT. IN SPITE OF THE CAST, HE SPENDS THE DAY DRAWING. HE WANTS TO BE A COMIC BOOK ARTIST SOME DAY.
GIMÉNEZ DRANK TWO GLASSES.
I CAN'T DRINK ANY-MORE!
BAH! YOU'RE A SISSY!
LUISITO DRANK SIX GLASSES...
...AND THREW UP AFTER THE SEVENTH...
"CODGER" HAS NINE GLASSES.
YOU'RE LYING DOWN? AREN'T YOU GOING TO CONTINUE THE CONTEST? OCTAVIANO IS BEATING YOU!
I DON'T CARE... MY STOMACH REALLY HURTS!

* "FET-JONS" (ON THE INFIRMARY SIGN) IS A SPANISH ACRONYM FOR THE ONLY POLITICAL PARTY PERMITTED DURING FRANCO'S RULE.

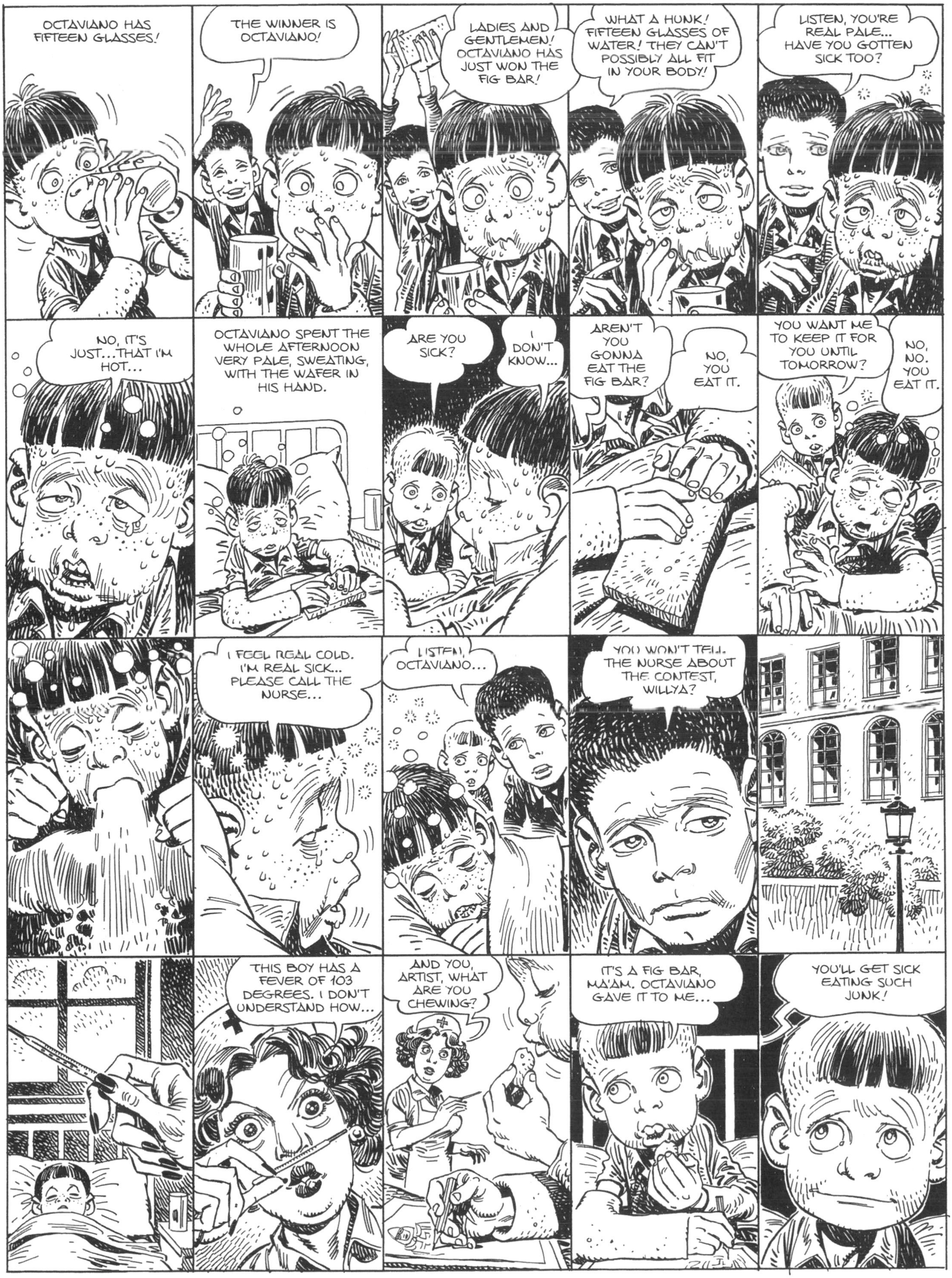

OCTAVIANO HAS FIFTEEN GLASSES!
THE WINNER IS OCTAVIANO!
LADIES AND GENTLEMEN! OCTAVIANO HAS JUST WON THE FIG BAR!
WHAT A HUNK! FIFTEEN GLASSES OF WATER! THEY CAN'T POSSIBLY ALL FIT IN YOUR BODY!
LISTEN, YOU'RE REAL PALE... HAVE YOU GOTTEN SICK TOO?
NO, IT'S JUST...THAT I'M HOT...
OCTAVIANO SPENT THE WHOLE AFTERNOON VERY PALE, SWEATING, WITH THE WAFER IN HIS HAND.
ARE YOU SICK?
I DON'T KNOW...
AREN'T YOU GONNA EAT THE FIG BAR?
NO, YOU EAT IT.
YOU WANT ME TO KEEP IT FOR YOU UNTIL TOMORROW?
NO, NO. YOU EAT IT.
I FEEL REAL COLD. I'M REAL SICK... PLEASE CALL THE NURSE...
LISTEN, OCTAVIANO...
YOU WON'T TELL THE NURSE ABOUT THE CONTEST, WILLYA?
THIS BOY HAS A FEVER OF 103 DEGREES. I DON'T UNDERSTAND HOW...
AND YOU, ARTIST, WHAT ARE YOU CHEWING?
IT'S A FIG BAR, MA'AM. OCTAVIANO GAVE IT TO ME...
YOU'LL GET SICK EATING SUCH JUNK!

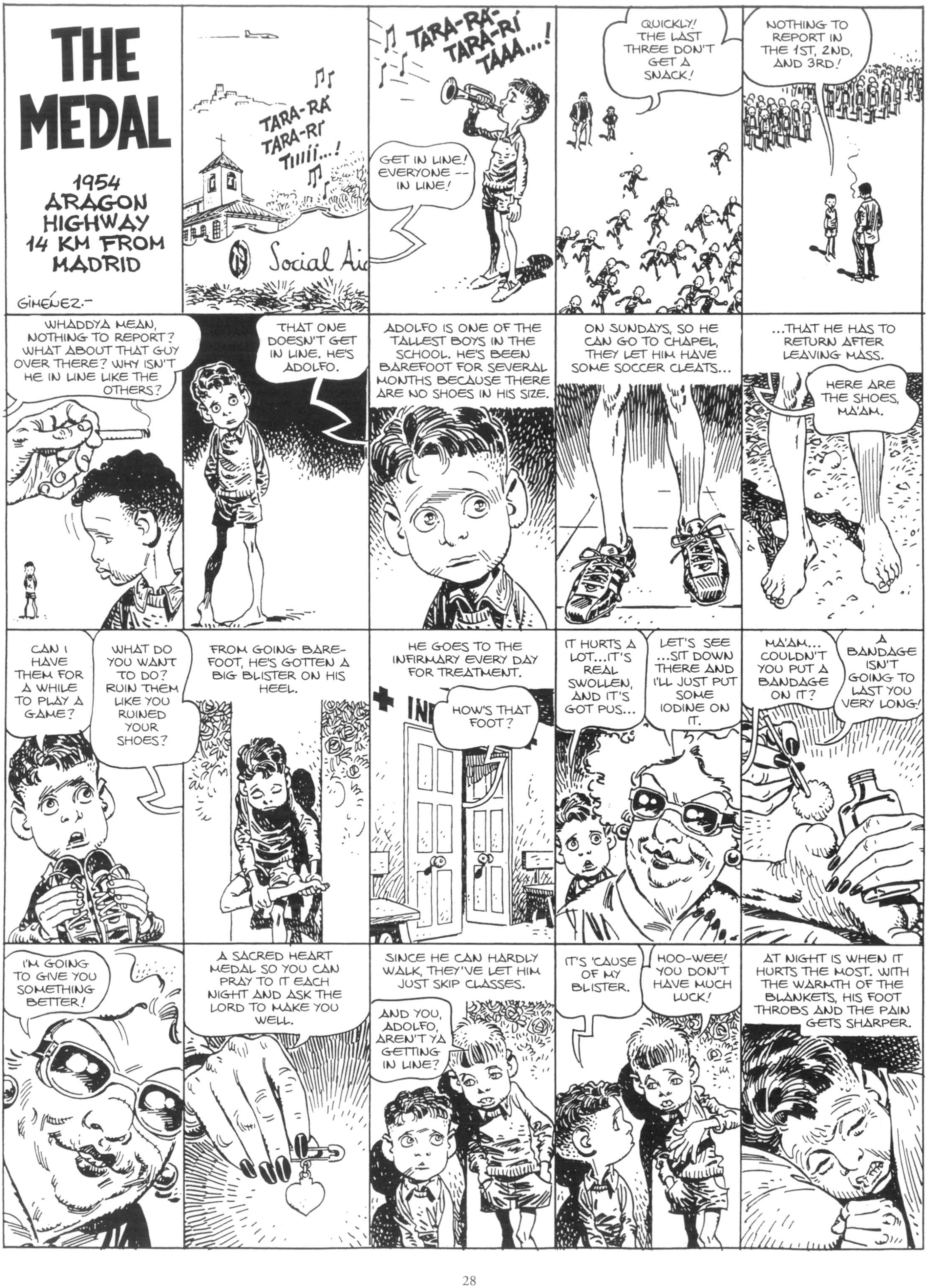

THE MEDAL
1954 ARAGON HIGHWAY 14 KM FROM MADRID
GIMÉNEZ.-
TARA-RÁ TARA-RÍ TIIIíí...!
Social Ai
TARA-RÁ- TARA-RÍ TAAA...!
GET IN LINE! EVERYONE -- IN LINE!
QUICKLY! THE LAST THREE DON'T GET A SNACK!
NOTHING TO REPORT IN THE 1ST, 2ND, AND 3RD!
WHADDYA MEAN, NOTHING TO REPORT? WHAT ABOUT THAT GUY OVER THERE? WHY ISN'T HE IN LINE LIKE THE OTHERS?
THAT ONE DOESN'T GET IN LINE. HE'S ADOLFO.
ADOLFO IS ONE OF THE TALLEST BOYS IN THE SCHOOL. HE'S BEEN BAREFOOT FOR SEVERAL MONTHS BECAUSE THERE ARE NO SHOES IN HIS SIZE.
ON SUNDAYS, SO HE CAN GO TO CHAPEL, THEY LET HIM HAVE SOME SOCCER CLEATS...
...THAT HE HAS TO RETURN AFTER LEAVING MASS.
HERE ARE THE SHOES, MA'AM.
CAN I HAVE THEM FOR A WHILE TO PLAY A GAME?
WHAT DO YOU WANT TO DO? RUIN THEM LIKE YOU RUINED YOUR SHOES?
FROM GOING BAREFOOT, HE'S GOTTEN A BIG BLISTER ON HIS HEEL.
HE GOES TO THE INFIRMARY EVERY DAY FOR TREATMENT.
HOW'S THAT FOOT?
IT HURTS A LOT...IT'S REAL SWOLLEN, AND IT'S GOT PUS...
LET'S SEE ...SIT DOWN THERE AND I'LL JUST PUT SOME IODINE ON IT.
MA'AM... COULDN'T YOU PUT A BANDAGE ON IT?
A BANDAGE ISN'T GOING TO LAST YOU VERY LONG!
I'M GOING TO GIVE YOU SOMETHING BETTER!
A SACRED HEART MEDAL SO YOU CAN PRAY TO IT EACH NIGHT AND ASK THE LORD TO MAKE YOU WELL.
SINCE HE CAN HARDLY WALK, THEY'VE LET HIM JUST SKIP CLASSES.
AND YOU, ADOLFO, AREN'T YA GETTING IN LINE?
IT'S 'CAUSE OF MY BLISTER.
HOO-WEE! YOU DON'T HAVE MUCH LUCK!
AT NIGHT IS WHEN IT HURTS THE MOST. WITH THE WARMTH OF THE BLANKETS, HIS FOOT THROBS AND THE PAIN GETS SHARPER.

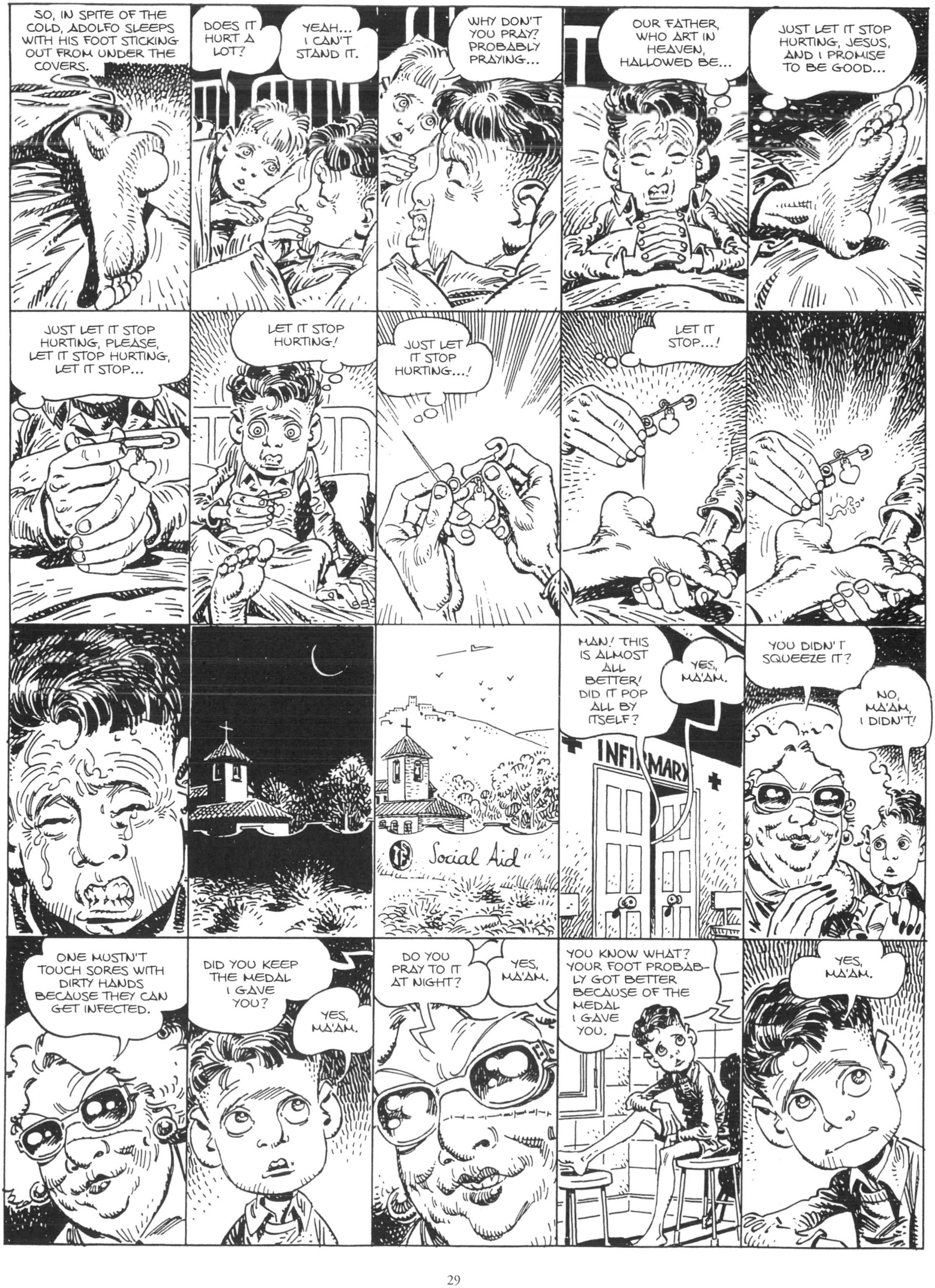
SO, IN SPITE OF THE COLD, ADOLFO SLEEPS WITH HIS FOOT STICKING OUT FROM UNDER THE COVERS.
DOES IT HURT A LOT?
YEAH... I CAN'T STAND IT.
WHY DON'T YOU PRAY? PROBABLY PRAYING...
OUR FATHER, WHO ART IN HEAVEN, HALLOWED BE...
JUST LET IT STOP HURTING, JESUS, AND I PROMISE TO BE GOOD...
JUST LET IT STOP HURTING, PLEASE, LET IT STOP HURTING, LET IT STOP...
LET IT STOP HURTING!
JUST LET IT STOP HURTING...!
LET IT STOP...!
Social Aid
MAN! THIS IS ALMOST ALL BETTER! DID IT POP ALL BY ITSELF?
YES, MA'AM.
INFIRMARY
YOU DIDN'T SQUEEZE IT?
NO, MA'AM, I DIDN'T!
ONE MUSTN'T TOUCH SORES WITH DIRTY HANDS BECAUSE THEY CAN GET INFECTED.
DID YOU KEEP THE MEDAL I GAVE YOU?
YES, MA'AM.
DO YOU PRAY TO IT AT NIGHT?
YES, MA'AM.
YOU KNOW WHAT? YOUR FOOT PROBABLY GOT BETTER BECAUSE OF THE MEDAL I GAVE YOU.
YES, MA'AM.

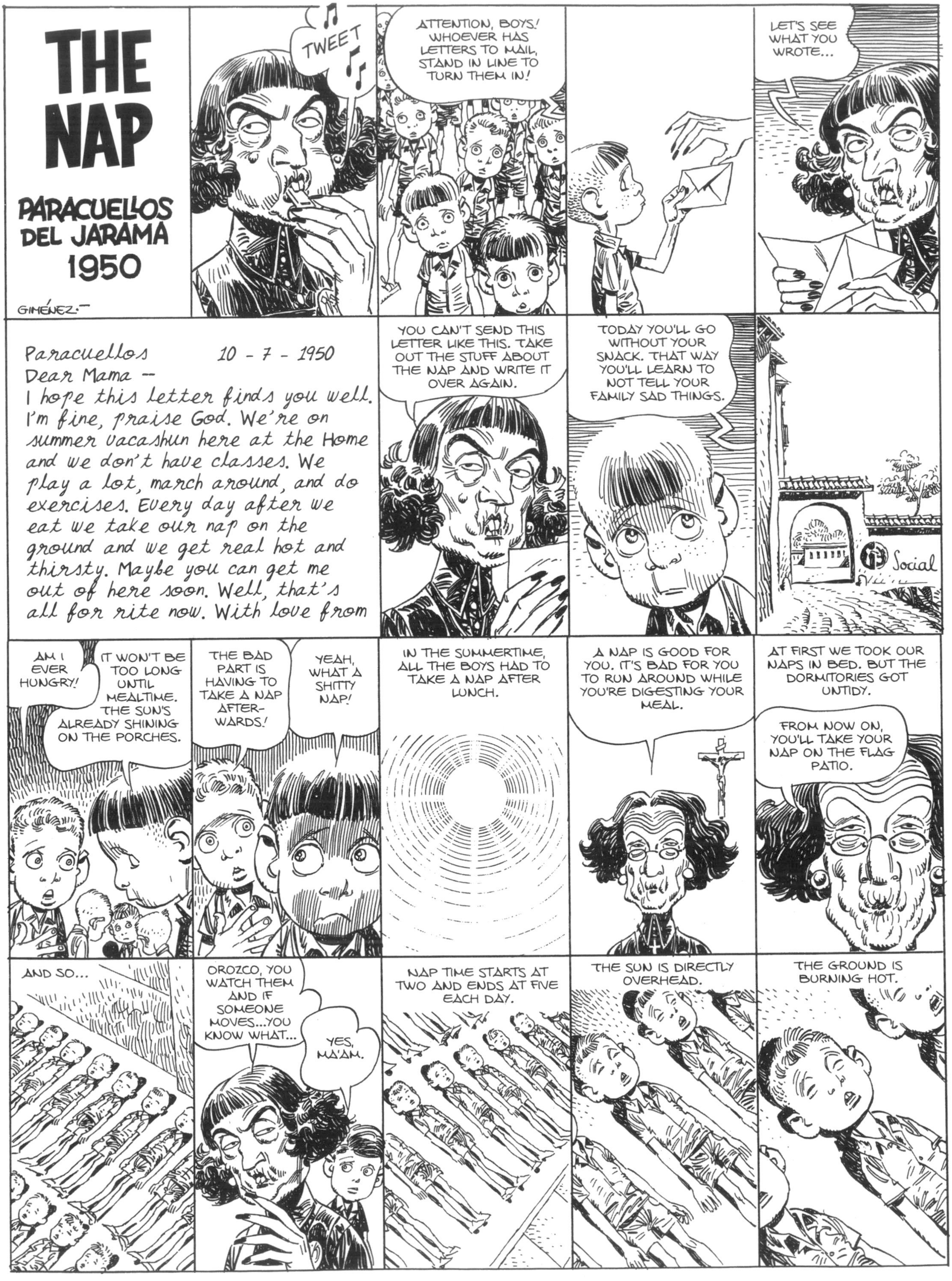
THE NAP
PARACUELLOS DEL JARAMA 1950
GIMÉNEZ
TWEET
ATTENTION, BOYS! WHOEVER HAS LETTERS TO MAIL, STAND IN LINE TO TURN THEM IN!
LET'S SEE WHAT YOU WROTE...
Paracuellos 10 - 7 - 1950
Dear Mama --
I hope this letter finds you well. I'm fine, praise God. We're on summer vacashun here at the Home and we don't have classes. We play a lot, march around, and do exercises. Every day after we eat we take our nap on the ground and we get real hot and thirsty. Maybe you can get me out of here soon. Well, that's all for rite now. With love from
YOU CAN'T SEND THIS LETTER LIKE THIS. TAKE OUT THE STUFF ABOUT THE NAP AND WRITE IT OVER AGAIN.
TODAY YOU'LL GO WITHOUT YOUR SNACK. THAT WAY YOU'LL LEARN TO NOT TELL YOUR FAMILY SAD THINGS.
Social
AM I EVER HUNGRY!
IT WON'T BE TOO LONG UNTIL MEALTIME. THE SUN'S ALREADY SHINING ON THE PORCHES.
THE BAD PART IS HAVING TO TAKE A NAP AFTER-WARDS!
YEAH, WHAT A SHITTY NAP!
IN THE SUMMERTIME, ALL THE BOYS HAD TO TAKE A NAP AFTER LUNCH.
A NAP IS GOOD FOR YOU. IT'S BAD FOR YOU TO RUN AROUND WHILE YOU'RE DIGESTING YOUR MEAL.
AT FIRST WE TOOK OUR NAPS IN BED. BUT THE DORMITORIES GOT UNTIDY.
FROM NOW ON, YOU'LL TAKE YOUR NAP ON THE FLAG PATIO.
AND SO...
OROZCO, YOU WATCH THEM AND IF SOMEONE MOVES...YOU KNOW WHAT...
YES, MA'AM.
NAP TIME STARTS AT TWO AND ENDS AT FIVE EACH DAY.
THE SUN IS DIRECTLY OVERHEAD.
THE GROUND IS BURNING HOT.

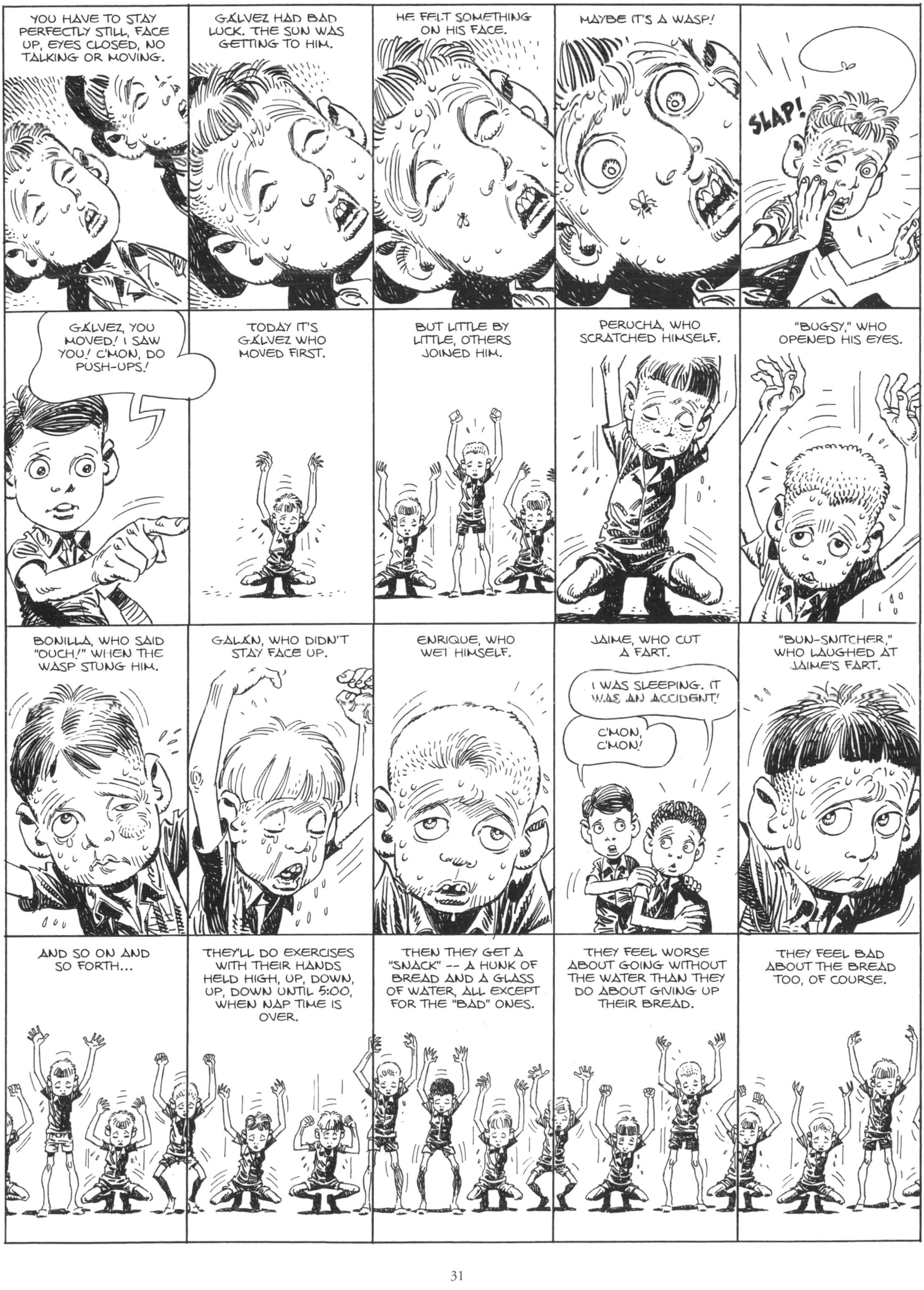
YOU HAVE TO STAY PERFECTLY STILL, FACE UP, EYES CLOSED, NO TALKING OR MOVING.
GÁLVEZ HAD BAD LUCK. THE SUN WAS GETTING TO HIM.
HE FELT SOMETHING ON HIS FACE.
MAYBE IT'S A WASP!
SLAP!
GÁLVEZ, YOU MOVED! I SAW YOU! C'MON, DO PUSH-UPS!
TODAY IT'S GÁLVEZ WHO MOVED FIRST.
BUT LITTLE BY LITTLE, OTHERS JOINED HIM.
PERUCHA, WHO SCRATCHED HIMSELF.
"BUGSY," WHO OPENED HIS EYES.
BONILLA, WHO SAID "OUCH!" WHEN THE WASP STUNG HIM.
GALÁN, WHO DIDN'T STAY FACE UP.
ENRIQUE, WHO WET HIMSELF.
JAIME, WHO CUT A FART.
I WAS SLEEPING. IT WAS AN ACCIDENT!
C'MON, C'MON!
"BUN-SNITCHER," WHO LAUGHED AT JAIME'S FART.
AND SO ON AND SO FORTH...
THEY'LL DO EXERCISES WITH THEIR HANDS HELD HIGH, UP, DOWN, UP, DOWN UNTIL 5:00, WHEN NAP TIME IS OVER.
THEN THEY GET A "SNACK" -- A HUNK OF BREAD AND A GLASS OF WATER, ALL EXCEPT FOR THE "BAD" ONES.
THEY FEEL WORSE ABOUT GOING WITHOUT THE WATER THAN THEY DO ABOUT GIVING UP THEIR BREAD.
THEY FEEL BAD ABOUT THE BREAD TOO, OF COURSE.

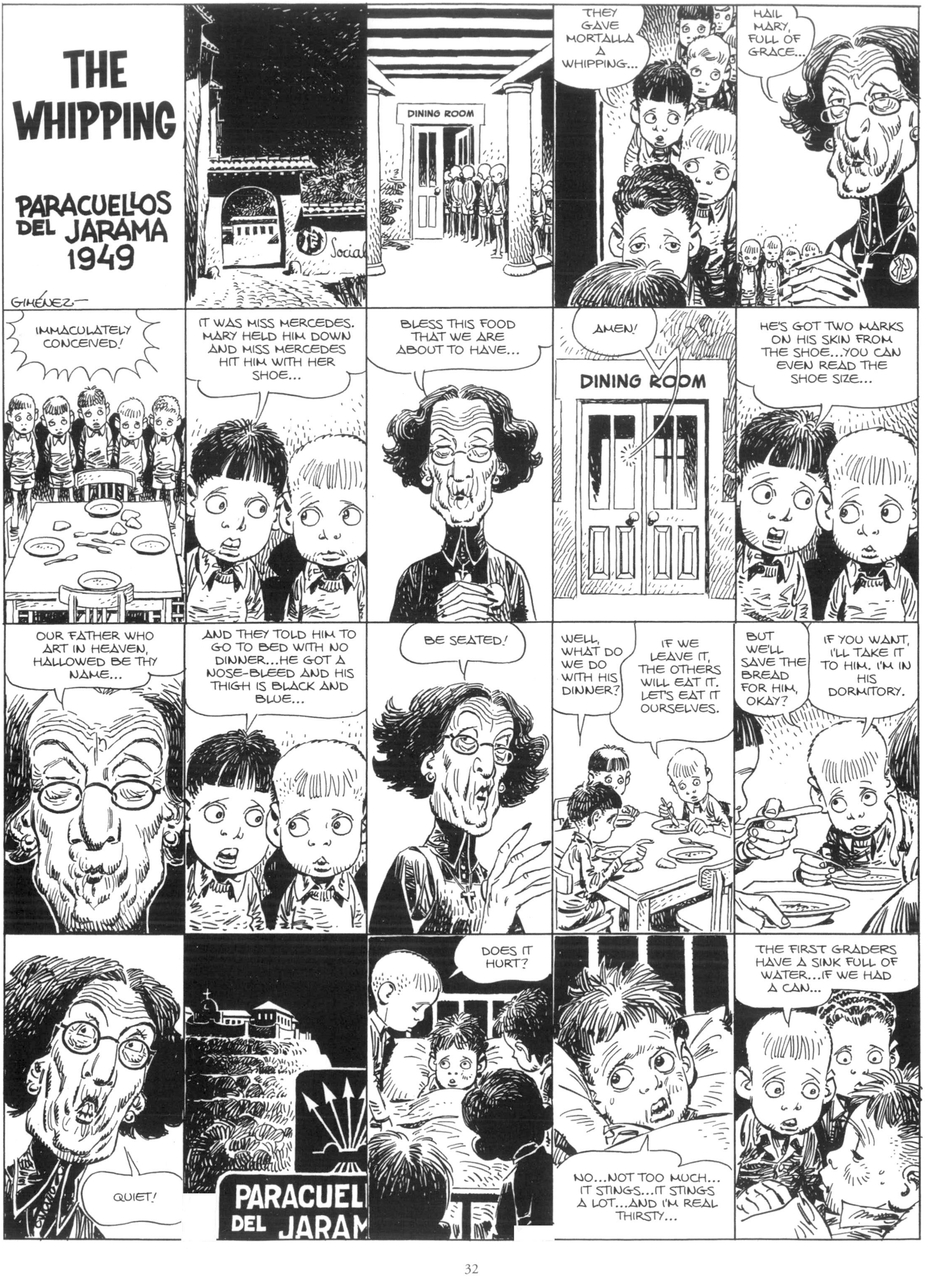
THE WHIPPING
PARACUELLOS DEL JARAMA 1949
GIMÉNEZ
DINING ROOM
THEY GAVE MORTALLA A WHIPPING...
HAIL MARY, FULL OF GRACE...
IMMACULATELY CONCEIVED!
IT WAS MISS MERCEDES. MARY HELD HIM DOWN AND MISS MERCEDES HIT HIM WITH HER SHOE...
BLESS THIS FOOD THAT WE ARE ABOUT TO HAVE...
AMEN!
DINING ROOM
HE'S GOT TWO MARKS ON HIS SKIN FROM THE SHOE...YOU CAN EVEN READ THE SHOE SIZE...
OUR FATHER WHO ART IN HEAVEN, HALLOWED BE THY NAME...
AND THEY TOLD HIM TO GO TO BED WITH NO DINNER...HE GOT A NOSE-BLEED AND HIS THIGH IS BLACK AND BLUE...
BE SEATED!
WELL, WHAT DO WE DO WITH HIS DINNER?
IF WE LEAVE IT, THE OTHERS WILL EAT IT. LET'S EAT IT OURSELVES.
BUT WE'LL SAVE THE BREAD FOR HIM, OKAY?
IF YOU WANT, I'LL TAKE IT TO HIM. I'M IN HIS DORMITORY.
QUIET!
PARACUELL
DEL JARAM
DOES IT HURT?
NO...NOT TOO MUCH...IT STINGS...IT STINGS A LOT...AND I'M REAL THIRSTY...
THE FIRST GRADERS HAVE A SINK FULL OF WATER...IF WE HAD A CAN...

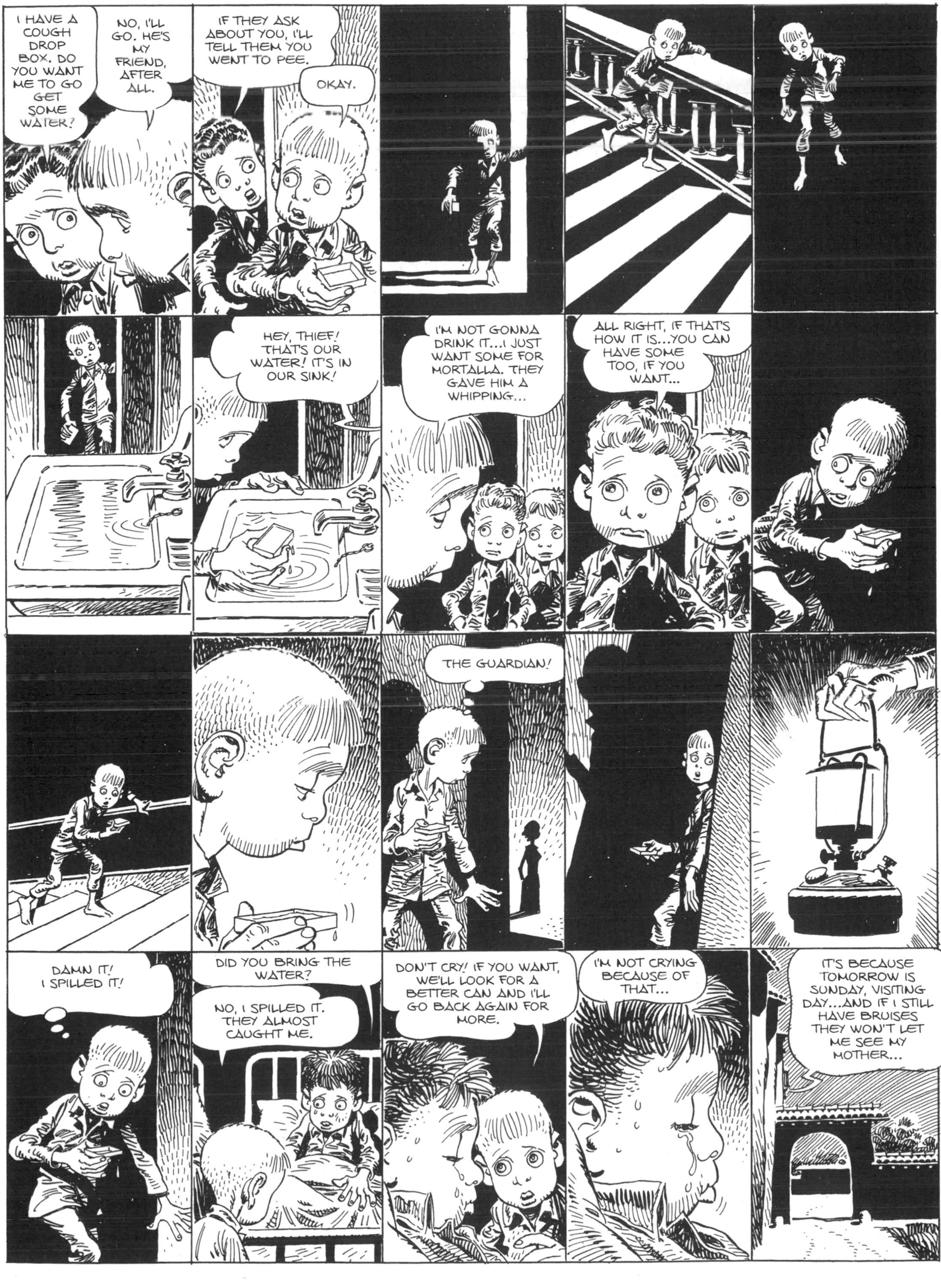

I HAVE A COUGH DROP BOX. DO YOU WANT ME TO GO GET SOME WATER?
NO, I'LL GO. HE'S MY FRIEND, AFTER ALL.
IF THEY ASK ABOUT YOU, I'LL TELL THEM YOU WENT TO PEE.
OKAY.
HEY, THIEF! THAT'S OUR WATER! IT'S IN OUR SINK!
I'M NOT GONNA DRINK IT...I JUST WANT SOME FOR MORTALLA. THEY GAVE HIM A WHIPPING...
ALL RIGHT, IF THAT'S HOW IT IS...YOU CAN HAVE SOME TOO, IF YOU WANT...
THE GUARDIAN!
DAMN IT! I SPILLED IT!
DID YOU BRING THE WATER?
NO, I SPILLED IT. THEY ALMOST CAUGHT ME.
DON'T CRY! IF YOU WANT, WE'LL LOOK FOR A BETTER CAN AND I'LL GO BACK AGAIN FOR MORE.
I'M NOT CRYING BECAUSE OF THAT...
IT'S BECAUSE TOMORROW IS SUNDAY, VISITING DAY...AND IF I STILL HAVE BRUISES THEY WON'T LET ME SEE MY MOTHER...

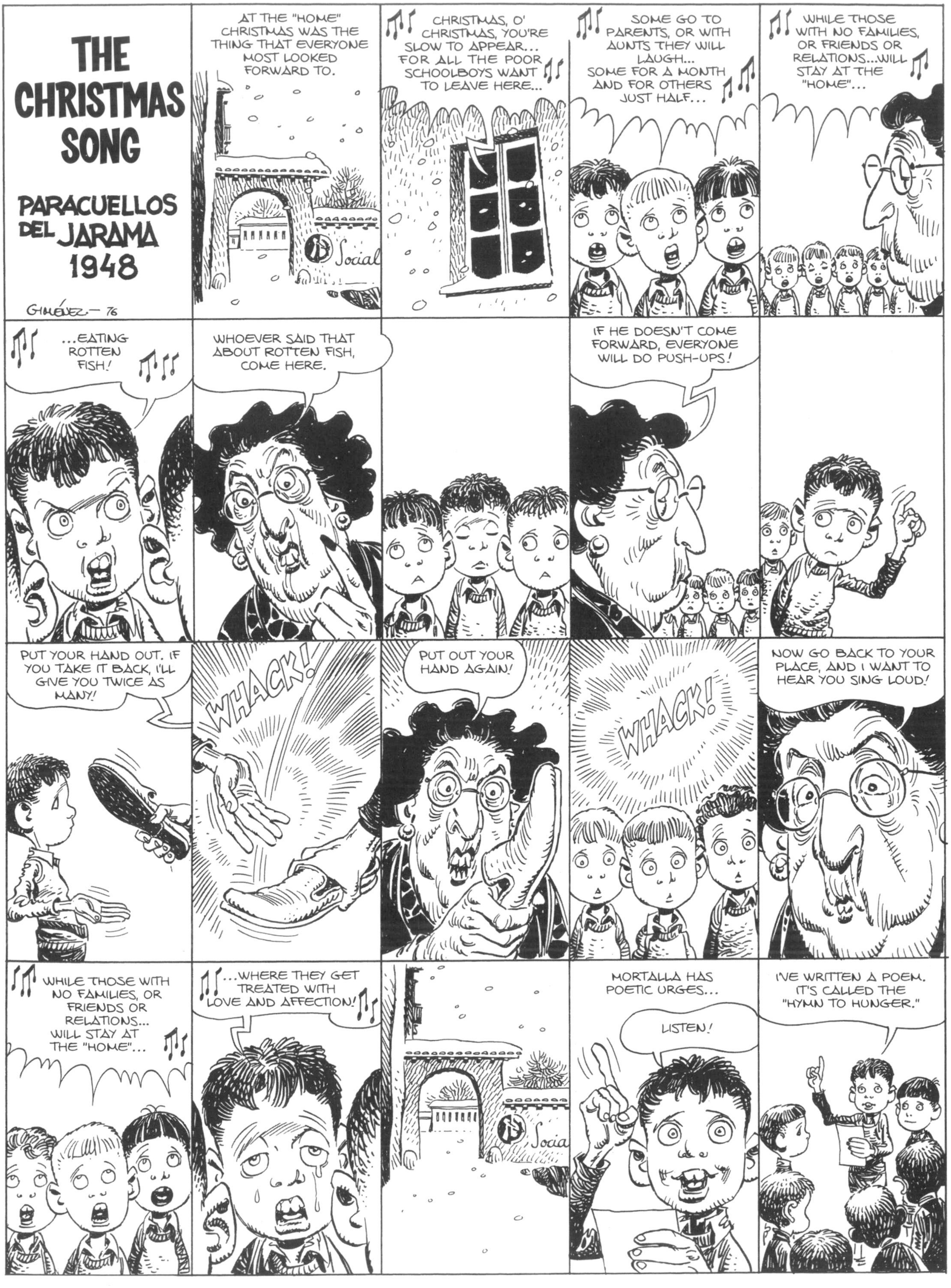
THE CHRISTMAS SONG
PARACUELLOS DEL JARAMA 1948
GIMÉNEZ — 76
AT THE "HOME" CHRISTMAS WAS THE THING THAT EVERYONE MOST LOOKED FORWARD TO.
Social
CHRISTMAS, O' CHRISTMAS, YOU'RE SLOW TO APPEAR... FOR ALL THE POOR SCHOOLBOYS WANT TO LEAVE HERE...
SOME GO TO PARENTS, OR WITH AUNTS THEY WILL LAUGH... SOME FOR A MONTH AND FOR OTHERS JUST HALF...
WHILE THOSE WITH NO FAMILIES, OR FRIENDS OR RELATIONS...WILL STAY AT THE "HOME"...
...EATING ROTTEN FISH!
WHOEVER SAID THAT ABOUT ROTTEN FISH, COME HERE.
IF HE DOESN'T COME FORWARD, EVERYONE WILL DO PUSH-UPS!
PUT YOUR HAND OUT. IF YOU TAKE IT BACK, I'LL GIVE YOU TWICE AS MANY!
WHACK!
PUT OUT YOUR HAND AGAIN!
WHACK!
NOW GO BACK TO YOUR PLACE, AND I WANT TO HEAR YOU SING LOUD!
WHILE THOSE WITH NO FAMILIES, OR FRIENDS OR RELATIONS... WILL STAY AT THE "HOME"...
...WHERE THEY GET TREATED WITH LOVE AND AFFECTION!
Social
MORTALLA HAS POETIC URGES...
LISTEN!
I'VE WRITTEN A POEM. IT'S CALLED THE "HYMN TO HUNGER."

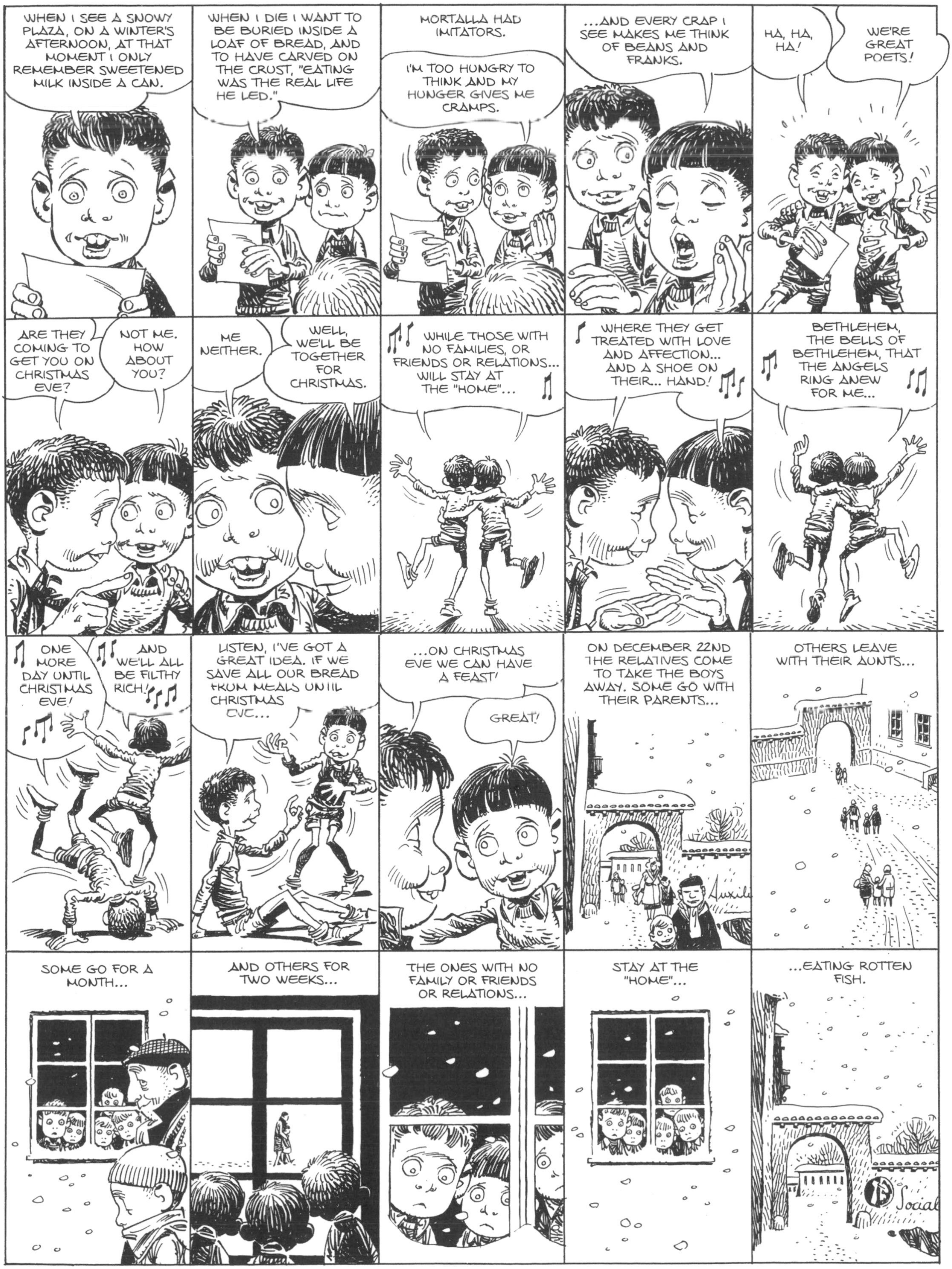
WHEN I SEE A SNOWY PLAZA, ON A WINTER'S AFTERNOON, AT THAT MOMENT I ONLY REMEMBER SWEETENED MILK INSIDE A CAN.
WHEN I DIE I WANT TO BE BURIED INSIDE A LOAF OF BREAD, AND TO HAVE CARVED ON THE CRUST, "EATING WAS THE REAL LIFE HE LED."
MORTALLA HAD IMITATORS.
I'M TOO HUNGRY TO THINK AND MY HUNGER GIVES ME CRAMPS.
...AND EVERY CRAP I SEE MAKES ME THINK OF BEANS AND FRANKS.
HA, HA, HA!
WE'RE GREAT POETS!
ARE THEY COMING TO GET YOU ON CHRISTMAS EVE?
NOT ME. HOW ABOUT YOU?
ME NEITHER.
WELL, WE'LL BE TOGETHER FOR CHRISTMAS.
WHILE THOSE WITH NO FAMILIES, OR FRIENDS OR RELATIONS... WILL STAY AT THE "HOME"...
WHERE THEY GET TREATED WITH LOVE AND AFFECTION... AND A SHOE ON THEIR... HAND!
BETHLEHEM, THE BELLS OF BETHLEHEM, THAT THE ANGELS RING ANEW FOR ME...
ONE MORE DAY UNTIL CHRISTMAS EVE!
AND WE'LL ALL BE FILTHY RICH!
LISTEN, I'VE GOT A GREAT IDEA. IF WE SAVE ALL OUR BREAD FROM MEALS UNTIL CHRISTMAS EVE...
...ON CHRISTMAS EVE WE CAN HAVE A FEAST!
GREAT!
ON DECEMBER 22ND THE RELATIVES COME TO TAKE THE BOYS AWAY. SOME GO WITH THEIR PARENTS...
Auxili
OTHERS LEAVE WITH THEIR AUNTS...
SOME GO FOR A MONTH...
AND OTHERS FOR TWO WEEKS...
THE ONES WITH NO FAMILY OR FRIENDS OR RELATIONS...
STAY AT THE "HOME"...
...EATING ROTTEN FISH.
Social

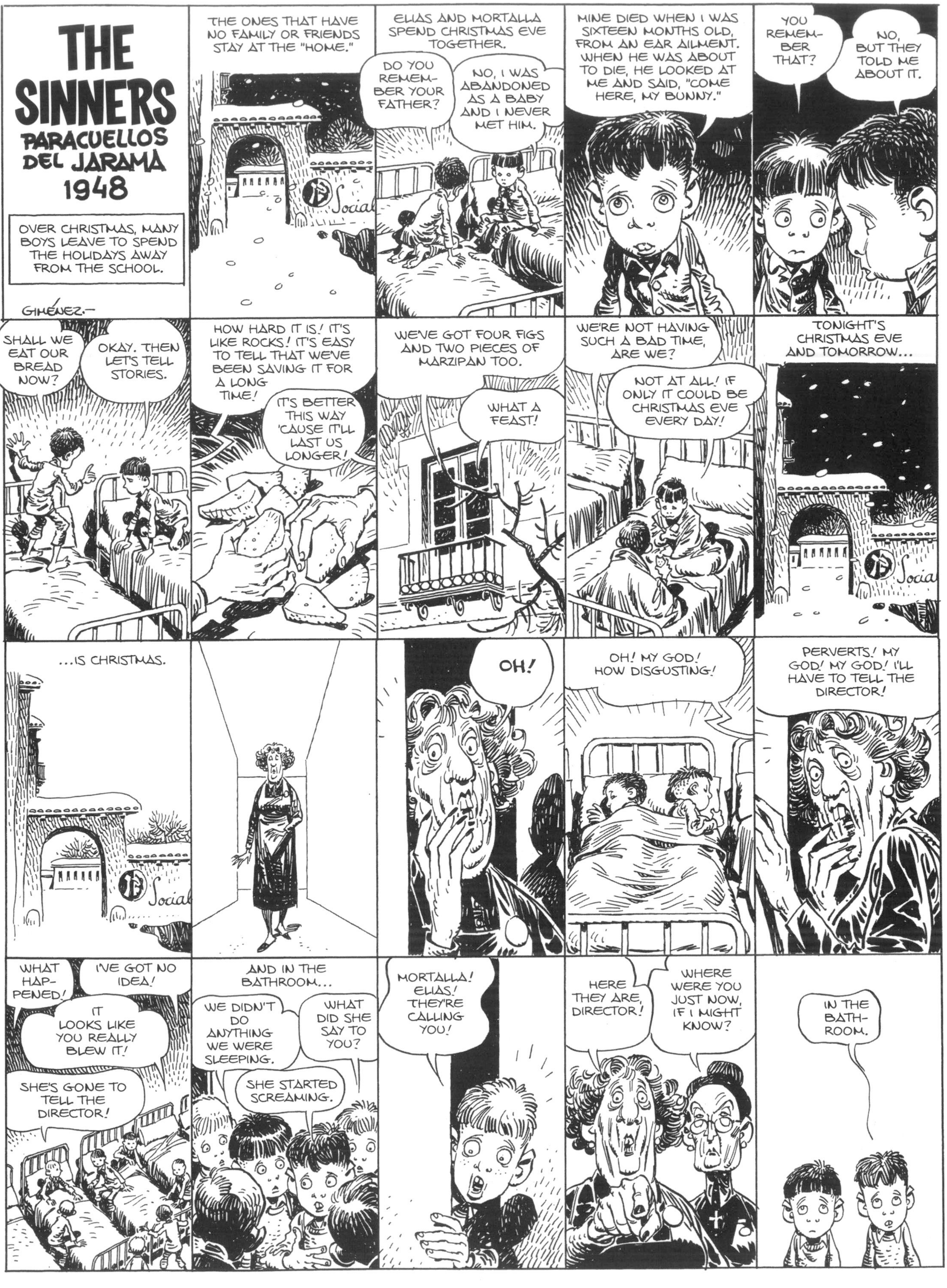
THE SINNERS
PARACUELLOS DEL JARAMA
1948
OVER CHRISTMAS, MANY BOYS LEAVE TO SPEND THE HOLIDAYS AWAY FROM THE SCHOOL.
GIMÉNEZ.-
THE ONES THAT HAVE NO FAMILY OR FRIENDS STAY AT THE "HOME."
ELIAS AND MORTALLA SPEND CHRISTMAS EVE TOGETHER.
DO YOU REMEMBER YOUR FATHER?
NO, I WAS ABANDONED AS A BABY AND I NEVER MET HIM.
MINE DIED WHEN I WAS SIXTEEN MONTHS OLD, FROM AN EAR AILMENT. WHEN HE WAS ABOUT TO DIE, HE LOOKED AT ME AND SAID, "COME HERE, MY BUNNY."
YOU REMEMBER THAT?
NO, BUT THEY TOLD ME ABOUT IT.
SHALL WE EAT OUR BREAD NOW?
OKAY. THEN LET'S TELL STORIES.
HOW HARD IT IS! IT'S LIKE ROCKS! IT'S EASY TO TELL THAT WE'VE BEEN SAVING IT FOR A LONG TIME!
IT'S BETTER THIS WAY 'CAUSE IT'LL LAST US LONGER!
WE'VE GOT FOUR FIGS AND TWO PIECES OF MARZIPAN TOO.
WHAT A FEAST!
WE'RE NOT HAVING SUCH A BAD TIME, ARE WE?
NOT AT ALL! IF ONLY IT COULD BE CHRISTMAS EVE EVERY DAY!
TONIGHT'S CHRISTMAS EVE AND TOMORROW...
...IS CHRISTMAS.
OH!
OH! MY GOD! HOW DISGUSTING!
PERVERTS! MY GOD! I'LL HAVE TO TELL THE DIRECTOR!
WHAT HAPPENED!
I'VE GOT NO IDEA!
IT LOOKS LIKE YOU REALLY BLEW IT!
SHE'S GONE TO TELL THE DIRECTOR!
AND IN THE BATHROOM...
WE DIDN'T DO ANYTHING WE WERE SLEEPING.
WHAT DID SHE SAY TO YOU?
SHE STARTED SCREAMING.
MORTALLA! ELIAS! THEY'RE CALLING YOU!
HERE THEY ARE, DIRECTOR!
WHERE WERE YOU JUST NOW, IF I MIGHT KNOW?
IN THE BATHROOM.

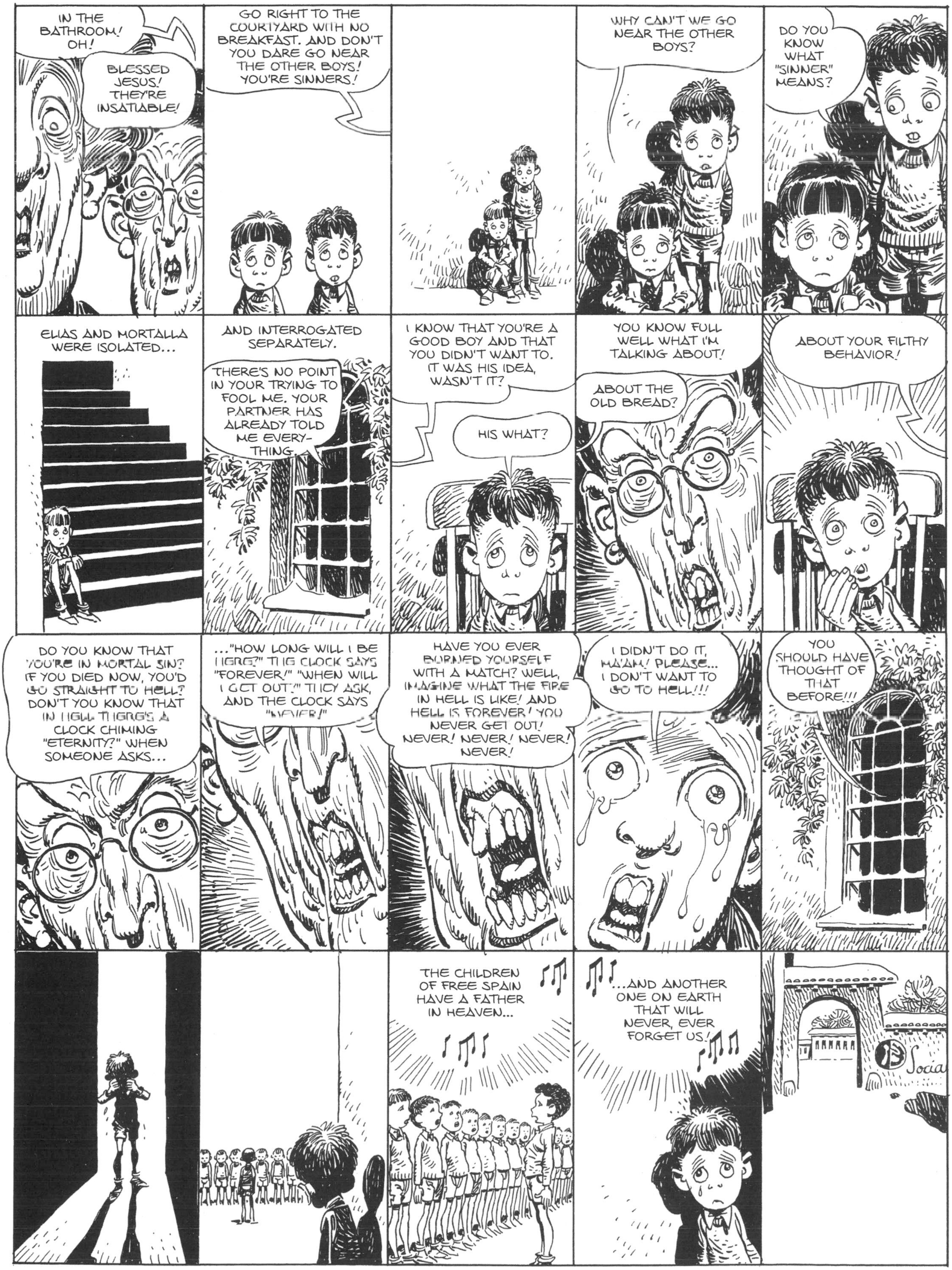

IN THE BATHROOM! OH!
BLESSED JESUS! THEY'RE INSATIABLE!
GO RIGHT TO THE COURTYARD WITH NO BREAKFAST. AND DON'T YOU DARE GO NEAR THE OTHER BOYS! YOU'RE SINNERS!
WHY CAN'T WE GO NEAR THE OTHER BOYS?
DO YOU KNOW WHAT "SINNER" MEANS?
ELIAS AND MORTALLA WERE ISOLATED...
AND INTERROGATED SEPARATELY.
THERE'S NO POINT IN YOUR TRYING TO FOOL ME. YOUR PARTNER HAS ALREADY TOLD ME EVERYTHING.
I KNOW THAT YOU'RE A GOOD BOY AND THAT YOU DIDN'T WANT TO. IT WAS HIS IDEA, WASN'T IT?
HIS WHAT?
YOU KNOW FULL WELL WHAT I'M TALKING ABOUT!
ABOUT THE OLD BREAD?
ABOUT YOUR FILTHY BEHAVIOR!
DO YOU KNOW THAT YOU'RE IN MORTAL SIN? IF YOU DIED NOW, YOU'D GO STRAIGHT TO HELL? DON'T YOU KNOW THAT IN HELL THERE'S A CLOCK CHIMING "ETERNITY?" WHEN SOMEONE ASKS...
..."HOW LONG WILL I BE HERE?" THE CLOCK SAYS "FOREVER!" "WHEN WILL I GET OUT?" THEY ASK, AND THE CLOCK SAYS "NEVER!"
HAVE YOU EVER BURNED YOURSELF WITH A MATCH? WELL, IMAGINE WHAT THE FIRE IN HELL IS LIKE! AND HELL IS FOREVER! YOU NEVER GET OUT! NEVER! NEVER! NEVER! NEVER!
I DIDN'T DO IT, MA'AM! PLEASE... I DON'T WANT TO GO TO HELL!!!
YOU SHOULD HAVE THOUGHT OF THAT BEFORE!!!
THE CHILDREN OF FREE SPAIN HAVE A FATHER IN HEAVEN...
...AND ANOTHER ONE ON EARTH THAT WILL NEVER, EVER FORGET US!

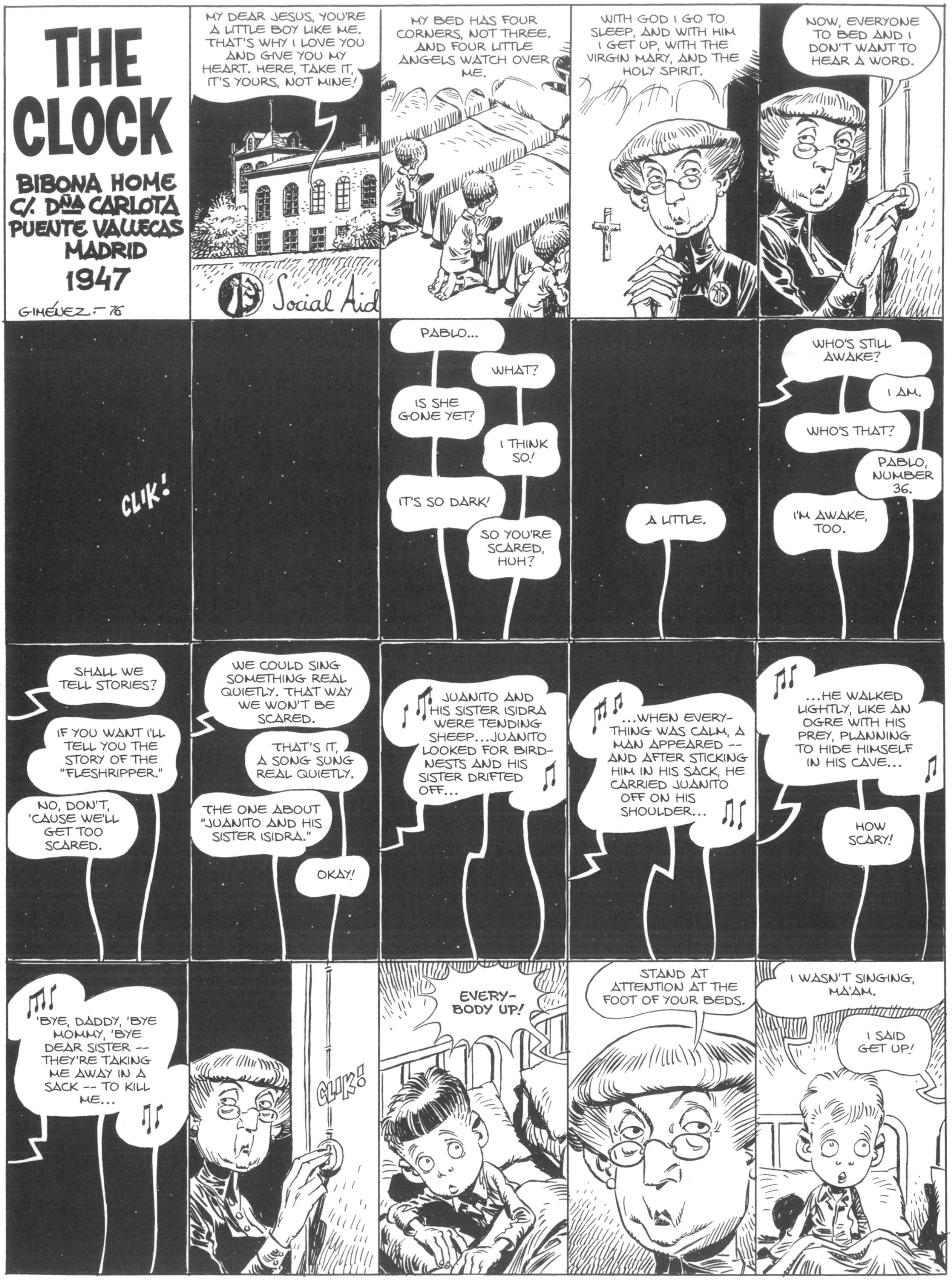
THE CLOCK
BIBONA HOME
C/. DÑA CARLOTA
PUENTE VALLECAS
MADRID
1947
GIMÉNEZ - 76
MY DEAR JESUS, YOU'RE A LITTLE BOY LIKE ME. THAT'S WHY I LOVE YOU AND GIVE YOU MY HEART. HERE, TAKE IT, IT'S YOURS, NOT MINE!
Social Aid
MY BED HAS FOUR CORNERS, NOT THREE. AND FOUR LITTLE ANGELS WATCH OVER ME.
WITH GOD I GO TO SLEEP, AND WITH HIM I GET UP, WITH THE VIRGIN MARY, AND THE HOLY SPIRIT.
NOW, EVERYONE TO BED AND I DON'T WANT TO HEAR A WORD.
CLIK!
PABLO...
WHAT?
IS SHE GONE YET?
I THINK SO!
IT'S SO DARK!
SO YOU'RE SCARED, HUH?
A LITTLE.
WHO'S STILL AWAKE?
I AM.
WHO'S THAT?
PABLO, NUMBER 36.
I'M AWAKE, TOO.
SHALL WE TELL STORIES?
IF YOU WANT I'LL TELL YOU THE STORY OF THE "FLESHRIPPER."
NO, DON'T, 'CAUSE WE'LL GET TOO SCARED.
WE COULD SING SOMETHING REAL QUIETLY. THAT WAY WE WON'T BE SCARED.
THAT'S IT, A SONG SUNG REAL QUIETLY.
THE ONE ABOUT "JUANITO AND HIS SISTER ISIDRA."
OKAY!
JUANITO AND HIS SISTER ISIDRA WERE TENDING SHEEP...JUANITO LOOKED FOR BIRD-NESTS AND HIS SISTER DRIFTED OFF...
...WHEN EVERY-THING WAS CALM, A MAN APPEARED -- AND AFTER STICKING HIM IN HIS SACK, HE CARRIED JUANITO OFF ON HIS SHOULDER...
...HE WALKED LIGHTLY, LIKE AN OGRE WITH HIS PREY, PLANNING TO HIDE HIMSELF IN HIS CAVE...
HOW SCARY!
'BYE, DADDY, 'BYE MOMMY, 'BYE DEAR SISTER -- THEY'RE TAKING ME AWAY IN A SACK -- TO KILL ME...
CLIK!
EVERY-BODY UP!
STAND AT ATTENTION AT THE FOOT OF YOUR BEDS.
I WASN'T SINGING, MA'AM.
I SAID GET UP!

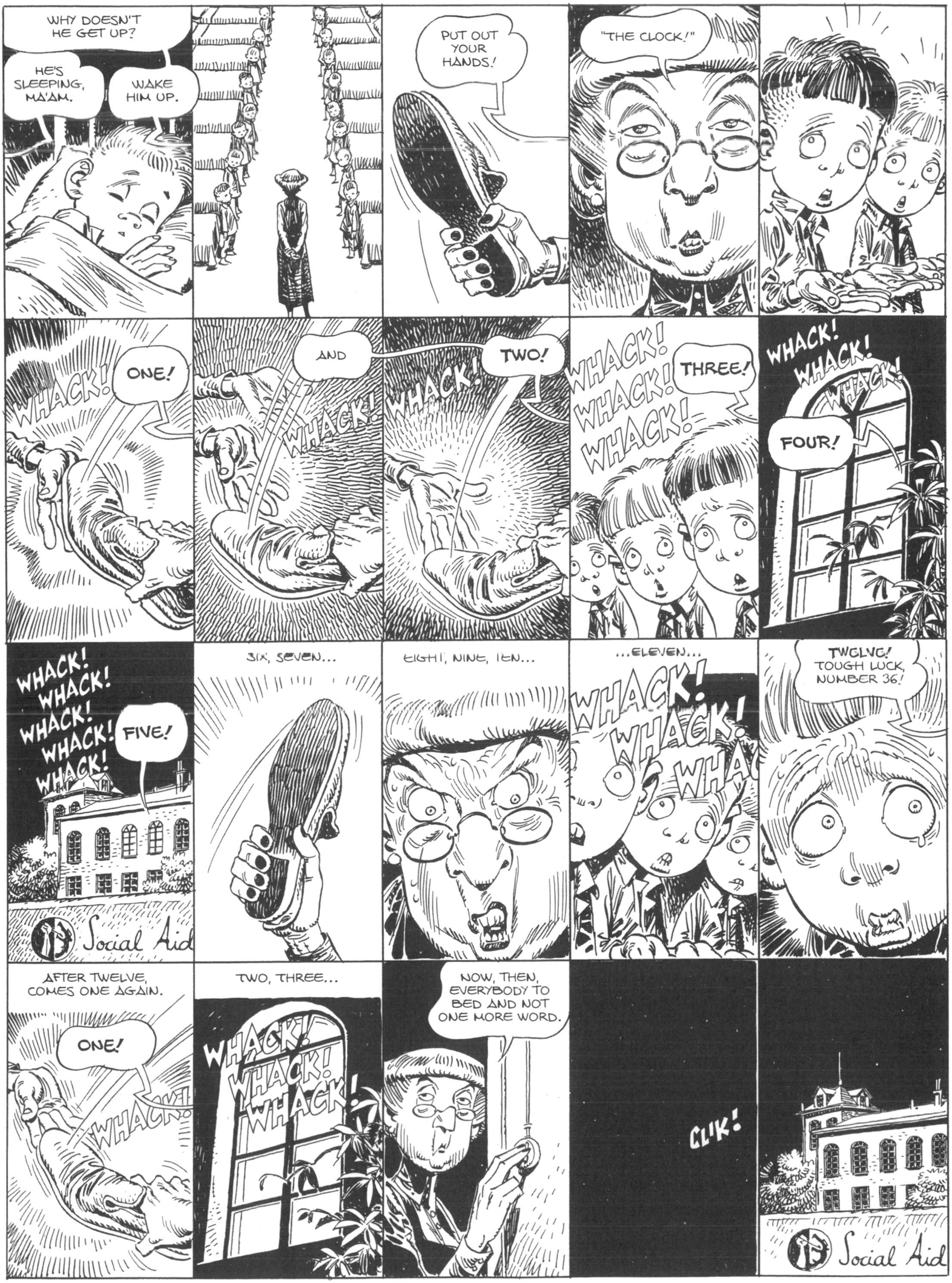
WHY DOESN'T HE GET UP?
HE'S SLEEPING, MA'AM.
WAKE HIM UP.
PUT OUT YOUR HANDS!
"THE CLOCK!"
WHACK!
ONE!
AND
WHACK!
WHACK!
TWO!
WHACK! WHACK! WHACK!
THREE!
WHACK! WHACK! WHACK!
FOUR!
WHACK! WHACK! WHACK! WHACK! WHACK!
FIVE!
Social Aid
SIX, SEVEN...
EIGHT, NINE, TEN...
...ELEVEN...
WHACK! WHACK!
TWELVE! TOUGH LUCK, NUMBER 36!
AFTER TWELVE, COMES ONE AGAIN.
ONE!
TWO, THREE...
WHACK! WHACK! WHACK!
NOW, THEN, EVERYBODY TO BED AND NOT ONE MORE WORD.
CLIK!
Social Aid

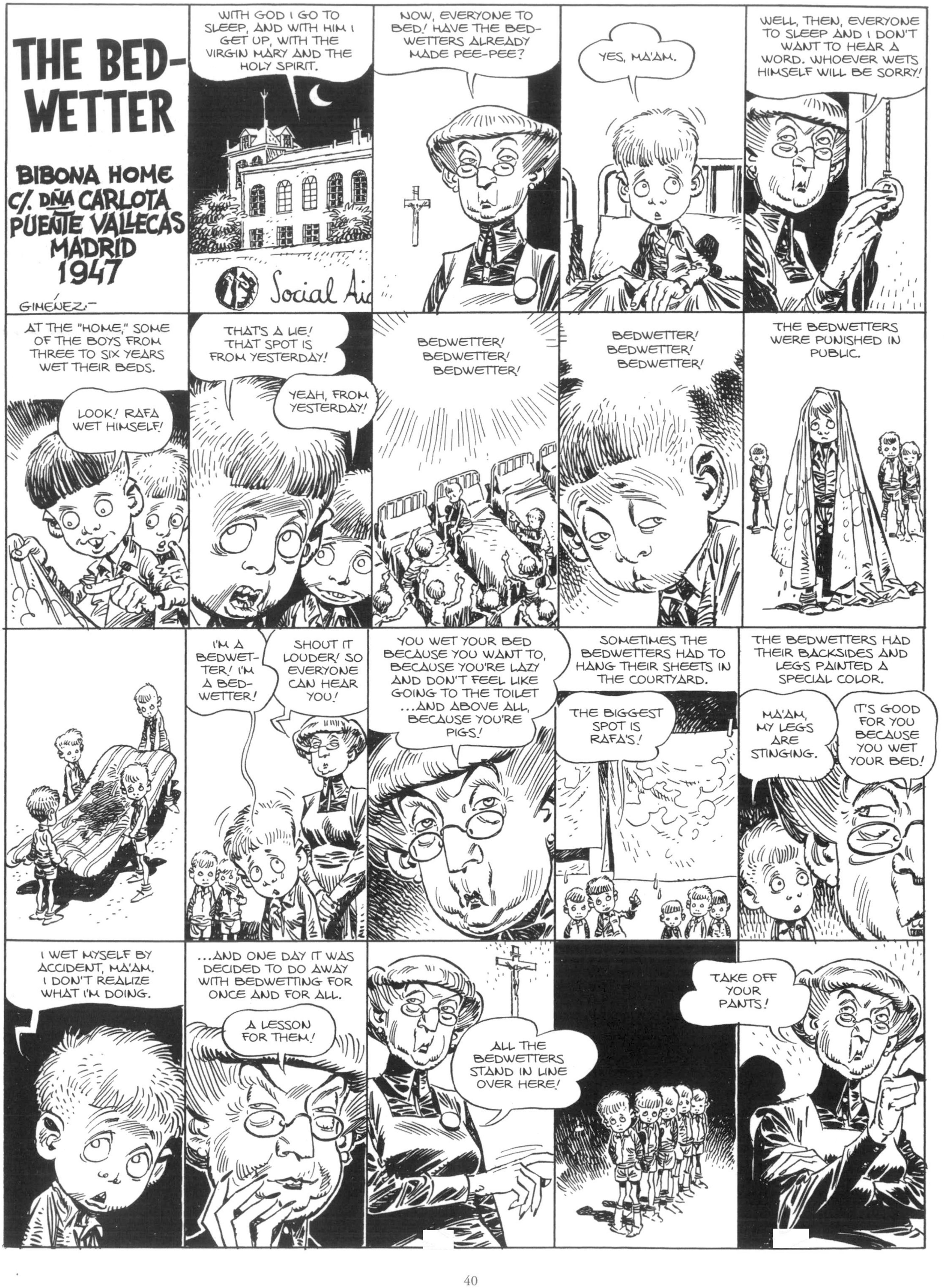
THE BED-WETTER
BIBONA HOME
C/. DÑA CARLOTA
PUENTE VALLECAS
MADRID
1947
GIMÉNEZ
WITH GOD I GO TO SLEEP, AND WITH HIM I GET UP, WITH THE VIRGIN MARY AND THE HOLY SPIRIT.
Social Aid
NOW, EVERYONE TO BED! HAVE THE BED-WETTERS ALREADY MADE PEE-PEE?
YES, MA'AM.
WELL, THEN, EVERYONE TO SLEEP AND I DON'T WANT TO HEAR A WORD. WHOEVER WETS HIMSELF WILL BE SORRY!
AT THE "HOME," SOME OF THE BOYS FROM THREE TO SIX YEARS WET THEIR BEDS.
LOOK! RAFA WET HIMSELF!
THAT'S A LIE! THAT SPOT IS FROM YESTERDAY!
YEAH, FROM YESTERDAY!
BEDWETTER! BEDWETTER! BEDWETTER!
BEDWETTER! BEDWETTER! BEDWETTER!
THE BEDWETTERS WERE PUNISHED IN PUBLIC.
I'M A BEDWETTER! I'M A BEDWETTER!
SHOUT IT LOUDER! SO EVERYONE CAN HEAR YOU!
YOU WET YOUR BED BECAUSE YOU WANT TO, BECAUSE YOU'RE LAZY AND DON'T FEEL LIKE GOING TO THE TOILET ...AND ABOVE ALL, BECAUSE YOU'RE PIGS!
SOMETIMES THE BEDWETTERS HAD TO HANG THEIR SHEETS IN THE COURTYARD.
THE BIGGEST SPOT IS RAFA'S!
THE BEDWETTERS HAD THEIR BACKSIDES AND LEGS PAINTED A SPECIAL COLOR.
MA'AM, MY LEGS ARE STINGING.
IT'S GOOD FOR YOU BECAUSE YOU WET YOUR BED!
I WET MYSELF BY ACCIDENT, MA'AM. I DON'T REALIZE WHAT I'M DOING.
...AND ONE DAY IT WAS DECIDED TO DO AWAY WITH BEDWETTING FOR ONCE AND FOR ALL.
A LESSON FOR THEM!
ALL THE BEDWETTERS STAND IN LINE OVER HERE!
TAKE OFF YOUR PANTS!

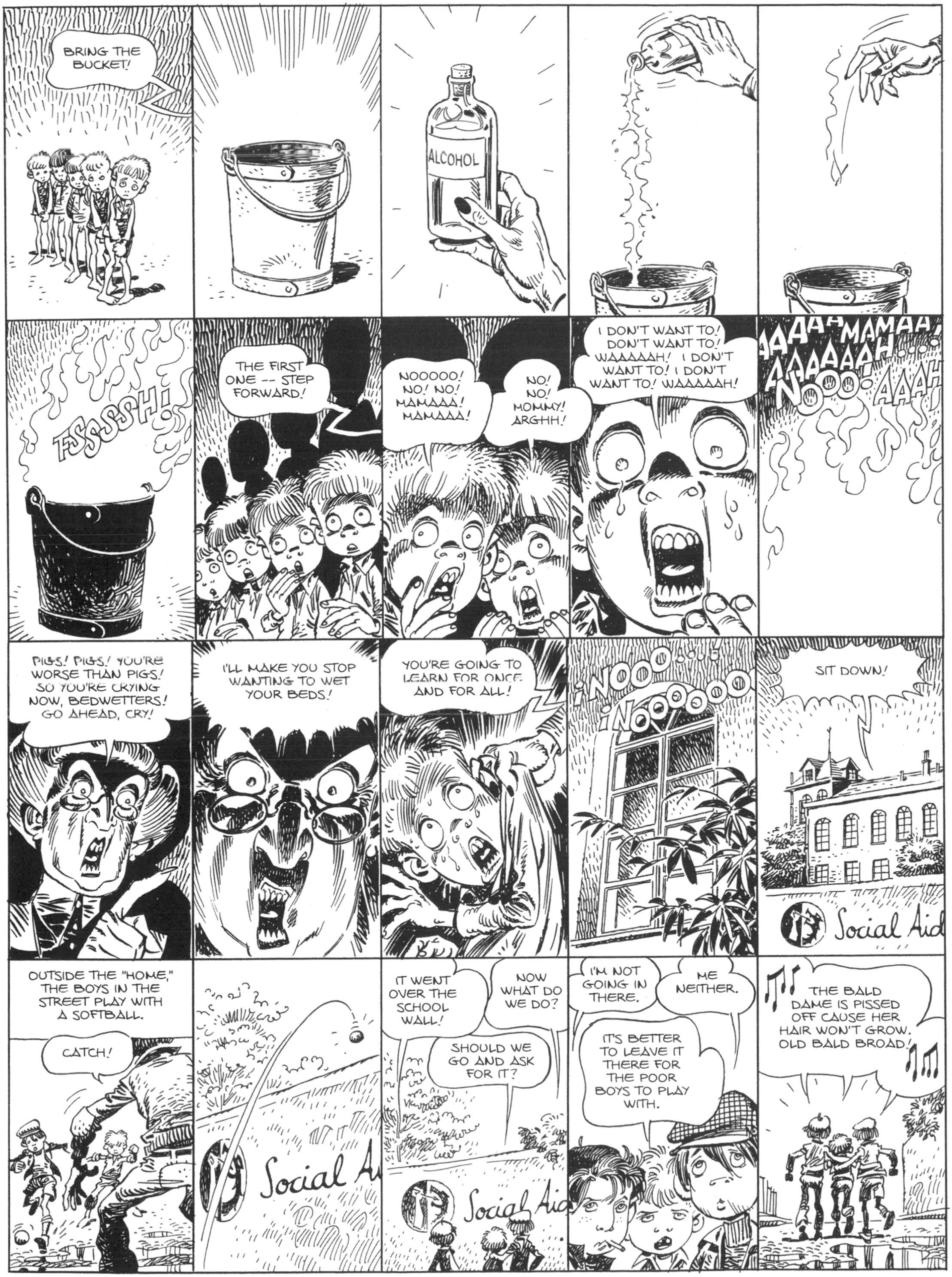
BRING THE BUCKET!
ALCOHOL
FSSSSH!
THE FIRST ONE -- STEP FORWARD!
NOOOOO! NO! NO! MAMAAA! MAMAAA!
NO! NO! MOMMY! ARGHH!
I DON'T WANT TO! DON'T WANT TO! WAAAAAH! I DON'T WANT TO! I DON'T WANT TO! WAAAAAH!
AAAAAMAMAA, AAAAAAH... NOOO! AAAH
PIGS! PIGS! YOU'RE WORSE THAN PIGS! SO YOU'RE CRYING NOW, BEDWETTERS! GO AHEAD, CRY!
I'LL MAKE YOU STOP WANTING TO WET YOUR BEDS!
YOU'RE GOING TO LEARN FOR ONCE AND FOR ALL!
¡NOOO ¡NOOOOOO
SIT DOWN!
Social Aid
OUTSIDE THE "HOME," THE BOYS IN THE STREET PLAY WITH A SOFTBALL.
CATCH!
IT WENT OVER THE SCHOOL WALL!
NOW WHAT DO WE DO?
SHOULD WE GO AND ASK FOR IT?
Social Aid
I'M NOT GOING IN THERE.
ME NEITHER.
IT'S BETTER TO LEAVE IT THERE FOR THE POOR BOYS TO PLAY WITH.
THE BALD DAME IS PISSED OFF CAUSE HER HAIR WON'T GROW. OLD BALD BROAD!

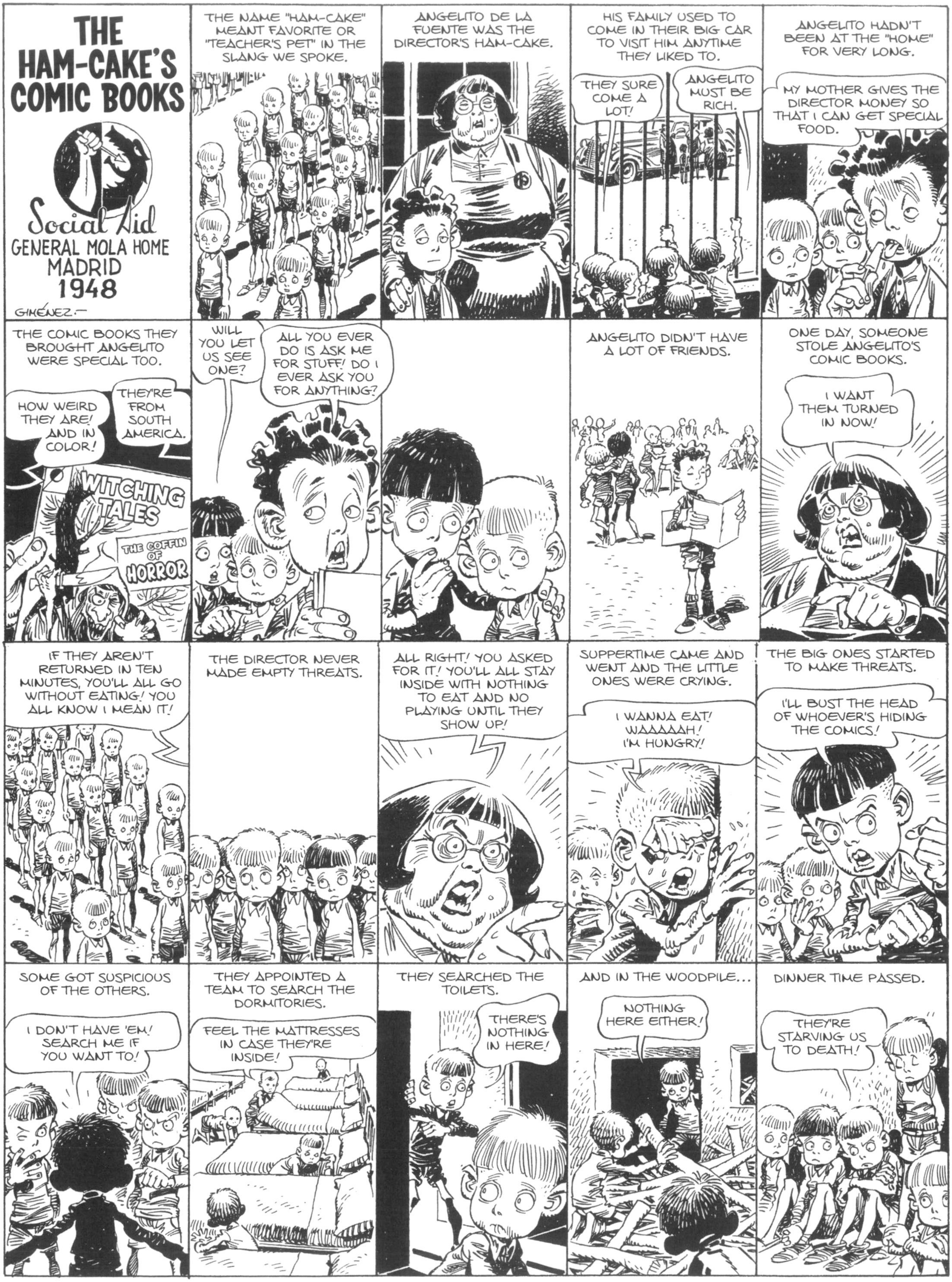
THE HAM-CAKE'S COMIC BOOKS
Social Aid
GENERAL MOLA HOME
MADRID
1948
GIMÉNEZ
THE NAME "HAM-CAKE" MEANT FAVORITE OR "TEACHER'S PET" IN THE SLANG WE SPOKE.
ANGELITO DE LA FUENTE WAS THE DIRECTOR'S HAM-CAKE.
HIS FAMILY USED TO COME IN THEIR BIG CAR TO VISIT HIM ANYTIME THEY LIKED TO.
THEY SURE COME A LOT!
ANGELITO MUST BE RICH.
ANGELITO HADN'T BEEN AT THE "HOME" FOR VERY LONG.
MY MOTHER GIVES THE DIRECTOR MONEY SO THAT I CAN GET SPECIAL FOOD.
THE COMIC BOOKS THEY BROUGHT ANGELITO WERE SPECIAL TOO.
HOW WEIRD THEY ARE! AND IN COLOR!
THEY'RE FROM SOUTH AMERICA.
WITCHING TALES
THE COFFIN OF HORROR
WILL YOU LET US SEE ONE?
ALL YOU EVER DO IS ASK ME FOR STUFF! DO I EVER ASK YOU FOR ANYTHING?
ANGELITO DIDN'T HAVE A LOT OF FRIENDS.
ONE DAY, SOMEONE STOLE ANGELITO'S COMIC BOOKS.
I WANT THEM TURNED IN NOW!
IF THEY AREN'T RETURNED IN TEN MINUTES, YOU'LL ALL GO WITHOUT EATING! YOU ALL KNOW I MEAN IT!
THE DIRECTOR NEVER MADE EMPTY THREATS.
ALL RIGHT! YOU ASKED FOR IT! YOU'LL ALL STAY INSIDE WITH NOTHING TO EAT AND NO PLAYING UNTIL THEY SHOW UP!
SUPPERTIME CAME AND WENT AND THE LITTLE ONES WERE CRYING.
I WANNA EAT! WAAAAAH! I'M HUNGRY!
THE BIG ONES STARTED TO MAKE THREATS.
I'LL BUST THE HEAD OF WHOEVER'S HIDING THE COMICS!
SOME GOT SUSPICIOUS OF THE OTHERS.
I DON'T HAVE 'EM! SEARCH ME IF YOU WANT TO!
THEY APPOINTED A TEAM TO SEARCH THE DORMITORIES.
FEEL THE MATTRESSES IN CASE THEY'RE INSIDE!
THEY SEARCHED THE TOILETS.
THERE'S NOTHING IN HERE!
AND IN THE WOODPILE...
NOTHING HERE EITHER!
DINNER TIME PASSED.
THEY'RE STARVING US TO DEATH!

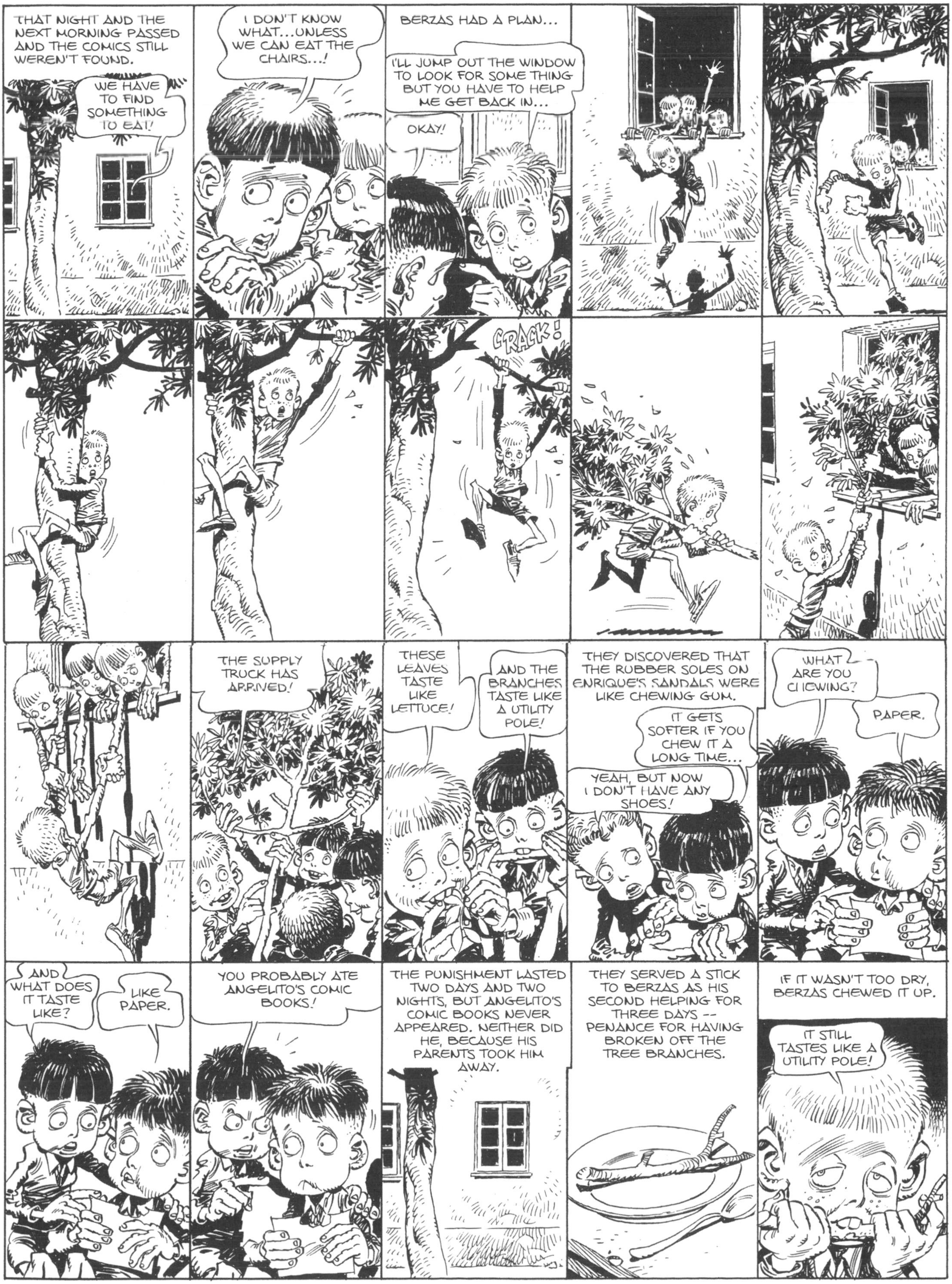
THAT NIGHT AND THE NEXT MORNING PASSED AND THE COMICS STILL WEREN'T FOUND.
WE HAVE TO FIND SOMETHING TO EAT!
I DON'T KNOW WHAT...UNLESS WE CAN EAT THE CHAIRS...!
BERZAS HAD A PLAN...
I'LL JUMP OUT THE WINDOW TO LOOK FOR SOME THING BUT YOU HAVE TO HELP ME GET BACK IN...
OKAY!
CRACK!
THE SUPPLY TRUCK HAS ARRIVED!
THESE LEAVES TASTE LIKE LETTUCE!
AND THE BRANCHES TASTE LIKE A UTILITY POLE!
THEY DISCOVERED THAT THE RUBBER SOLES ON ENRIQUE'S SANDALS WERE LIKE CHEWING GUM.
IT GETS SOFTER IF YOU CHEW IT A LONG TIME...
YEAH, BUT NOW I DON'T HAVE ANY SHOES!
WHAT ARE YOU CHEWING?
PAPER.
AND WHAT DOES IT TASTE LIKE?
LIKE PAPER.
YOU PROBABLY ATE ANGELITO'S COMIC BOOKS!
THE PUNISHMENT LASTED TWO DAYS AND TWO NIGHTS, BUT ANGELITO'S COMIC BOOKS NEVER APPEARED. NEITHER DID HE, BECAUSE HIS PARENTS TOOK HIM AWAY.
THEY SERVED A STICK TO BERZAS AS HIS SECOND HELPING FOR THREE DAYS -- PENANCE FOR HAVING BROKEN OFF THE TREE BRANCHES.
IF IT WASN'T TOO DRY, BERZAS CHEWED IT UP.
IT STILL TASTES LIKE A UTILITY POLE!

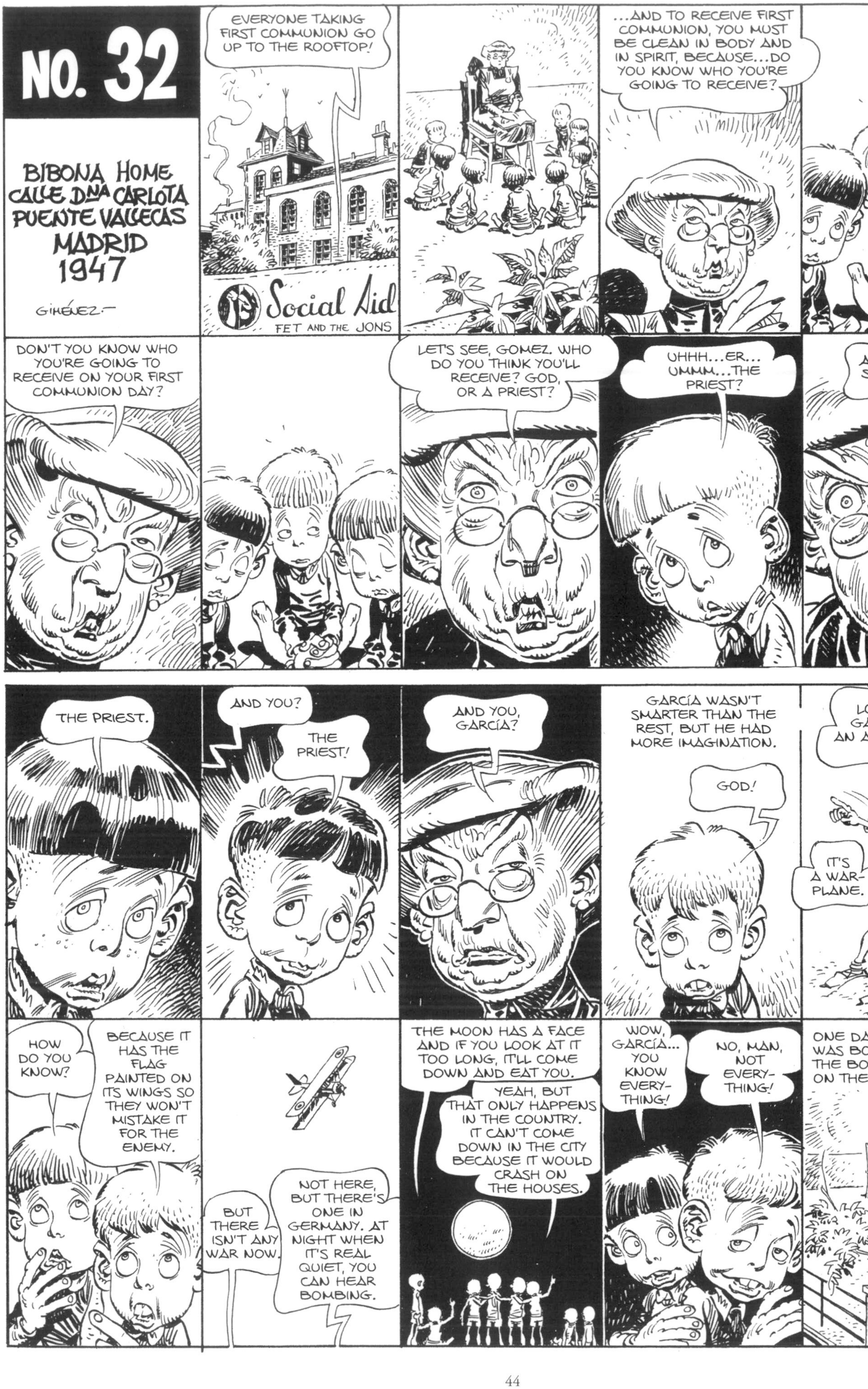
NO. 32
BIBONA HOME
CALLE DNA CARLOTA
PUENTE VALLECAS
MADRID
1947
GIMÉNEZ
EVERYONE TAKING FIRST COMMUNION GO UP TO THE ROOFTOP!
Social Aid
FET AND THE JONS
...AND TO RECEIVE FIRST COMMUNION, YOU MUST BE CLEAN IN BODY AND IN SPIRIT, BECAUSE...DO YOU KNOW WHO YOU'RE GOING TO RECEIVE?
DON'T YOU KNOW WHO YOU'RE GOING TO RECEIVE ON YOUR FIRST COMMUNION DAY?
LET'S SEE, GOMEZ. WHO DO YOU THINK YOU'LL RECEIVE? GOD, OR A PRIEST?
UHHH...ER... UMMM...THE PRIEST?
AND YOU, SANCHEZ?
THE PRIEST.
AND YOU?
THE PRIEST!
AND YOU, GARCÍA?
GARCÍA WASN'T SMARTER THAN THE REST, BUT HE HAD MORE IMAGINATION.
GOD!
LOOK, GARCÍA, AN AIRPLANE!
IT'S A WAR-PLANE.
HOW DO YOU KNOW?
BECAUSE IT HAS THE FLAG PAINTED ON ITS WINGS SO THEY WON'T MISTAKE IT FOR THE ENEMY.
BUT THERE ISN'T ANY WAR NOW.
NOT HERE, BUT THERE'S ONE IN GERMANY. AT NIGHT WHEN IT'S REAL QUIET, YOU CAN HEAR BOMBING.
THE MOON HAS A FACE AND IF YOU LOOK AT IT TOO LONG, IT'LL COME DOWN AND EAT YOU.
YEAH, BUT THAT ONLY HAPPENS IN THE COUNTRY. IT CAN'T COME DOWN IN THE CITY BECAUSE IT WOULD CRASH ON THE HOUSES.
WOW, GARCÍA... YOU KNOW EVERY-THING!
NO, MAN, NOT EVERY-THING!
ONE DAY THE GUARDIAN WAS BORED. SHE MADE THE BOYS GET INTO LINE ON THE ROOFTOP...

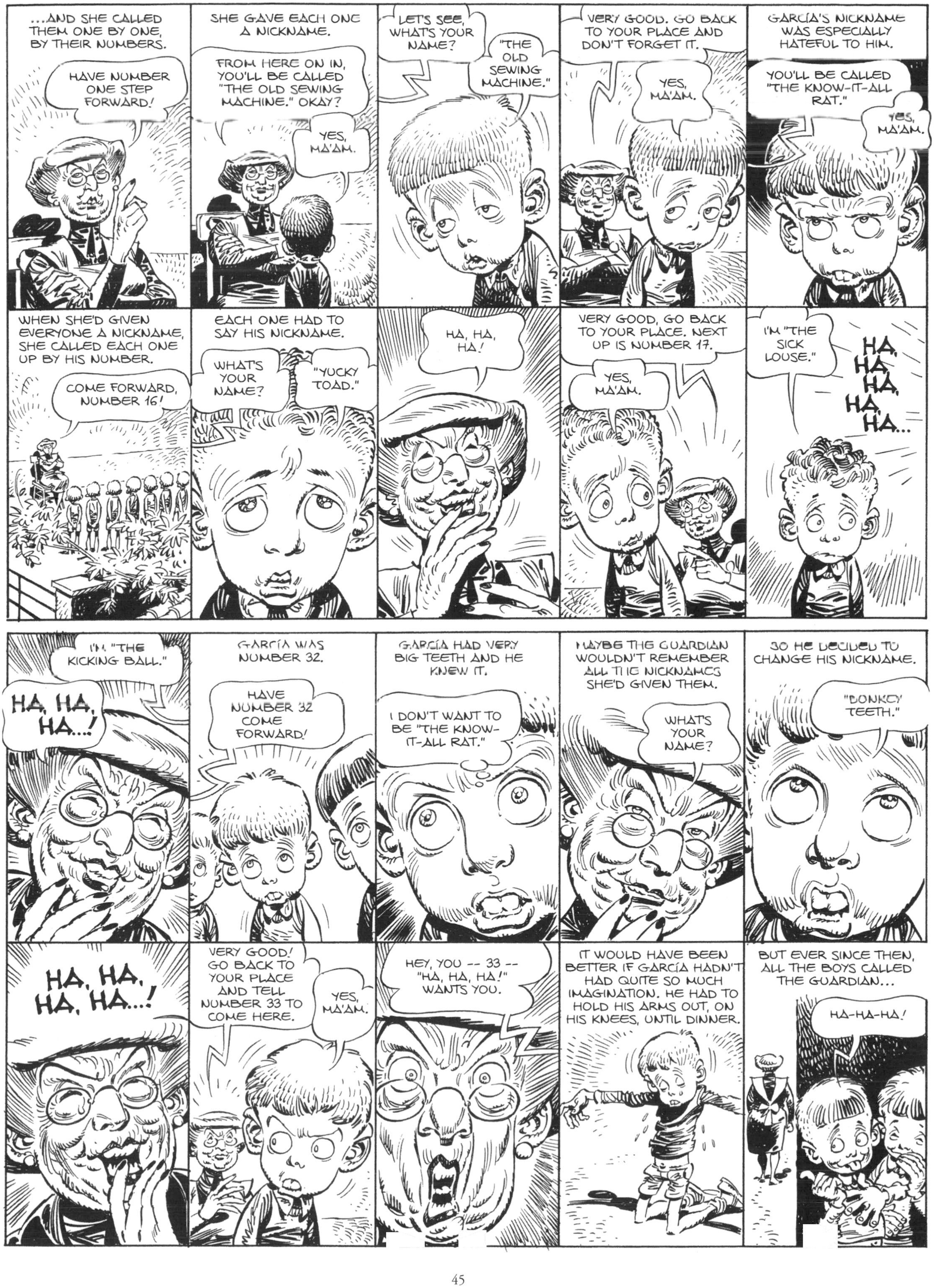
...AND SHE CALLED THEM ONE BY ONE, BY THEIR NUMBERS.
HAVE NUMBER ONE STEP FORWARD!
SHE GAVE EACH ONE A NICKNAME.
FROM HERE ON IN, YOU'LL BE CALLED "THE OLD SEWING MACHINE." OKAY?
YES, MA'AM.
LET'S SEE, WHAT'S YOUR NAME?
"THE OLD SEWING MACHINE."
VERY GOOD. GO BACK TO YOUR PLACE AND DON'T FORGET IT.
YES, MA'AM.
GARCÍA'S NICKNAME WAS ESPECIALLY HATEFUL TO HIM.
YOU'LL BE CALLED "THE KNOW-IT-ALL RAT."
YES, MA'AM.
WHEN SHE'D GIVEN EVERYONE A NICKNAME, SHE CALLED EACH ONE UP BY HIS NUMBER.
COME FORWARD, NUMBER 16!
EACH ONE HAD TO SAY HIS NICKNAME.
WHAT'S YOUR NAME?
"YUCKY TOAD."
HA, HA, HA!
VERY GOOD, GO BACK TO YOUR PLACE. NEXT UP IS NUMBER 17.
YES, MA'AM.
I'M "THE SICK LOUSE."
HA, HA, HA, HA, HA...
I'M "THE KICKING BALL."
HA, HA, HA...!
GARCÍA WAS NUMBER 32.
HAVE NUMBER 32 COME FORWARD!
GARCÍA HAD VERY BIG TEETH AND HE KNEW IT.
I DON'T WANT TO BE "THE KNOW-IT-ALL RAT."
MAYBE THE GUARDIAN WOULDN'T REMEMBER ALL THE NICKNAMES SHE'D GIVEN THEM.
WHAT'S YOUR NAME?
SO HE DECIDED TO CHANGE HIS NICKNAME.
"DONKEY TEETH."
HA, HA, HA, HA...!
VERY GOOD! GO BACK TO YOUR PLACE AND TELL NUMBER 33 TO COME HERE.
YES, MA'AM.
HEY, YOU -- 33 -- "HA, HA, HA!" WANTS YOU.
IT WOULD HAVE BEEN BETTER IF GARCÍA HADN'T HAD QUITE SO MUCH IMAGINATION. HE HAD TO HOLD HIS ARMS OUT, ON HIS KNEES, UNTIL DINNER.
BUT EVER SINCE THEN, ALL THE BOYS CALLED THE GUARDIAN...
HA-HA-HA!

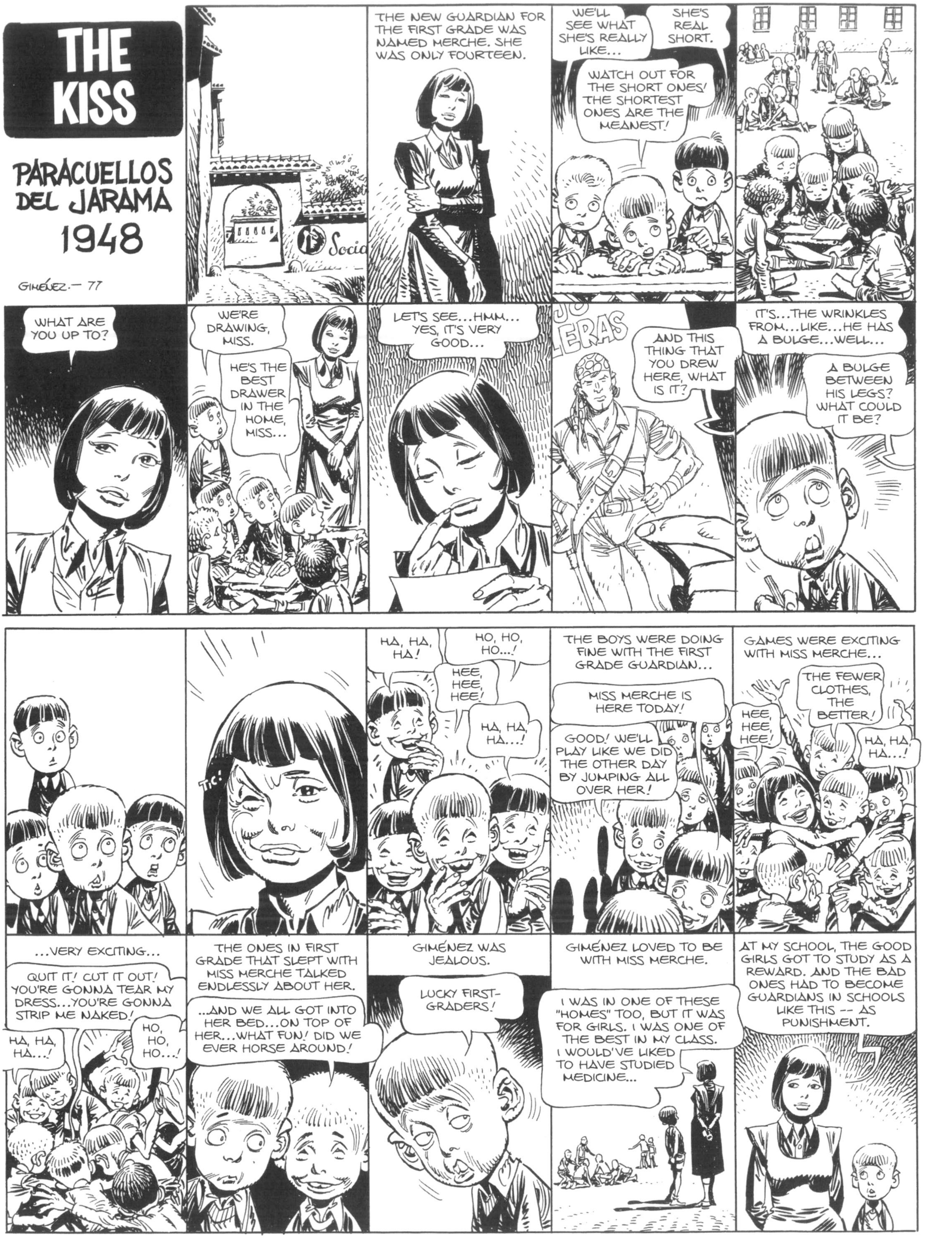
THE KISS
PARACUELLOS DEL JARAMA
1948
GIMÉNEZ.— 77
Socia
THE NEW GUARDIAN FOR THE FIRST GRADE WAS NAMED MERCHE. SHE WAS ONLY FOURTEEN.
WE'LL SEE WHAT SHE'S REALLY LIKE...
SHE'S REAL SHORT.
WATCH OUT FOR THE SHORT ONES! THE SHORTEST ONES ARE THE MEANEST!
WHAT ARE YOU UP TO?
WE'RE DRAWING, MISS.
HE'S THE BEST DRAWER IN THE HOME, MISS...
LET'S SEE... HMM... YES, IT'S VERY GOOD...
AND THIS THING THAT YOU DREW HERE, WHAT IS IT?
IT'S... THE WRINKLES FROM... LIKE... HE HAS A BULGE... WELL...
A BULGE BETWEEN HIS LEGS? WHAT COULD IT BE?
HA, HA, HA!
HO, HO, HO...!
HEE, HEE, HEE!
HA, HA, HA...!
THE BOYS WERE DOING FINE WITH THE FIRST GRADE GUARDIAN...
MISS MERCHE IS HERE TODAY!
GOOD! WE'LL PLAY LIKE WE DID THE OTHER DAY BY JUMPING ALL OVER HER!
GAMES WERE EXCITING WITH MISS MERCHE...
THE FEWER CLOTHES, THE BETTER!
HEE, HEE, HEE!
HA, HA, HA...!
...VERY EXCITING...
QUIT IT! CUT IT OUT! YOU'RE GONNA TEAR MY DRESS... YOU'RE GONNA STRIP ME NAKED!
HA, HA, HA...!
HO, HO, HO...!
THE ONES IN FIRST GRADE THAT SLEPT WITH MISS MERCHE TALKED ENDLESSLY ABOUT HER.
...AND WE ALL GOT INTO HER BED... ON TOP OF HER... WHAT FUN! DID WE EVER HORSE AROUND!
GIMÉNEZ WAS JEALOUS.
LUCKY FIRST-GRADERS!
GIMÉNEZ LOVED TO BE WITH MISS MERCHE.
I WAS IN ONE OF THESE "HOMES" TOO, BUT IT WAS FOR GIRLS. I WAS ONE OF THE BEST IN MY CLASS. I WOULD'VE LIKED TO HAVE STUDIED MEDICINE...
AT MY SCHOOL, THE GOOD GIRLS GOT TO STUDY AS A REWARD. AND THE BAD ONES HAD TO BECOME GUARDIANS IN SCHOOLS LIKE THIS -- AS PUNISHMENT.

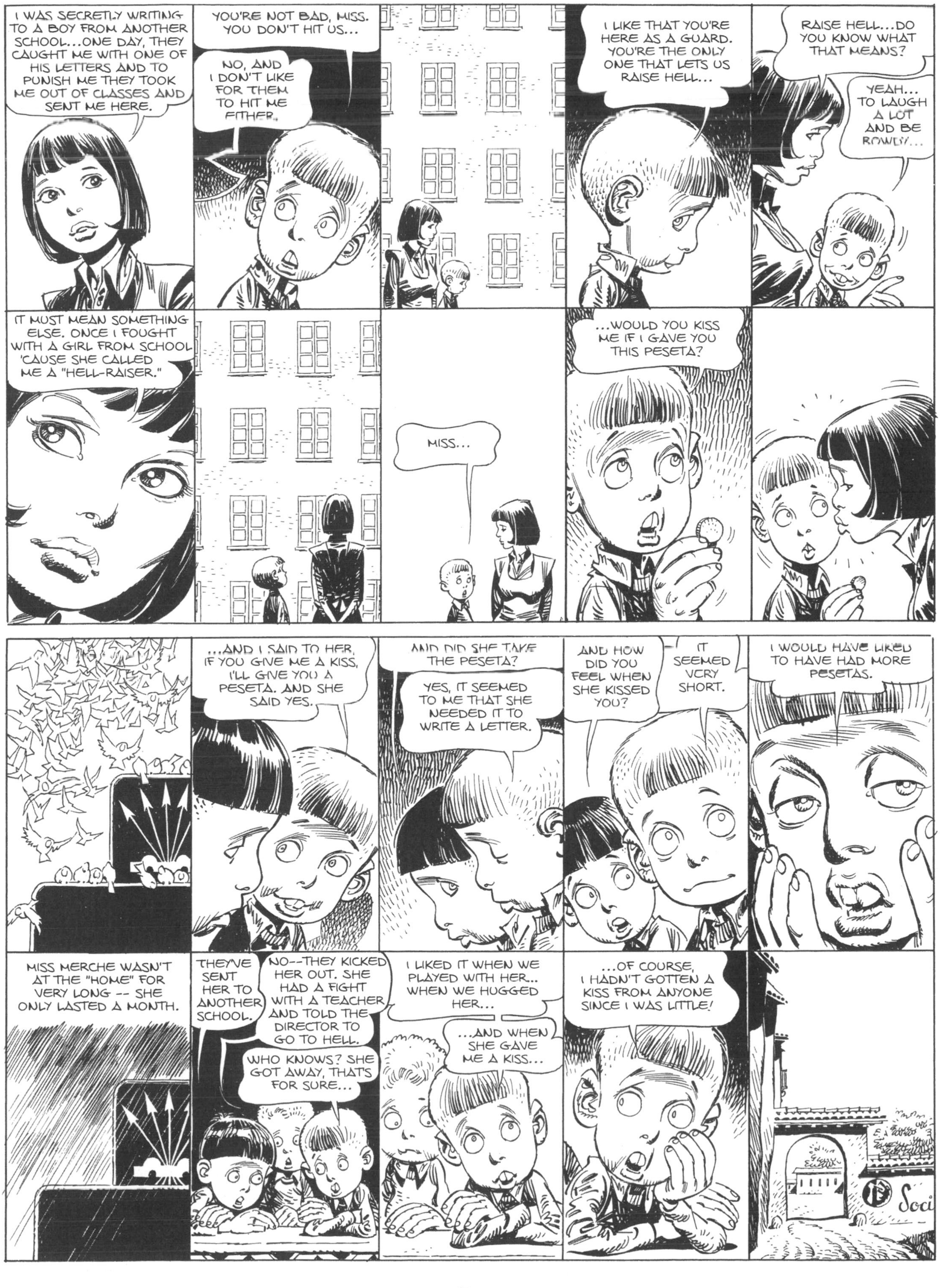

I WAS SECRETLY WRITING TO A BOY FROM ANOTHER SCHOOL...ONE DAY, THEY CAUGHT ME WITH ONE OF HIS LETTERS AND TO PUNISH ME THEY TOOK ME OUT OF CLASSES AND SENT ME HERE.
YOU'RE NOT BAD, MISS. YOU DON'T HIT US...
NO, AND I DON'T LIKE FOR THEM TO HIT ME EITHER.
I LIKE THAT YOU'RE HERE AS A GUARD. YOU'RE THE ONLY ONE THAT LETS US RAISE HELL...
RAISE HELL...DO YOU KNOW WHAT THAT MEANS?
YEAH... TO LAUGH A LOT AND BE ROWDY...
IT MUST MEAN SOMETHING ELSE. ONCE I FOUGHT WITH A GIRL FROM SCHOOL 'CAUSE SHE CALLED ME A "HELL-RAISER."
MISS...
...WOULD YOU KISS ME IF I GAVE YOU THIS PESETA?
...AND I SAID TO HER, IF YOU GIVE ME A KISS, I'LL GIVE YOU A PESETA. AND SHE SAID YES.
AND DID SHE TAKE THE PESETA?
YES, IT SEEMED TO ME THAT SHE NEEDED IT TO WRITE A LETTER.
AND HOW DID YOU FEEL WHEN SHE KISSED YOU?
IT SEEMED VERY SHORT.
I WOULD HAVE LIKED TO HAVE HAD MORE PESETAS.
MISS MERCHE WASN'T AT THE "HOME" FOR VERY LONG -- SHE ONLY LASTED A MONTH.
THEY'VE SENT HER TO ANOTHER SCHOOL.
NO--THEY KICKED HER OUT. SHE HAD A FIGHT WITH A TEACHER AND TOLD THE DIRECTOR TO GO TO HELL.
WHO KNOWS? SHE GOT AWAY, THAT'S FOR SURE...
I LIKED IT WHEN WE PLAYED WITH HER... WHEN WE HUGGED HER...
...AND WHEN SHE GAVE ME A KISS...
...OF COURSE, I HADN'T GOTTEN A KISS FROM ANYONE SINCE I WAS LITTLE!

SEX

MADRID
1953

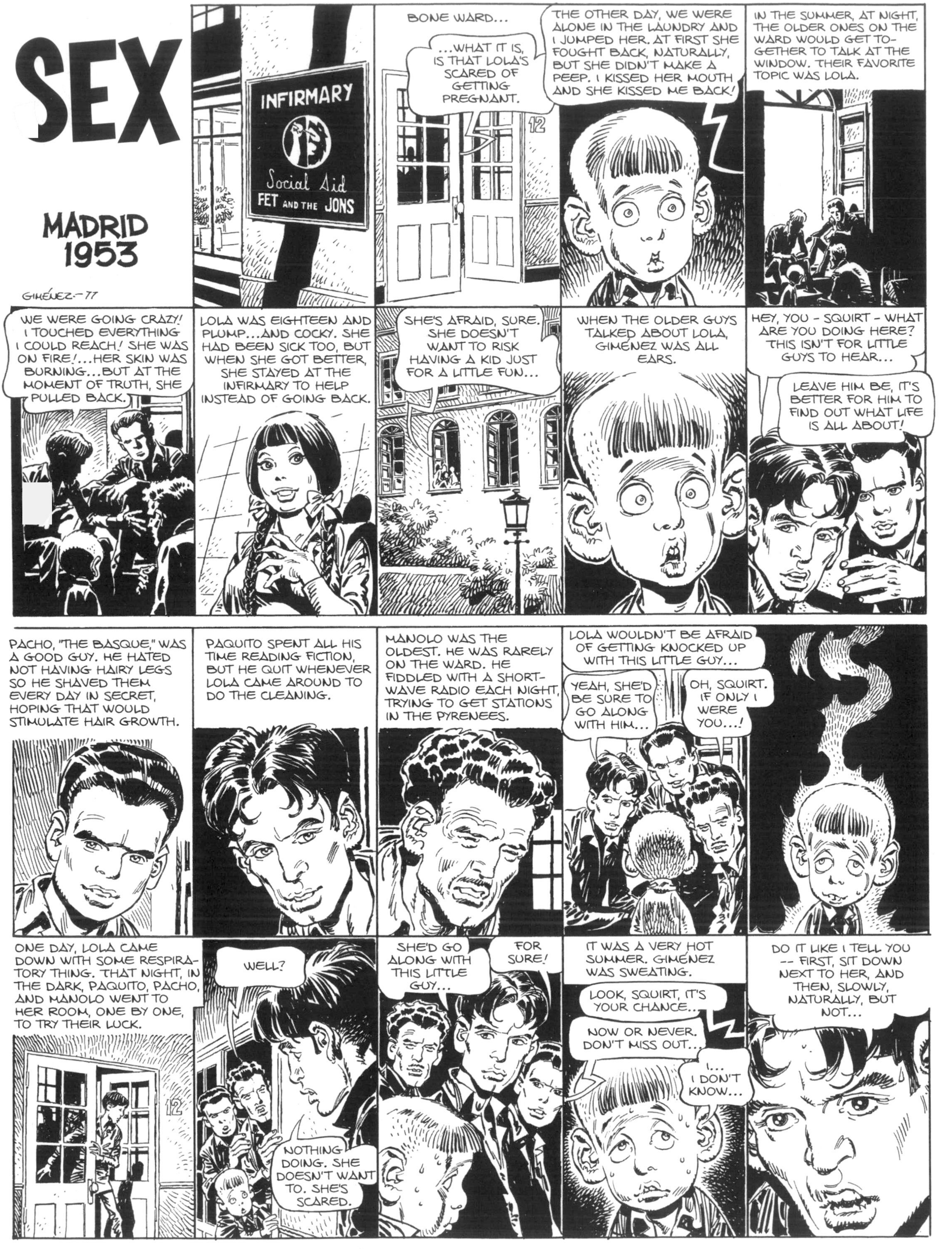
GIMÉNEZ-77
INFIRMARY
Social Aid
FET AND THE JONS
BONE WARD...
...WHAT IT IS, IS THAT LOLA'S SCARED OF GETTING PREGNANT.
12
THE OTHER DAY, WE WERE ALONE IN THE LAUNDRY AND I JUMPED HER. AT FIRST SHE FOUGHT BACK, NATURALLY, BUT SHE DIDN'T MAKE A PEEP. I KISSED HER MOUTH AND SHE KISSED ME BACK!
IN THE SUMMER, AT NIGHT, THE OLDER ONES ON THE WARD WOULD GET TOGETHER TO TALK AT THE WINDOW. THEIR FAVORITE TOPIC WAS LOLA.
WE WERE GOING CRAZY! I TOUCHED EVERYTHING I COULD REACH! SHE WAS ON FIRE!...HER SKIN WAS BURNING...BUT AT THE MOMENT OF TRUTH, SHE PULLED BACK.
LOLA WAS EIGHTEEN AND PLUMP...AND COCKY. SHE HAD BEEN SICK TOO, BUT WHEN SHE GOT BETTER, SHE STAYED AT THE INFIRMARY TO HELP INSTEAD OF GOING BACK.
SHE'S AFRAID, SURE. SHE DOESN'T WANT TO RISK HAVING A KID JUST FOR A LITTLE FUN...
WHEN THE OLDER GUYS TALKED ABOUT LOLA, GIMENEZ WAS ALL EARS.
HEY, YOU - SQUIRT - WHAT ARE YOU DOING HERE? THIS ISN'T FOR LITTLE GUYS TO HEAR...
LEAVE HIM BE, IT'S BETTER FOR HIM TO FIND OUT WHAT LIFE IS ALL ABOUT!
PACHO, "THE BASQUE," WAS A GOOD GUY. HE HATED NOT HAVING HAIRY LEGS SO HE SHAVED THEM EVERY DAY IN SECRET, HOPING THAT WOULD STIMULATE HAIR GROWTH.
PAQUITO SPENT ALL HIS TIME READING FICTION, BUT HE QUIT WHENEVER LOLA CAME AROUND TO DO THE CLEANING.
MANOLO WAS THE OLDEST. HE WAS RARELY ON THE WARD. HE FIDDLED WITH A SHORT-WAVE RADIO EACH NIGHT, TRYING TO GET STATIONS IN THE PYRENEES.
LOLA WOULDN'T BE AFRAID OF GETTING KNOCKED UP WITH THIS LITTLE GUY...
YEAH, SHE'D BE SURE TO GO ALONG WITH HIM...
OH, SQUIRT. IF ONLY I WERE YOU...!
ONE DAY, LOLA CAME DOWN WITH SOME RESPIRATORY THING. THAT NIGHT, IN THE DARK, PAQUITO, PACHO, AND MANOLO WENT TO HER ROOM, ONE BY ONE, TO TRY THEIR LUCK.
12
WELL?
NOTHING DOING. SHE DOESN'T WANT TO. SHE'S SCARED.
SHE'D GO ALONG WITH THIS LITTLE GUY...
FOR SURE!
IT WAS A VERY HOT SUMMER. GIMÉNEZ WAS SWEATING.
LOOK, SQUIRT, IT'S YOUR CHANCE...
NOW OR NEVER. DON'T MISS OUT...
I... I DON'T KNOW...
DO IT LIKE I TELL YOU -- FIRST, SIT DOWN NEXT TO HER, AND THEN, SLOWLY, NATURALLY, BUT NOT...

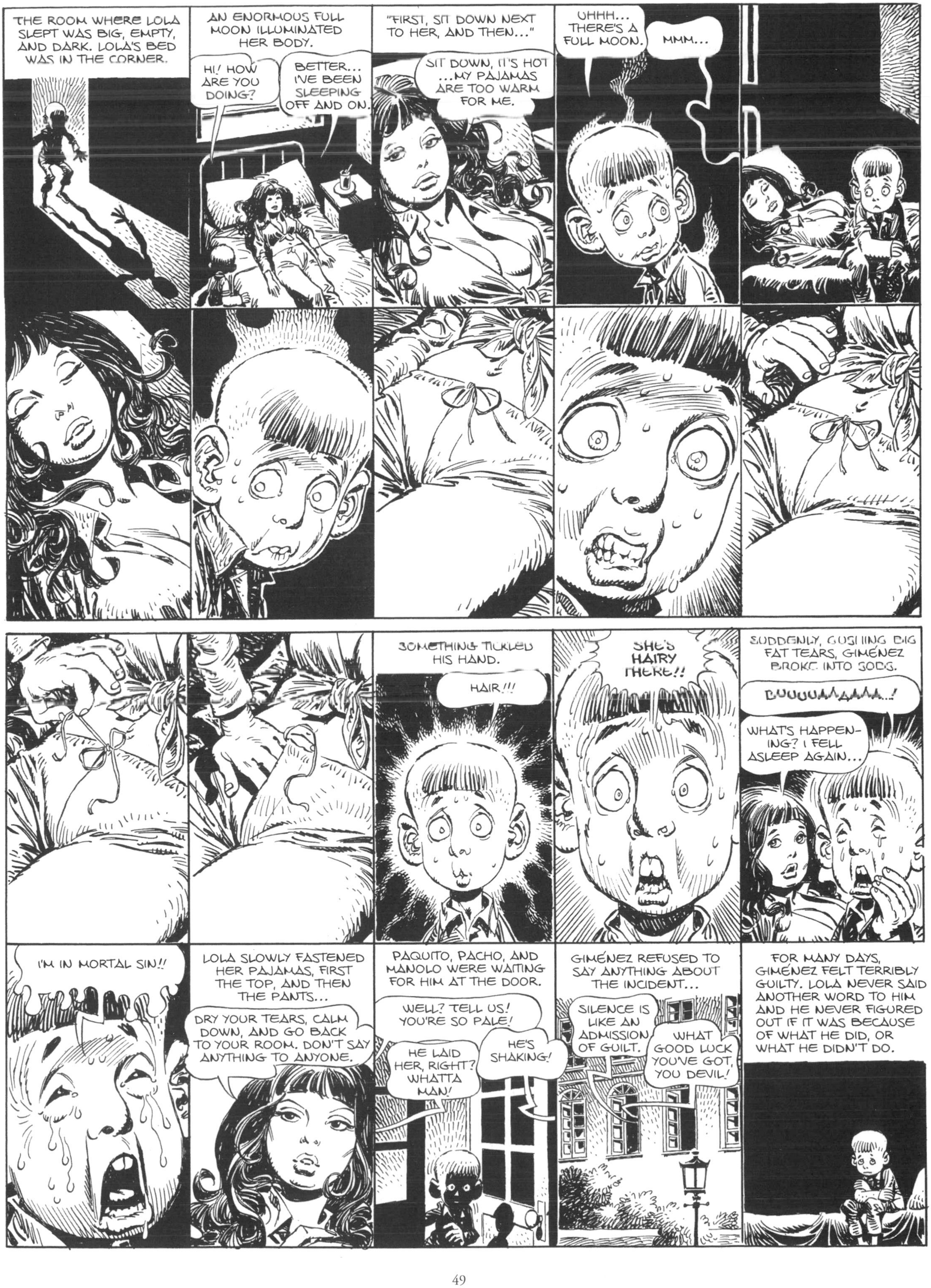
THE ROOM WHERE LOLA SLEPT WAS BIG, EMPTY, AND DARK. LOLA'S BED WAS IN THE CORNER.
AN ENORMOUS FULL MOON ILLUMINATED HER BODY.
HI! HOW ARE YOU DOING?
BETTER... I'VE BEEN SLEEPING OFF AND ON.
"FIRST, SIT DOWN NEXT TO HER, AND THEN..."
SIT DOWN, IT'S HOT ...MY PAJAMAS ARE TOO WARM FOR ME.
UHHH... THERE'S A FULL MOON.
MMM...
SOMETHING TICKLED HIS HAND.
HAIR!!!
SHE'S HAIRY THERE!!
SUDDENLY, GUSHING BIG FAT TEARS, GIMÉNEZ BROKE INTO SOBS.
BUUUUAAAAA...!
WHAT'S HAPPENING? I FELL ASLEEP AGAIN...
I'M IN MORTAL SIN!!
LOLA SLOWLY FASTENED HER PAJAMAS, FIRST THE TOP, AND THEN THE PANTS...
DRY YOUR TEARS, CALM DOWN, AND GO BACK TO YOUR ROOM. DON'T SAY ANYTHING TO ANYONE.
PAQUITO, PACHO, AND MANOLO WERE WAITING FOR HIM AT THE DOOR.
WELL? TELL US! YOU'RE SO PALE!
HE LAID HER, RIGHT? WHATTA MAN!
HE'S SHAKING!
GIMÉNEZ REFUSED TO SAY ANYTHING ABOUT THE INCIDENT...
SILENCE IS LIKE AN ADMISSION OF GUILT.
WHAT GOOD LUCK YOU'VE GOT, YOU DEVIL!
FOR MANY DAYS, GIMÉNEZ FELT TERRIBLY GUILTY. LOLA NEVER SAID ANOTHER WORD TO HIM AND HE NEVER FIGURED OUT IF IT WAS BECAUSE OF WHAT HE DID, OR WHAT HE DIDN'T DO.

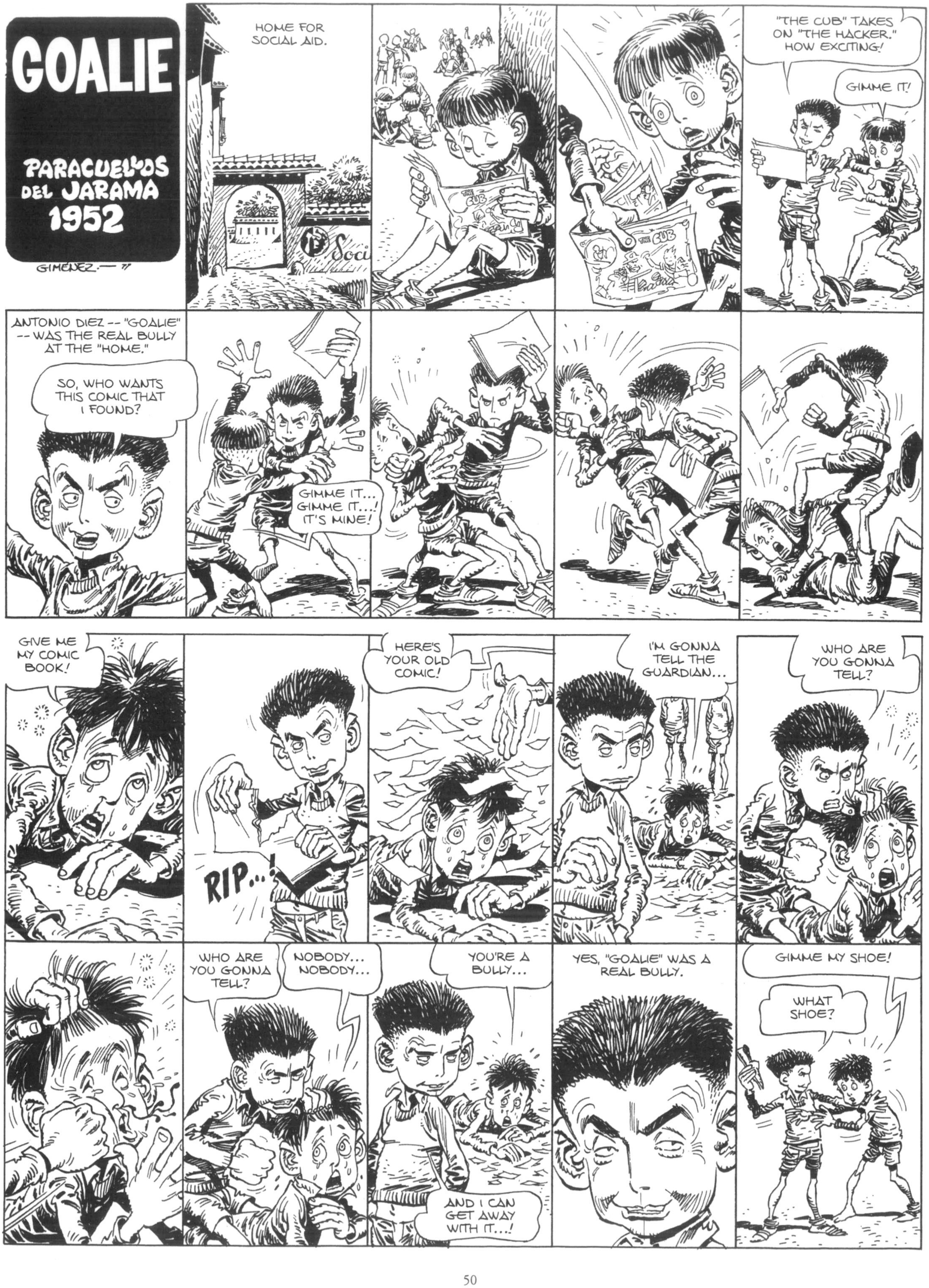
GOALIE
PARACUELLOS DEL JARAMA 1952
GIMENEZ — 77
HOME FOR SOCIAL AID.
"THE CUB" TAKES ON "THE HACKER." HOW EXCITING!
GIMME IT!
ANTONIO DIEZ -- "GOALIE" -- WAS THE REAL BULLY AT THE "HOME."
SO, WHO WANTS THIS COMIC THAT I FOUND?
GIMME IT... GIMME IT...! IT'S MINE!
GIVE ME MY COMIC BOOK!
RIP...!
HERE'S YOUR OLD COMIC!
I'M GONNA TELL THE GUARDIAN...
WHO ARE YOU GONNA TELL?
WHO ARE YOU GONNA TELL?
NOBODY... NOBODY...
YOU'RE A BULLY...
AND I CAN GET AWAY WITH IT...!
YES, "GOALIE" WAS A REAL BULLY.
GIMME MY SHOE!
WHAT SHOE?

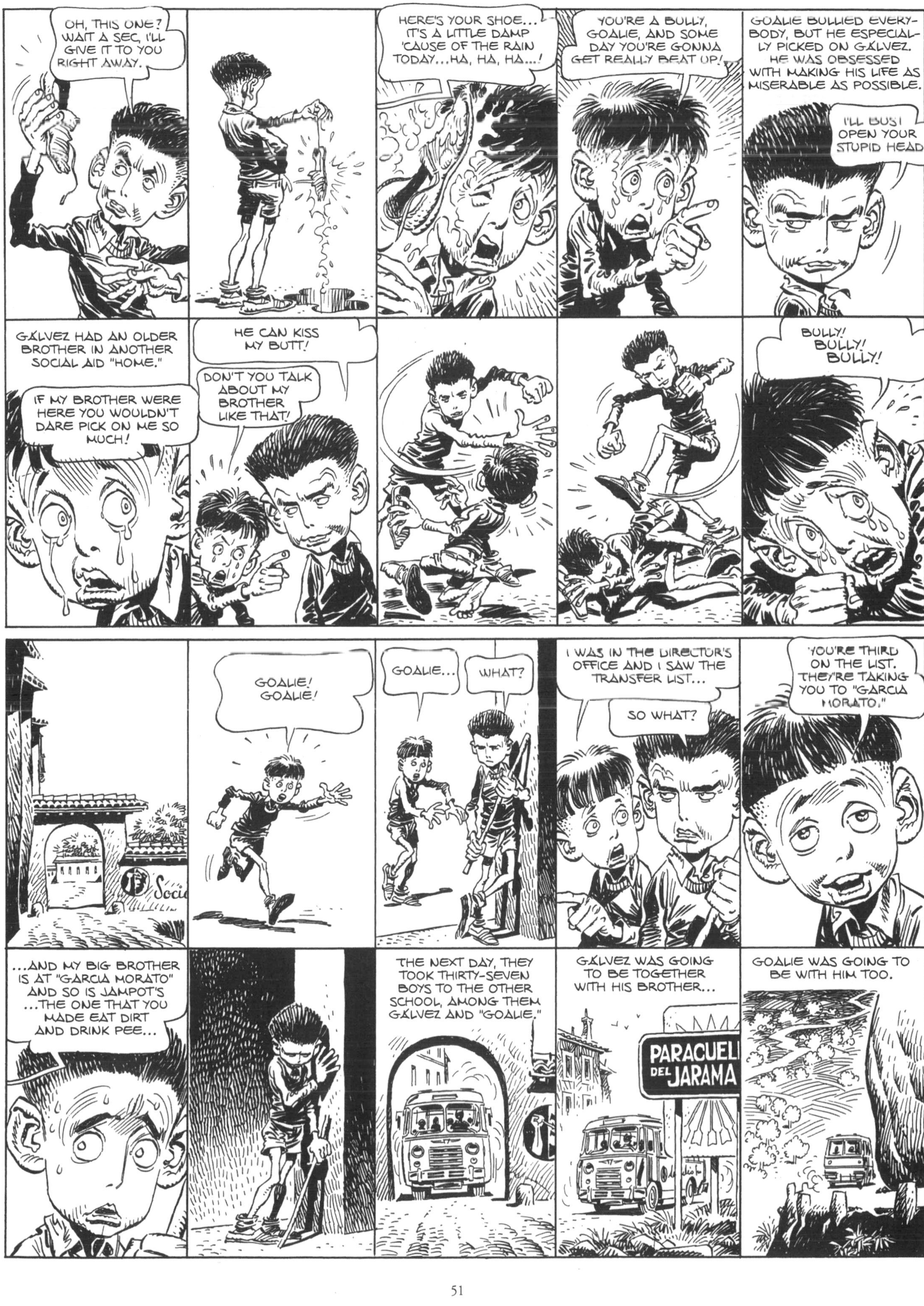

OH, THIS ONE? WAIT A SEC, I'LL GIVE IT TO YOU RIGHT AWAY.
HERE'S YOUR SHOE... IT'S A LITTLE DAMP 'CAUSE OF THE RAIN TODAY...HA, HA, HA...!
YOU'RE A BULLY, GOALIE, AND SOME DAY YOU'RE GONNA GET REALLY BEAT UP!
GOALIE BULLIED EVERYBODY, BUT HE ESPECIALLY PICKED ON GÁLVEZ. HE WAS OBSESSED WITH MAKING HIS LIFE AS MISERABLE AS POSSIBLE.
I'LL BUST OPEN YOUR STUPID HEAD!
GÁLVEZ HAD AN OLDER BROTHER IN ANOTHER SOCIAL AID "HOME."
IF MY BROTHER WERE HERE YOU WOULDN'T DARE PICK ON ME SO MUCH!
HE CAN KISS MY BUTT!
DON'T YOU TALK ABOUT MY BROTHER LIKE THAT!
BULLY! BULLY! BULLY!
GOALIE! GOALIE!
GOALIE...
WHAT?
I WAS IN THE DIRECTOR'S OFFICE AND I SAW THE TRANSFER LIST...
SO WHAT?
YOU'RE THIRD ON THE LIST. THEY'RE TAKING YOU TO "GARCIA MORATO."
...AND MY BIG BROTHER IS AT "GARCIA MORATO" AND SO IS JAMPOT'S ...THE ONE THAT YOU MADE EAT DIRT AND DRINK PEE...
THE NEXT DAY, THEY TOOK THIRTY-SEVEN BOYS TO THE OTHER SCHOOL, AMONG THEM GÁLVEZ AND "GOALIE."
GÁLVEZ WAS GOING TO BE TOGETHER WITH HIS BROTHER...
PARACUELL DEL JARAMA
GOALIE WAS GOING TO BE WITH HIM TOO.

PARACUELLOS
2

DEDICATION BY Carlos Giménez

I want to dedicate this book, first, to the memory of my "grandfather" Evelio. That's how I saw him.

Evelio was the gardener at the Social Aid "Home" named Battle of Jarama, where I spent part of the eight years that I was interned in these State institutions.

Grandfather Evelio would take me out of school whenever he could and take me to his home. This was usually during summer vacation, and above all, during Christmas break. He didn't only do it for me, but with all the boys that he could, the ones who didn't have anyone to come and see them. It hurt him that we were so small and alone, to see us so helpless. Sometimes on Sundays he'd bring me some fish-shaped buns that he'd made himself. Whenever I'd see him at school, I'd go up to him if I could and he'd pat me on the head and ask about my mother and brothers and what I was going to be when I grew up. He took it upon himself to write cheery letters to my mother, who was in a tuberculosis ward in Bilbao, telling her that I was a good boy and that everything was all right, and he even sent her photos of me and him together so that she could see what a fine lad I was turning into.

The few times that I got to leave school, clutching Grandfather Evelio's hand, I was tremendously happy. I called him Grandfather as if he really were. I loved him with all my heart. He was very kind and oozed tenderness out of every pore and absorbed my affection like a sponge. He took me home with him, to his children and grandchildren, and I was like a member of the family. He put a bed in a corner of a room for me, on top of a trunk, and for me it was heaven.

When they transferred me to another school in a town much farther away, Grandfather Evelio even went there on his donkey to look for me in the summer. He arranged the paperwork so they'd let me leave and took me home with him to his family which, in many ways, was mine, too.

My mother would write about him in her letters to me at school, saying, "Blessed be that good man."

I also want to dedicate this book to all those who in some way or another have helped me to bring it about.

To my friend and fellow classmate Cándido García who, in his long letters has reminded me of an infinity of details, figures, names, and anecdotes about the Social Aid "Homes." Also to my brother Antonio (Toñin in some of these stories) for the same reason.

To Meli, my wife, who has worked on this as much as I, helping me with correspondence, typing up the scripts and other writings, and above all, for putting up with me.

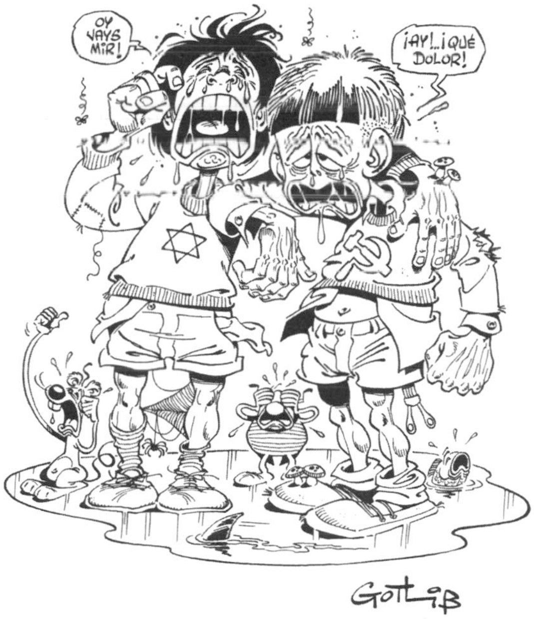
OY VAYS MIR!
¡AY!..¡QUÉ DOLOR!
GOTLIB

Carlos Giménez and the cartoonist Marcel Gotlib, who serialized *Paracuellos* in France.

To Adolfo Usero (what would I have done without Adolfo?) who by living with me in the different Social Aid "Homes" has been with me in every moment of my memory, and who moreover corrected my spelling and took charge of the "refreshments" problem.

To Manolo E. Darías from Tenerife, who always believed in this series and constantly cheered me on.

To Antonio Arigita, Ramón González, Joan Navarro, and Agustín Sánchez, who all helped me by providing different sorts of documentation.

To Gotlib and Diament, who dared to publish *Paracuellos* in *Fluide Glacial*, a Belgian-French magazine designed to produce laughter, even though *Paracuellos* is meant to cause tears, an act that could have sunk their magazine.

I also want to dedicate this book to those who were my friends at Social Aid: to Carabantes, who had the *Purk, the Man of Steel* collection; to Bene, who was a phenomenal soccer player; to Marcos Tablero, who drew wonderfully, especially racing cars; to "Pelines," who was one of the best students in class and wet his bed and everything else because he couldn't hold it and was always hopping around when he couldn't piss; to Benito Guzmán; to the Delso brothers; to my good friend Antonio Sánchez, a kind, likable fellow with a sharp sense of humor that led him to invent his own jokes; to good old "Shakey" who had ears that stuck way out ("What is the wind? Shakeee's ears flapping!"); to "Grape," who was a real scrapper; to Gil Pérez, whom we called "Perejil" (Spanish for "parsley"—it rhymes with "Gil") and who couldn't pronounce "rr"; to Alsina, who was all teeth; to Carballo, who never cried and made fun of everyone and who would stick out his elbows in such a way as to make whoever hit him get hurt themselves instead and who always would end up saying after a beating, "you didn't get me, even once..." and who they had to give up on as being simply impossible to discipline because it was exhausting to keep beating him all the time; to Julio Rubio who fell from the second floor and busted two flagstones; to Miguel Díez, who "owed his life" to Sancha; to Sancha, who patched our rubber balls; to Antonio Díaz, also known as "Cucufato Pi"; to Requena; to Cambón, who sang rancheras; to Segui; to Verbena, who was the package room boss; to Domiciano ("Snout"), to whom we sang "Domi, Domi, Domiciano..." in Kyrie Eleison style; to "Pickle," who had a head shaped like a small cucumber and would never let anyone hit him; to "Trolley," whose large intestine was herniated and would jut out like a streetcar exiting a tunnel; to "Sleepy," "Chameleon," Tárraga, and "Moon"; to Ángelito, who was a little bit retarded and came from a rich family that came with a chauffeur and everything to see him when it wasn't even visiting day; to "Dead Tuna"; to my friend Little Perucha who helped me get together the money for the "Cub" comics; to his brother Big Perucha; to our soccer team forwards: "Pichi," "Cacha,"

"Moro," "Guito" and Cano; to Luis Bueno, whom we called "Phenomenon" because he could stuff a half loaf of bread and two boiled eggs into his mouth; to dear old Felipe Díaz, who loved to draw even though he was awful at it; to Dionisio Polo; to "Little Flea," to Pasalodos; to "Chick" and to "Hunger," who ate a whole pot of rice once, enough for twenty-five boys, and was still hungry afterwards; to Ramón Gómez, who was a chatterbox and fond of inventing insults; to my good friend Manolo Yáñez, who, by the way, gave me the worst pounding of my life with a broomstick, and all because I threatened to let everyone know that he was sweet on Miss Esther. I told him, "If you hit me, I'm gonna tell." He then proceeded to give me a beating that left me half senseless and warned me, "If you snitch on me, I'll wallop you again." We made up that night and he sang a little song to me, the one that goes, "To be a good farmer you need a good horse..." He kind of warbled when he sang. I also want to include little Yáñez in this dedication, may he rest in peace.

And to Ormazábal, the fastest runner in the "Home"; he ran so fast that when we had a race he would take a handicap of half the distance and could, with a running start, take several bounds up a wall and touch the ceiling with his hand; to Emilio González Castellano, the "Frenchman"; to Luisito Barbeito, who had a wonderful mother who worked in the school to be near her son; to my good friend Juan Manuel Escribano, who had great big eyes that made more than one school-mistress into his patsy; to his brother Goyo; to José Luis Muñoz, who had a gorgeous mother who was an artist. I'd really like to see him again because I still have enormous affection for him. To his brother Gumersindo Apolinar, who was the bugle boy; to the elder Gálvez, who was always drawing comics, and, since he couldn't draw faces at all, invented characters without heads, such as "The Headless Man," "The Invisible Man," "The Hooded Man," "The Man in the Diving Suit"...; to the younger Gálvez; to "Ant"; to Bonilla, who was always in the kitchen; to "Demon," who cut his finger with a razor blade to be like the martyrs in the religious books; to "Pirracas," who ate flies and beetles and whose head was always buzzing; to "Bun Chomper" and to "Ladies' Man"; to Antolín, the albino whose skin, hair and eyes were all white, and who was blinded by sunlight but could see perfectly well in the dark; to "Goalie," who was a real mean fighter; to Enrique Mercado, who was like a young wild boar; to Orozco, who one day, with no warning whatsoever, gave me four tremendous slaps in the face and I still don't have any idea why; to Ernestín, who had the good luck to be handsome and who was the favorite of a bunch of the woman guards and teachers; to Emilio Pato; to Salvador; to Modesto Sánchez, who came to see me at my home not too long ago; to Elías with whom I decided to sleep in the same bed one Christmas Eve which caused a huge scandal because the teachers said that we had been doing something "filthy" and we had no idea of what it was; to Rudy, who got a beating for surprising a woman guard who was screwing this man who lit the furnaces; to José Antonio Trujillo, who had an operation for pleurisy and used to say that he had lead balls in his lungs; to his brother Javier; to Rehak, who was the son of a Czech and a Galician; to Lucio, who would get sympathy by bending his legs around behind his head and got visitors to give him treats; to Albiñana; to Vaquerizo; to Tomasín, who was lucky and got sent to study in Tinuca; to Vilches, who was a great sketcher and had a razor blade that he used to whittle the backs of the benches in the chapel during Rosary, carving names and drawings; to Sebastián, the cripple in the wheelchair; to "Gallur," who was from Gallur in Zaragoza; to my friend Orihuela, who was small, freckled, and a regular monkey; to Santiago García, who was lame; to Emilio Muñoz; to "Chuckles," who always smiled; to Parrondo, who stuttered; to Pascual Rubio; to Suárez, alias the "Fig," who was the best goalie in the "Home" and who, why I'll never know, I never liked; to Julito Carrascal; to Julito Mooya, a long time friend; to Herminio, who was from my old neighborhood, Lavapiés; to Higinio, the "Little Chinaman"; to Antonio López; to "Birdseed"; to José María Arranz; to Iglesias; to Heliodoro, "Chickpea," whose head was like a garbanzo bean; to Deogracias, who besides being blond and handsome played stupendous soccer and liked schmaltzy songs ("From the end of the pier/I came calling my mother/and when she didn't answer/I called the Virgin of Carmen"); to Pacheco; to Sacristán; to José Moreno; to Pablito, my great friend Pablito, who wore glasses and had a drifting eye; to Araújo, who had real ugly teeth and "influence" because he gathered grass for the Phalanx instructor's brother, Alfonso, who raised rabbits; to Antonio Novoa, who was very small; to Marianín; to Emilio Lorente; to Felisín, whom I bullied and did some really shitty things to (forgive me, Felisín); to Cándido, who had a paralyzed leg and wore a boot with metal taps and a very thick sole and who still had to stand in line to receive instruction like the rest; to Féliz Miguel, "Little Bird," who had a blind father, which did not prevent him to visit every Sunday; to Félix Gómex who, the same as Yáñez, was also in love with Miss Esther; to Zárate, who was a really big kid and still peed himself; to Boluda, who liked to draw; to Ángel García; to Bogas; to Rafael Hernández, who went with me down to the kitchen one night to look for leftovers; to Eduardo Puchol; to Hierro, who always stood watch for us; to Alfredo Muyo; to Agulló; to Antonio Gutiérrez; to "Mortadella"; to "Primitive Elm"; to Paco Rodríquez, who had a round head and was one of the boys who looked for grass for Alfonso; to the Ballestero brothers, Jaime and Enrique Ballestero; to Agustín Vega, who turned out to be the best drawer at the "Home"...ahem, that is, after I left; to Mariano del Amor; to Julián Gámez; to Demetrio Rodríguez, "Jam-pot" or "Jammie" to his buddies; to "Centipede"; to Félix Blanco; to Luis Cuadrado, the "Shrimp"; to Zorrilla, who had an evil temper; to Jacinto Oviedo; to Billarín; to "Baby-fish"; to Luis Hita; to Ruda; to Romo; to "Pinecone"; to Delgado; to "The Asturian," who also drew; to "The Cow"; to Paco and Carlos, "The Bananas"; to Gonzalo; to Gaspar; to "The Monkey"; to "The Old Lady"; to Mendoza...

To Adolfo, my inseparable friend Adolfo, the Adolfo of my comics, the Adolfo of my whole life, the one with whom I've wandered around the world since we were both eight years old and who is right here, at my side, helping me make this incredible list; Adolfo is more than a friend, something like a brother, but actually like a Siamese twin. And to Cruz Buendía, who was a good friend of Adolfo's.

To all the others, to all those who were my "Home" comrades, to the chewers, camels, dromedaries, monkeys, bed-wetters and pant-shitters, to the gluttons and teasers and masturbators, to the teachers' pets, to the stupid ones, to the clever ones, to the hypocrites, to the fittest and the flabbiest, to the stooges and those who "owed their lives," to the ones who had visitors and the ones who didn't, to the ones with "influence" who gathered grass, to the ones who always had a package, to the ones who ate weeds, to the altar-boys, to the ones who answered the door...

In short, to all those who, like me, were once Social Aid boys. Also to Miss Carmen, Luyisito Barbeito's mother, and to Miss Alicia Rodríguez, who spoiled me and let me read her books.

As part of his preparation for the publication of Paracuellos 2, *Carlos Giménez visited the sites of some of the former Social Aid "Homes" and reflected on what he discovered. This early 1980s report augments the overarching journey of recovered memory.*

Notes on the Social Aid "Homes" in which the *Paracuellos* and *Parcuellos 2* stories take place

The Battle of Jarama "Home" was a palace of the Dukes of Medinaceli before becoming a Social Aid school. The church and palace of the town of Paracuellos del Jarama date from the same year: 1587.

For many years the townspeople called the children at the home "The palace children."

This institution has been run by nuns for more than a dozen years.

In 1980, during a visit to this school, we witnessed profound changes: the children who board there enjoy great freedom, can walk around town whenever they wish, and can dress comfortably. They look very well and seem happy. The dormitories and the dining rooms appear to be impeccable and there are abundant books in the classes. In one of the classrooms, on top of one of the desks like an unmistakable sign of change, we saw a binder with a photo of Che Guevara on its covers.

Oddly, at the present time the two most neglected aspects of the "Home" are precisely the two places that most typified the old Social Aid's ideology: the Chapel and the Flag Courtyard, both of which are threatening to crumble into ruins.

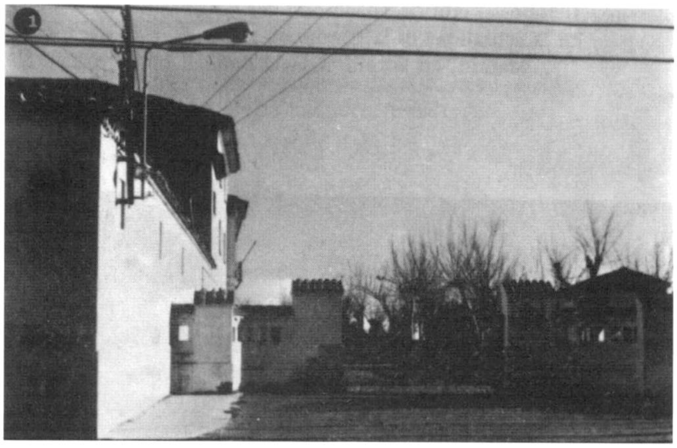

Photo #1: The Battle of Jarama "Home" is at the entrance to the town of Paracuellos del Jarama, at the corner of Santa Ana Alley. It opened in 1950 and housed three hundred boys from other schools, such as the the Blue "Home," The Battle of Brunete, and the General Mola.

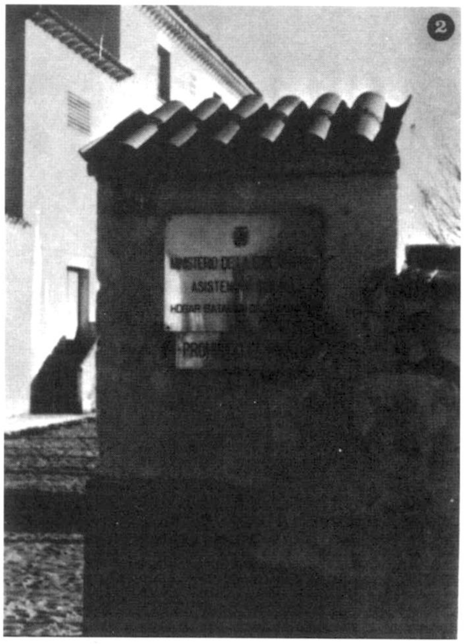

Photo #2: The old initials "F.E.T. and J.O.N.S." have disappeared, together with the Falangist emblems and the "Social Aid" name. The main door's entry arch has also disappeared, demolished during a fire in order to let the fire trucks pass through.

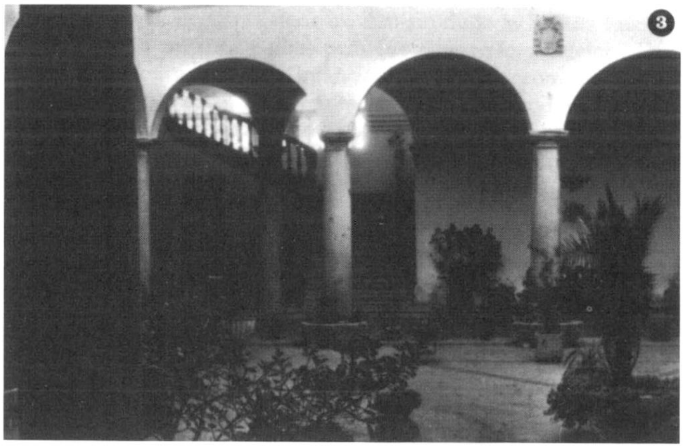

Photo #3: Battle of Jarama "Home." The palace's pillar courtyard as it now appears. An ancient coat of arms, perhaps of the Dukes of Medinaceli, can still be seen over the arches. The wide staircase leads to the dormitory halls.

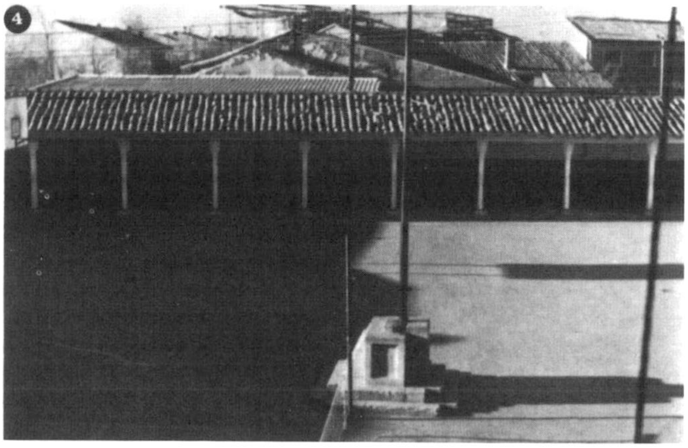

Photo #4: The flag courtyard where the boys raised and lowered the flag, exercised and did drills, sang "Faces to the Sun," and where, laying on their backs on the ground, in rigid formation, their faces exposed to the sun, they took naps during the hottest summer days.

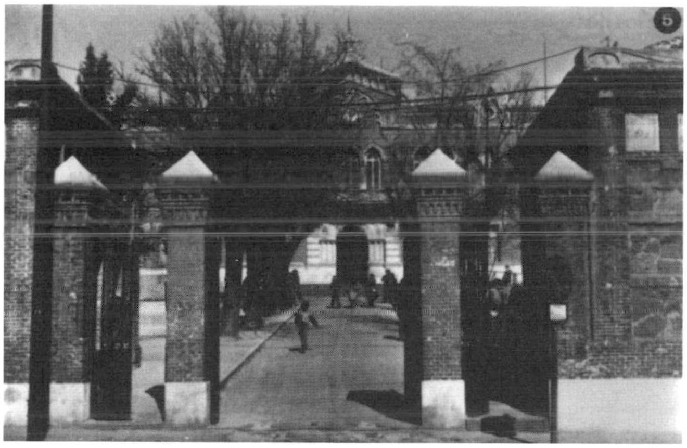

Photo #5: The former infirmary façade is practically unchanged. It was a friars' monastery before it was given to the State for a Social Aid hospital during the post-war period. In time the building was returned to the friars and is now the Caldeiro Foundation, located at No. 2 Rafaela Street in Madrid.

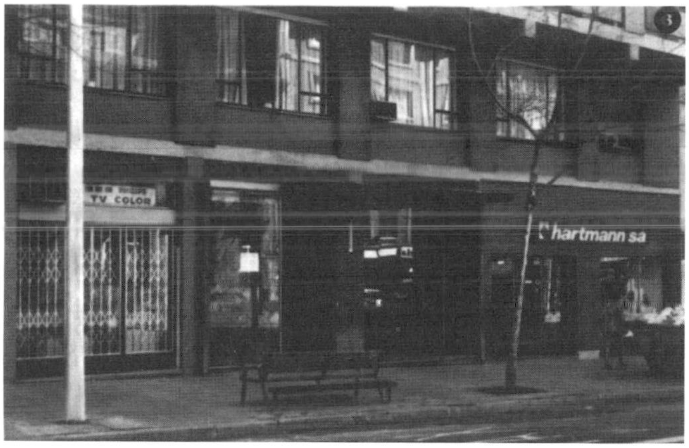
TV COLOR
hartmann sa

Photo #6: The General Mola "Home" was a girls' school called "María de Molina's Home." It was later occupied by small boys who were to be interned at the "Home" in Paracuellos del Jarama. It too was a privately owned building that was deeded to the State and is located at 82 General Mola Street in Madrid. It is now a residential building.

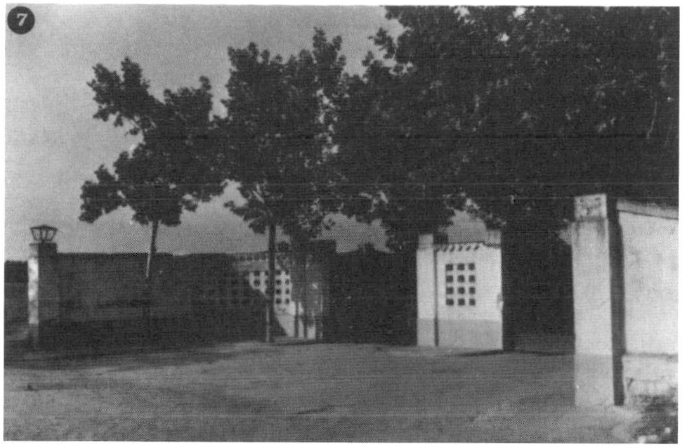

Photo #7: The entrance to the enormous walled compound of the Joaquín García "Home." It looks exactly as it did in the Fifties; it hasn't even been whitewashed since then. It is now the Barajas Child Development Center. A plaque at the entrance reads: Ministry of the Interior, National Institute of Social Assistance. It's located on the outskirts of Madrid, near the town of Barajas, fourteen kilometers from the Aragón Highway.

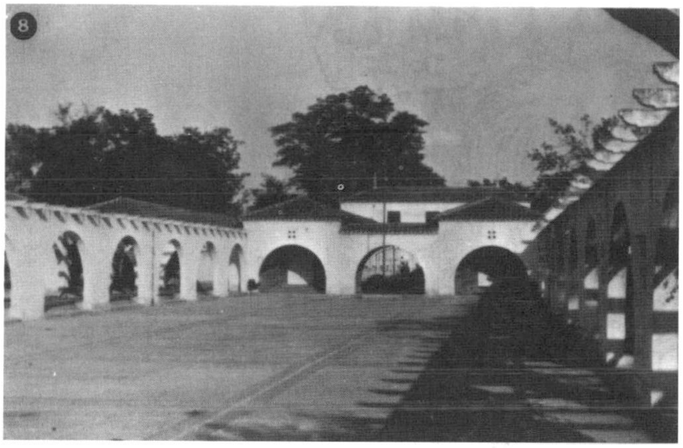

Photo #8: The García Morato "Home," now the Barajas Center, is a school for barely a dozen poorly dressed youngsters, according to what we were able to discern. During the Forties and Fifties it housed around three hundred boys. The school has been completely neglected and the majority of its structure has fallen into disuse. Some buildings, such as the chapel and the theater, no longer exist.

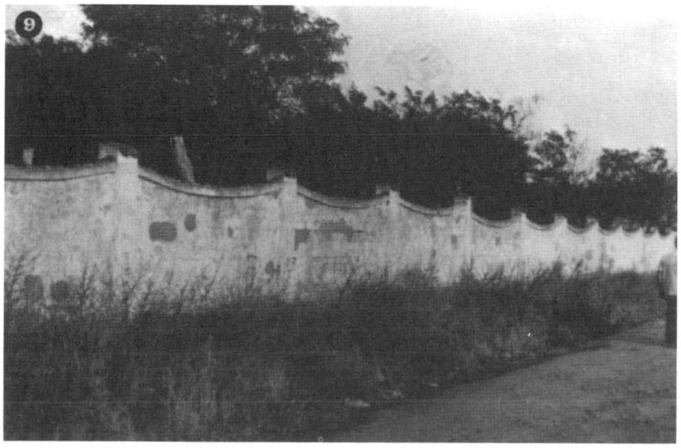

Photo #9: Behind these walls that are falling into ruins, are some stupendous structures: a pool, dormitories, laundry rooms, locker rooms, dining rooms, classrooms, parlors, residence halls, an infirmary, and an entire system of underground rooms. It's not known for whom or for what reason the subterranean quarters were constructed; except for one large white marble room in which the Social Aid authorities held a festive annual banquet, we don't recall the rooms ever being occupied.

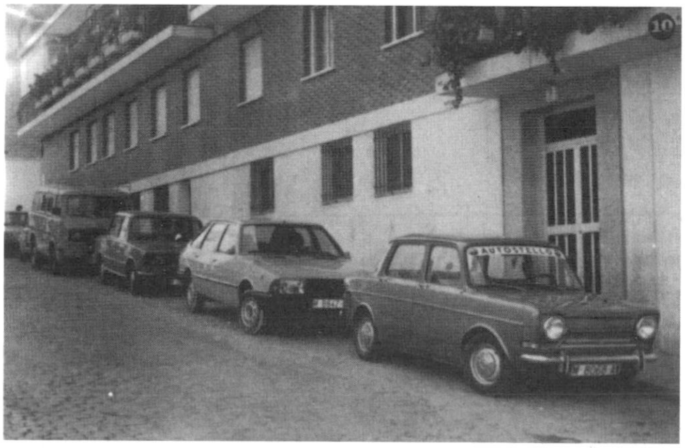

Photo #10: The Bibona "Home" near the Vallecas Bridge in Madrid that housed fifty boys from four to six years of age. It's located in the Doña Carlotta district at the end of Peña Prieta Street, at the corner of Manuel Arranz and San Florencio. It was an old estate, with an ancient ivy-covered building, garden paths, a pond, and some fruit trees. The grounds abutted the vegetable garden of a Mr. Juanito, who occasionally threw apples at the boys. It is now used for residential housing.

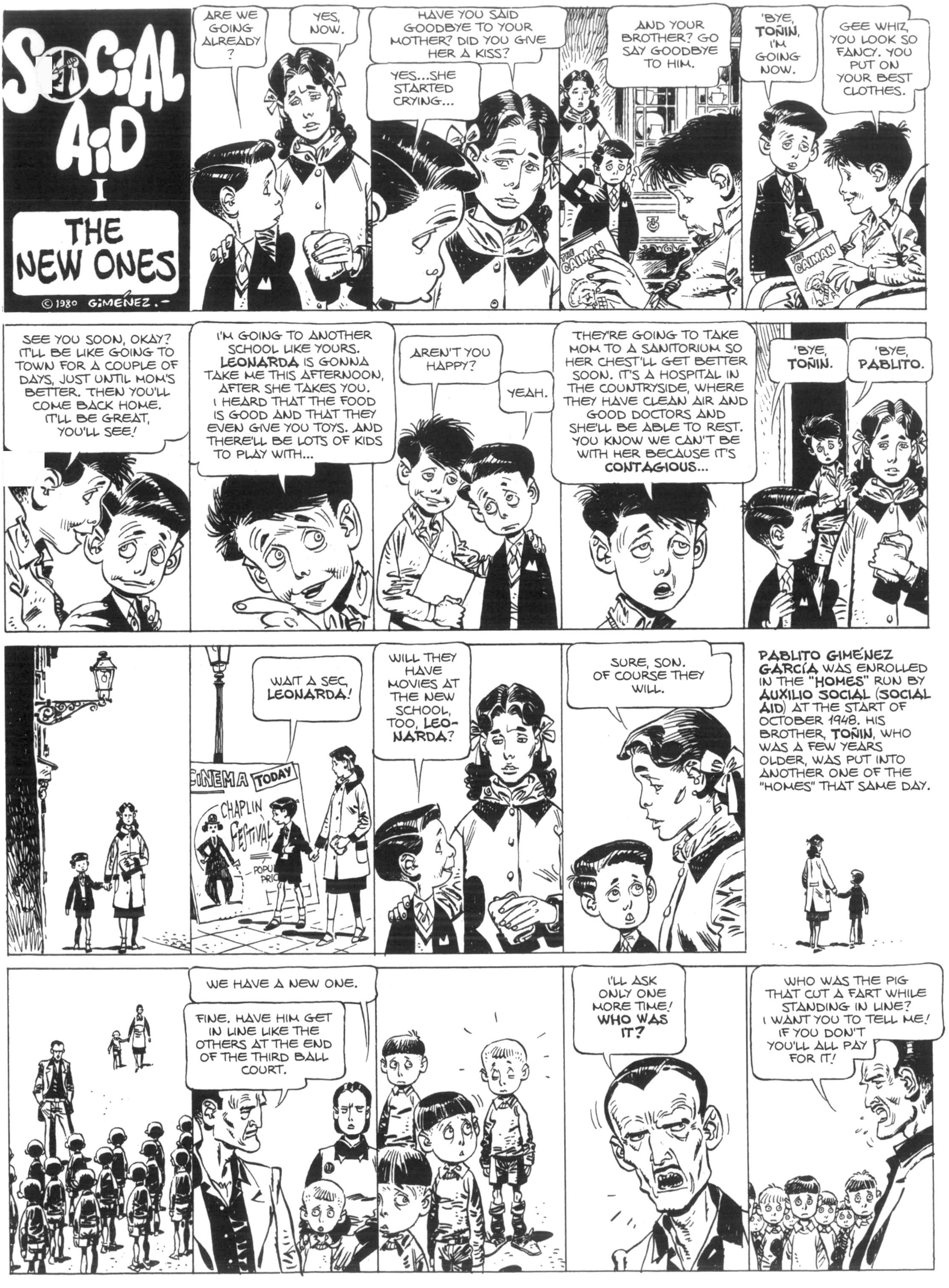
SOCIAL AID
I
THE NEW ONES
©1980 GIMENEZ.-
ARE WE GOING ALREADY ?
YES, NOW.
HAVE YOU SAID GOODBYE TO YOUR MOTHER? DID YOU GIVE HER A KISS?
YES...SHE STARTED CRYING...
AND YOUR BROTHER? GO SAY GOODBYE TO HIM.
THE CAIMAN
'BYE, TOÑIN, I'M GOING NOW.
GEE WHIZ, YOU LOOK SO FANCY. YOU PUT ON YOUR BEST CLOTHES.
THE CAIMAN
SEE YOU SOON, OKAY? IT'LL BE LIKE GOING TO TOWN FOR A COUPLE OF DAYS, JUST UNTIL MOM'S BETTER. THEN YOU'LL COME BACK HOME. IT'LL BE GREAT, YOU'LL SEE!
I'M GOING TO ANOTHER SCHOOL LIKE YOURS. LEONARDA IS GONNA TAKE ME THIS AFTERNOON, AFTER SHE TAKES YOU. I HEARD THAT THE FOOD IS GOOD AND THAT THEY EVEN GIVE YOU TOYS. AND THERE'LL BE LOTS OF KIDS TO PLAY WITH...
AREN'T YOU HAPPY?
YEAH.
THEY'RE GOING TO TAKE MOM TO A SANITORIUM SO HER CHEST'LL GET BETTER SOON. IT'S A HOSPITAL IN THE COUNTRYSIDE, WHERE THEY HAVE CLEAN AIR AND GOOD DOCTORS AND SHE'LL BE ABLE TO REST. YOU KNOW WE CAN'T BE WITH HER BECAUSE IT'S CONTAGIOUS...
'BYE, TOÑIN.
'BYE, PABLITO.
WAIT A SEC, LEONARDA!
CINEMA TODAY
CHAPLIN FESTIVAL
WILL THEY HAVE MOVIES AT THE NEW SCHOOL, TOO, LEONARDA?
SURE, SON. OF COURSE THEY WILL.
PABLITO GIMÉNEZ GARCÍA WAS ENROLLED IN THE "HOMES" RUN BY AUXILIO SOCIAL (SOCIAL AID) AT THE START OF OCTOBER 1948. HIS BROTHER, TOÑIN, WHO WAS A FEW YEARS OLDER, WAS PUT INTO ANOTHER ONE OF THE "HOMES" THAT SAME DAY.
WE HAVE A NEW ONE.
FINE. HAVE HIM GET IN LINE LIKE THE OTHERS AT THE END OF THE THIRD BALL COURT.
I'LL ASK ONLY ONE MORE TIME! WHO WAS IT?
WHO WAS THE PIG THAT CUT A FART WHILE STANDING IN LINE? I WANT YOU TO TELL ME! IF YOU DON'T YOU'LL ALL PAY FOR IT!

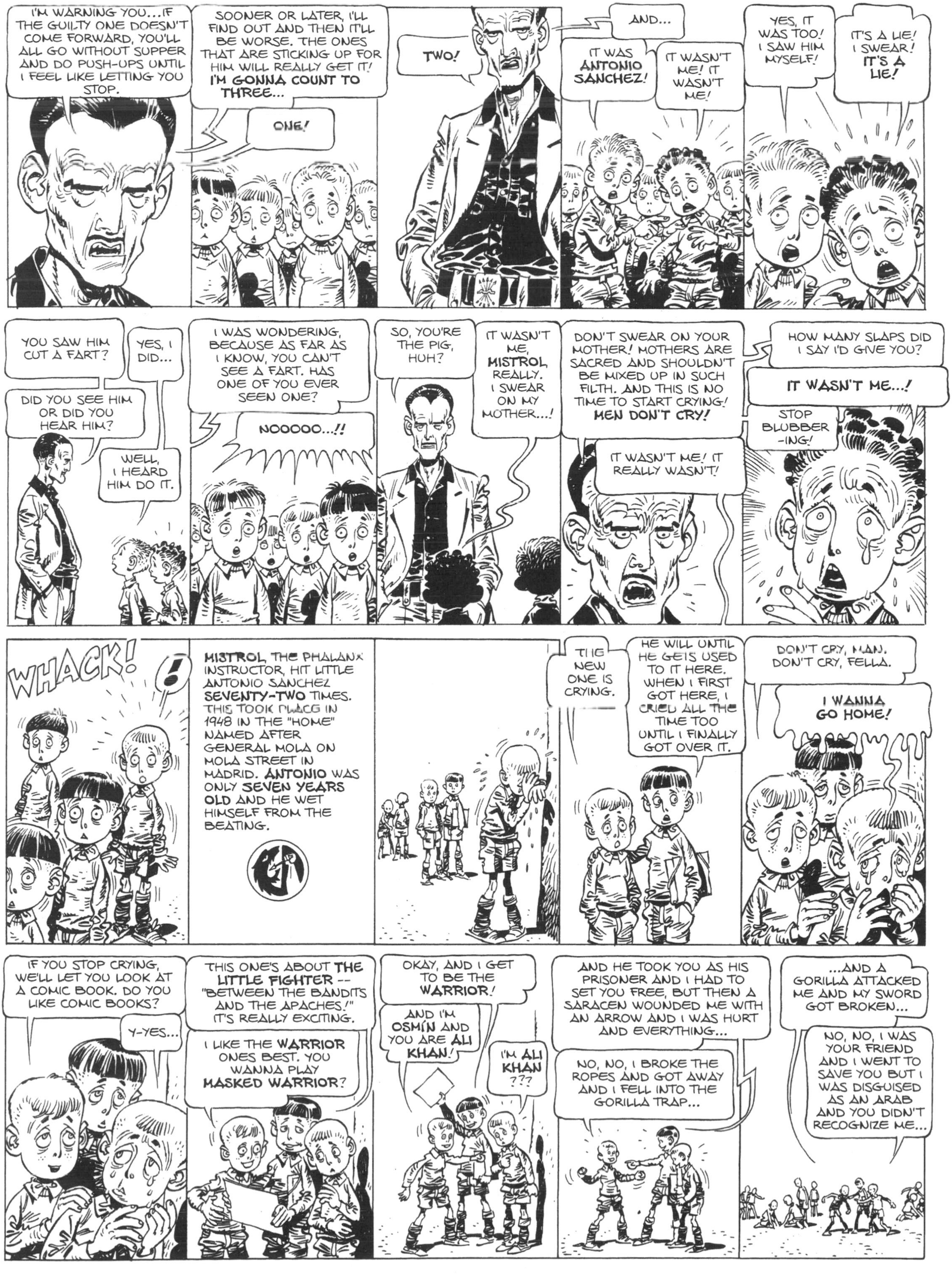
I'M WARNING YOU...IF THE GUILTY ONE DOESN'T COME FORWARD, YOU'LL ALL GO WITHOUT SUPPER AND DO PUSH-UPS UNTIL I FEEL LIKE LETTING YOU STOP.
SOONER OR LATER, I'LL FIND OUT AND THEN IT'LL BE WORSE. THE ONES THAT ARE STICKING UP FOR HIM WILL REALLY GET IT! I'M GONNA COUNT TO THREE...
ONE!
TWO!
AND...
IT WAS ANTONIO SANCHEZ!
IT WASN'T ME! IT WASN'T ME!
YES, IT WAS TOO! I SAW HIM MYSELF!
IT'S A LIE! I SWEAR! IT'S A LIE!
YOU SAW HIM CUT A FART?
YES, I DID...
DID YOU SEE HIM OR DID YOU HEAR HIM?
WELL, I HEARD HIM DO IT.
I WAS WONDERING, BECAUSE AS FAR AS I KNOW, YOU CAN'T SEE A FART. HAS ONE OF YOU EVER SEEN ONE?
NOOOOO...!!
SO, YOU'RE THE PIG, HUH?
IT WASN'T ME, MISTROL, REALLY. I SWEAR ON MY MOTHER...!
DON'T SWEAR ON YOUR MOTHER! MOTHERS ARE SACRED AND SHOULDN'T BE MIXED UP IN SUCH FILTH. AND THIS IS NO TIME TO START CRYING! MEN DON'T CRY!
IT WASN'T ME! IT REALLY WASN'T!
HOW MANY SLAPS DID I SAY I'D GIVE YOU?
IT WASN'T ME...!
STOP BLUBBER-ING!
WHACK!
!
MISTROL, THE PHALANX INSTRUCTOR, HIT LITTLE ANTONIO SANCHEZ SEVENTY-TWO TIMES. THIS TOOK PLACE IN 1948 IN THE "HOME" NAMED AFTER GENERAL MOLA ON MOLA STREET IN MADRID. ANTONIO WAS ONLY SEVEN YEARS OLD AND HE WET HIMSELF FROM THE BEATING.
THE NEW ONE IS CRYING.
HE WILL UNTIL HE GETS USED TO IT HERE. WHEN I FIRST GOT HERE, I CRIED ALL THE TIME TOO UNTIL I FINALLY GOT OVER IT.
DON'T CRY, MAN. DON'T CRY, FELLA.
I WANNA GO HOME!
IF YOU STOP CRYING, WE'LL LET YOU LOOK AT A COMIC BOOK. DO YOU LIKE COMIC BOOKS?
Y-YES...
THIS ONE'S ABOUT THE LITTLE FIGHTER -- "BETWEEN THE BANDITS AND THE APACHES!" IT'S REALLY EXCITING.
I LIKE THE WARRIOR ONES BEST. YOU WANNA PLAY MASKED WARRIOR?
OKAY, AND I GET TO BE THE WARRIOR!
AND I'M OSMÍN AND YOU ARE ALI KHAN!
I'M ALI KHAN ???
AND HE TOOK YOU AS HIS PRISONER AND I HAD TO SET YOU FREE, BUT THEN A SARACEN WOUNDED ME WITH AN ARROW AND I WAS HURT AND EVERYTHING...
NO, NO, I BROKE THE ROPES AND GOT AWAY AND I FELL INTO THE GORILLA TRAP...
...AND A GORILLA ATTACKED ME AND MY SWORD GOT BROKEN...
NO, NO, I WAS YOUR FRIEND AND I WENT TO SAVE YOU BUT I WAS DISGUISED AS AN ARAB AND YOU DIDN'T RECOGNIZE ME...

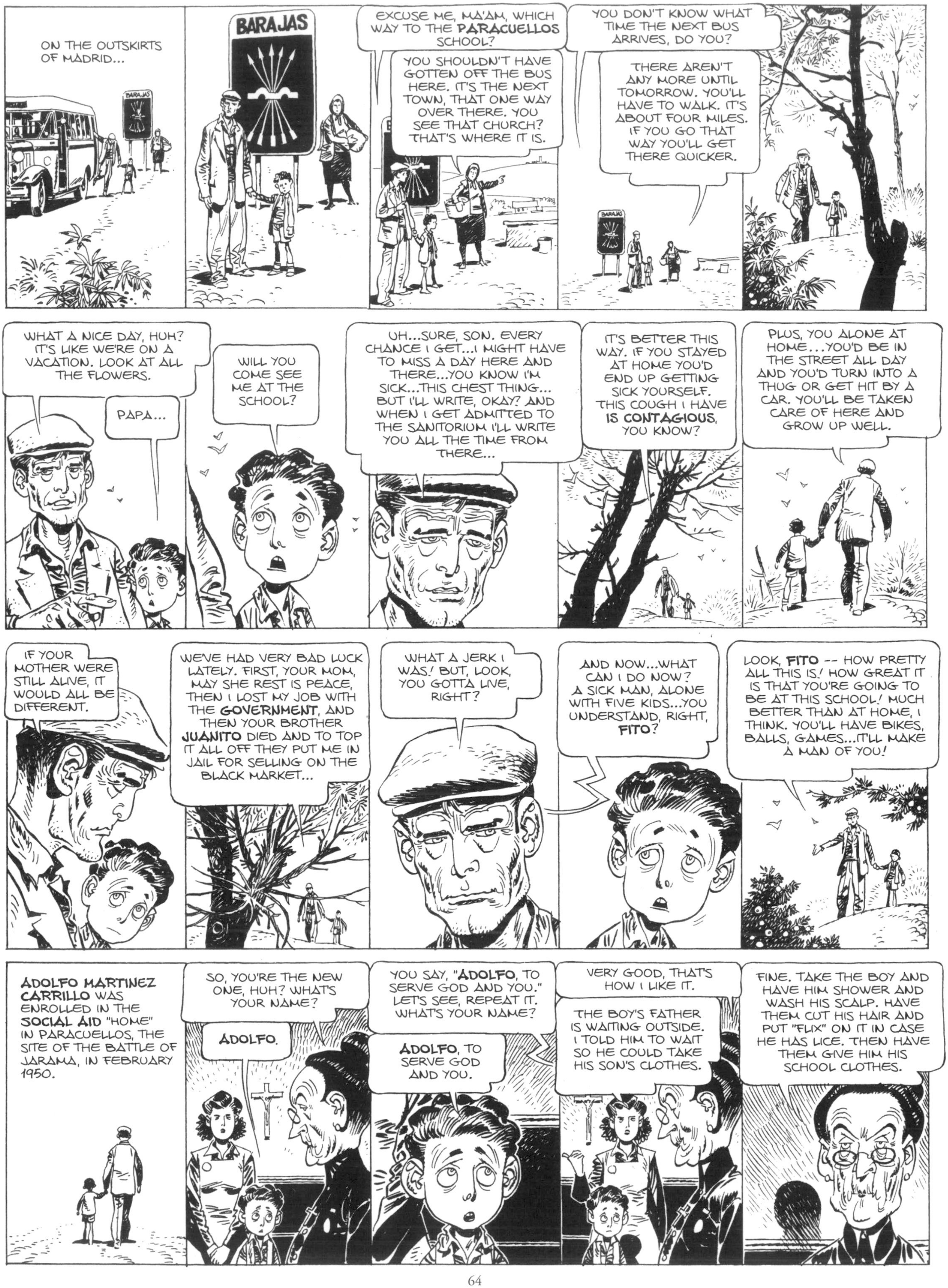

ON THE OUTSKIRTS OF MADRID...
BARAJAS
EXCUSE ME, MA'AM, WHICH WAY TO THE **PARACUELLOS** SCHOOL?
YOU SHOULDN'T HAVE GOTTEN OFF THE BUS HERE. IT'S THE NEXT TOWN, THAT ONE WAY OVER THERE. YOU SEE THAT CHURCH? THAT'S WHERE IT IS.
YOU DON'T KNOW WHAT TIME THE NEXT BUS ARRIVES, DO YOU?
THERE AREN'T ANY MORE UNTIL TOMORROW. YOU'LL HAVE TO WALK. IT'S ABOUT FOUR MILES. IF YOU GO THAT WAY YOU'LL GET THERE QUICKER.
WHAT A NICE DAY, HUH? IT'S LIKE WE'RE ON A VACATION. LOOK AT ALL THE FLOWERS.
PAPA...
WILL YOU COME SEE ME AT THE SCHOOL?
UH...SURE, SON. EVERY CHANCE I GET...I MIGHT HAVE TO MISS A DAY HERE AND THERE...YOU KNOW I'M SICK...THIS CHEST THING... BUT I'LL WRITE, OKAY? AND WHEN I GET ADMITTED TO THE SANITORIUM I'LL WRITE YOU ALL THE TIME FROM THERE...
IT'S BETTER THIS WAY. IF YOU STAYED AT HOME YOU'D END UP GETTING SICK YOURSELF. THIS COUGH I HAVE **IS CONTAGIOUS**, YOU KNOW?
PLUS, YOU ALONE AT HOME...YOU'D BE IN THE STREET ALL DAY AND YOU'D TURN INTO A THUG OR GET HIT BY A CAR. YOU'LL BE TAKEN CARE OF HERE AND GROW UP WELL.
IF YOUR MOTHER WERE STILL ALIVE, IT WOULD ALL BE DIFFERENT.
WE'VE HAD VERY BAD LUCK LATELY. FIRST, YOUR MOM, MAY SHE REST IS PEACE, THEN I LOST MY JOB WITH THE **GOVERNMENT**, AND THEN YOUR BROTHER **JUANITO** DIED AND TO TOP IT ALL OFF THEY PUT ME IN JAIL FOR SELLING ON THE BLACK MARKET...
WHAT A JERK I WAS! BUT, LOOK, YOU GOTTA LIVE, RIGHT?
AND NOW...WHAT CAN I DO NOW? A SICK MAN, ALONE WITH FIVE KIDS...YOU UNDERSTAND, RIGHT, **FITO**?
LOOK, **FITO** -- HOW PRETTY ALL THIS IS! HOW GREAT IT IS THAT YOU'RE GOING TO BE AT THIS SCHOOL! MUCH BETTER THAN AT HOME, I THINK. YOU'LL HAVE BIKES, BALLS, GAMES...IT'LL MAKE A MAN OF YOU!
ADOLFO MARTINEZ CARRILLO WAS ENROLLED IN THE **SOCIAL AID** "HOME" IN PARACUELLOS, THE SITE OF THE BATTLE OF JARAMA, IN FEBRUARY 1950.
SO, YOU'RE THE NEW ONE, HUH? WHAT'S YOUR NAME?
ADOLFO.
YOU SAY, "**ADOLFO**, TO SERVE GOD AND YOU." LET'S SEE, REPEAT IT. WHAT'S YOUR NAME?
ADOLFO, TO SERVE GOD AND YOU.
VERY GOOD, THAT'S HOW I LIKE IT.
THE BOY'S FATHER IS WAITING OUTSIDE. I TOLD HIM TO WAIT SO HE COULD TAKE HIS SON'S CLOTHES.
FINE. TAKE THE BOY AND HAVE HIM SHOWER AND WASH HIS SCALP. HAVE THEM CUT HIS HAIR AND PUT "FLIX" ON IT IN CASE HE HAS LICE. THEN HAVE THEM GIVE HIM HIS SCHOOL CLOTHES.

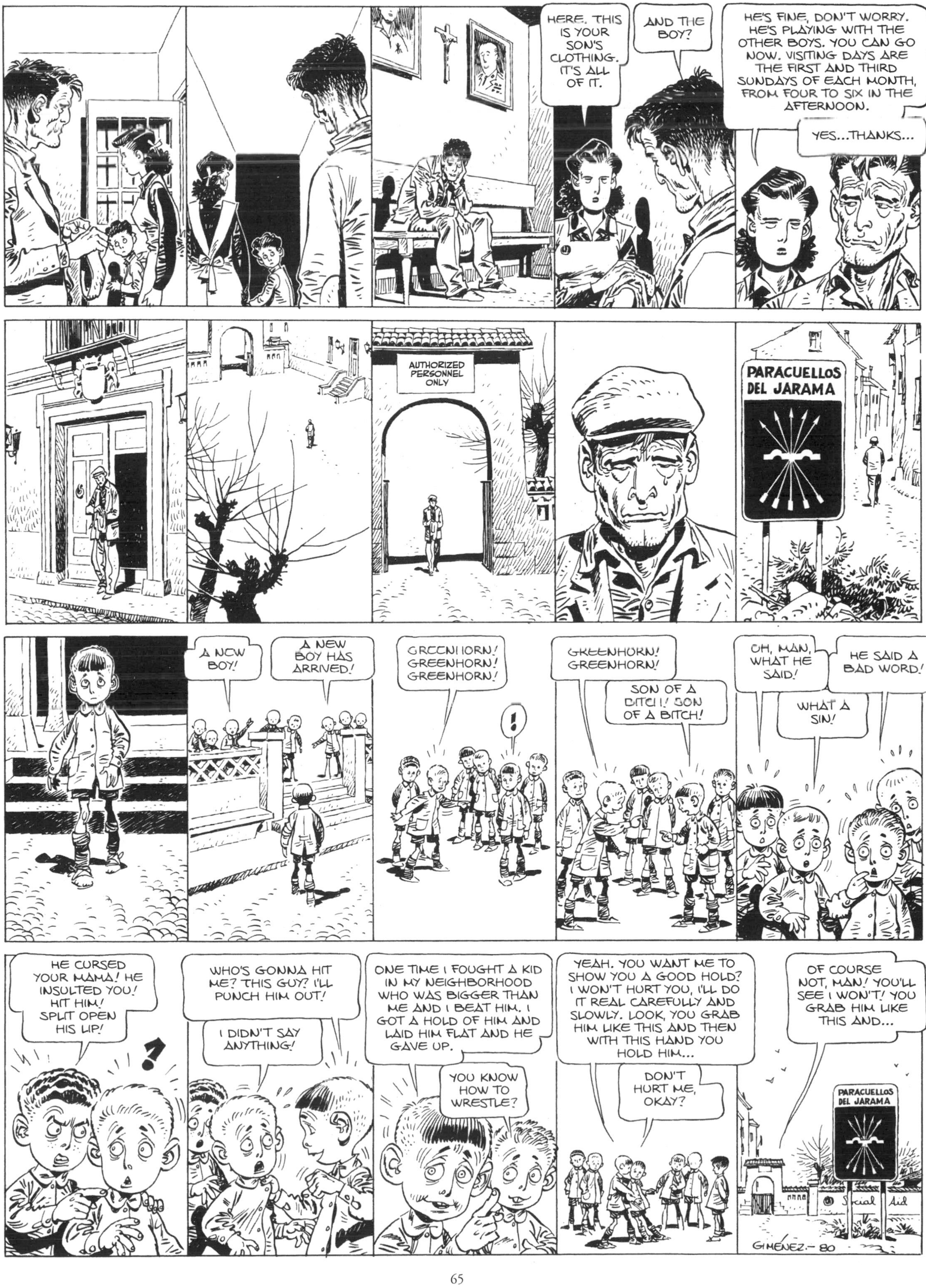
HERE. THIS IS YOUR SON'S CLOTHING. IT'S ALL OF IT.
AND THE BOY?
HE'S FINE, DON'T WORRY. HE'S PLAYING WITH THE OTHER BOYS. YOU CAN GO NOW. VISITING DAYS ARE THE FIRST AND THIRD SUNDAYS OF EACH MONTH, FROM FOUR TO SIX IN THE AFTERNOON.
YES...THANKS...
AUTHORIZED PERSONNEL ONLY
PARACUELLOS DEL JARAMA
A NEW BOY!
A NEW BOY HAS ARRIVED!
GREENHORN! GREENHORN! GREENHORN!
!
GREENHORN! GREENHORN!
SON OF A BITCH! SON OF A BITCH!
OH, MAN, WHAT HE SAID!
WHAT A SIN!
HE SAID A BAD WORD!
HE CURSED YOUR MAMA! HE INSULTED YOU! HIT HIM! SPLIT OPEN HIS LIP!
?
WHO'S GONNA HIT ME? THIS GUY? I'LL PUNCH HIM OUT!
I DIDN'T SAY ANYTHING!
ONE TIME I FOUGHT A KID IN MY NEIGHBORHOOD WHO WAS BIGGER THAN ME AND I BEAT HIM. I GOT A HOLD OF HIM AND LAID HIM FLAT AND HE GAVE UP.
YOU KNOW HOW TO WRESTLE?
YEAH. YOU WANT ME TO SHOW YOU A GOOD HOLD? I WON'T HURT YOU, I'LL DO IT REAL CAREFULLY AND SLOWLY. LOOK, YOU GRAB HIM LIKE THIS AND THEN WITH THIS HAND YOU HOLD HIM...
DON'T HURT ME, OKAY?
OF COURSE NOT, MAN! YOU'LL SEE I WON'T! YOU GRAB HIM LIKE THIS AND...
PARACUELLOS DEL JARAMA
Social Aid
GIMÉNEZ.- 80

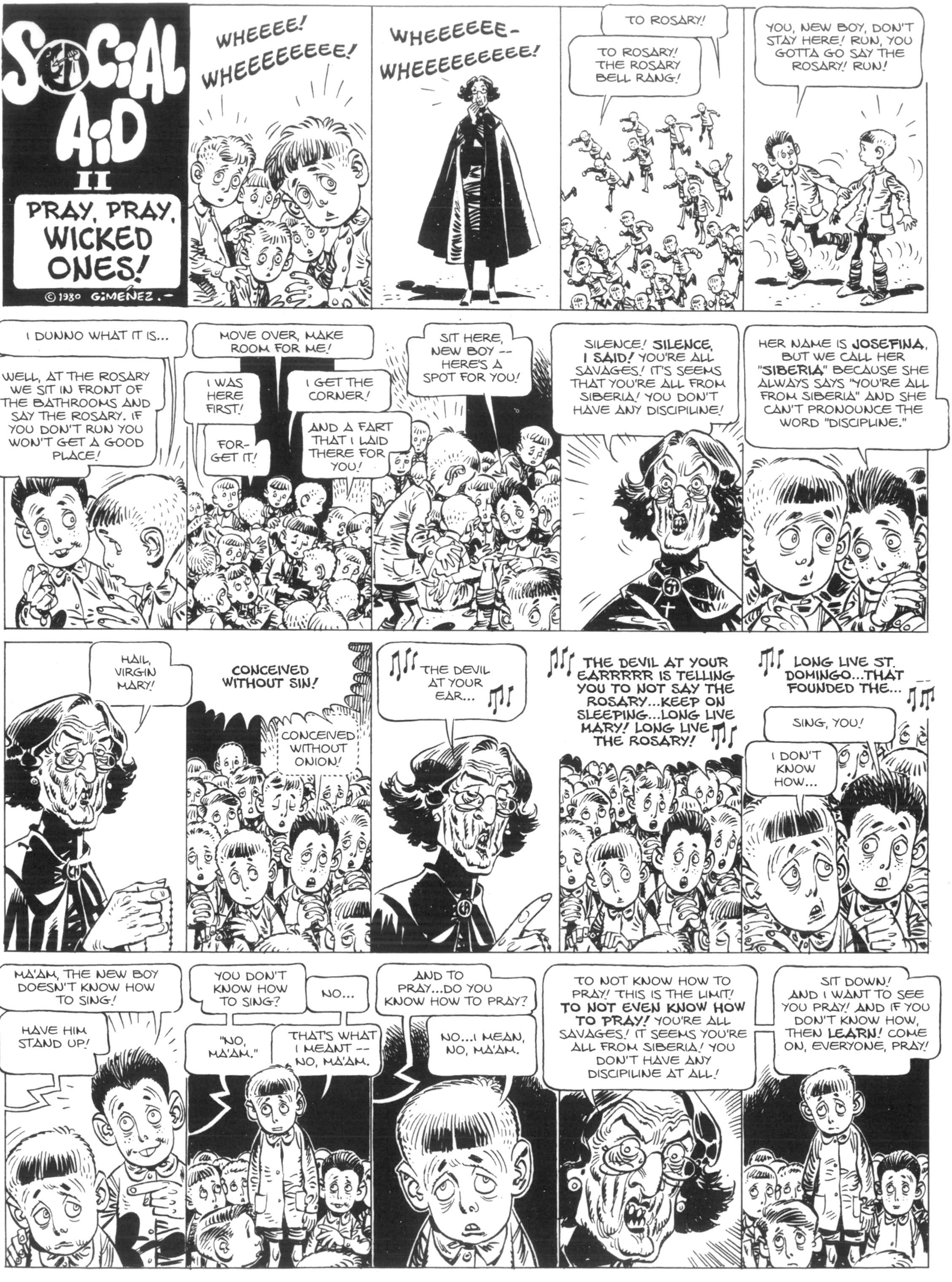

SOCIAL AID
II
PRAY, PRAY, WICKED ONES!
©1980 GIMENEZ.-
WHEEEE! WHEEEEEEEE!
WHEEEEEE-WHEEEEEEEEE!
TO ROSARY!
TO ROSARY! THE ROSARY BELL RANG!
YOU, NEW BOY, DON'T STAY HERE! RUN, YOU GOTTA GO SAY THE ROSARY! RUN!
I DUNNO WHAT IT IS...
WELL, AT THE ROSARY WE SIT IN FRONT OF THE BATHROOMS AND SAY THE ROSARY. IF YOU DON'T RUN YOU WON'T GET A GOOD PLACE!
MOVE OVER, MAKE ROOM FOR ME!
I WAS HERE FIRST!
FOR-GET IT!
I GET THE CORNER!
AND A FART THAT I LAID THERE FOR YOU!
SIT HERE, NEW BOY -- HERE'S A SPOT FOR YOU!
SILENCE! SILENCE, I SAID! YOU'RE ALL SAVAGES! IT'S SEEMS THAT YOU'RE ALL FROM SIBERIA! YOU DON'T HAVE ANY DISCIPILINE!
HER NAME IS JOSEFINA, BUT WE CALL HER "SIBERIA" BECAUSE SHE ALWAYS SAYS "YOU'RE ALL FROM SIBERIA" AND SHE CAN'T PRONOUNCE THE WORD "DISCIPLINE."
HAIL, VIRGIN MARY!
CONCEIVED WITHOUT SIN!
CONCEIVED WITHOUT ONION!
THE DEVIL AT YOUR EAR...
THE DEVIL AT YOUR EARRRRR IS TELLING YOU TO NOT SAY THE ROSARY...KEEP ON SLEEPING...LONG LIVE MARY! LONG LIVE THE ROSARY!
LONG LIVE ST. DOMINGO...THAT FOUNDED THE...
SING, YOU!
I DON'T KNOW HOW...
MA'AM, THE NEW BOY DOESN'T KNOW HOW TO SING!
HAVE HIM STAND UP!
YOU DON'T KNOW HOW TO SING?
NO...
"NO, MA'AM."
THAT'S WHAT I MEANT -- NO, MA'AM.
AND TO PRAY...DO YOU KNOW HOW TO PRAY?
NO...I MEAN, NO, MA'AM.
TO NOT KNOW HOW TO PRAY! THIS IS THE LIMIT! TO NOT EVEN KNOW HOW TO PRAY! YOU'RE ALL SAVAGES! IT SEEMS YOU'RE ALL FROM SIBERIA! YOU DON'T HAVE ANY DISCIPILINE AT ALL!
SIT DOWN! AND I WANT TO SEE YOU PRAY! AND IF YOU DON'T KNOW HOW, THEN LEARN! COME ON, EVERYONE, PRAY!

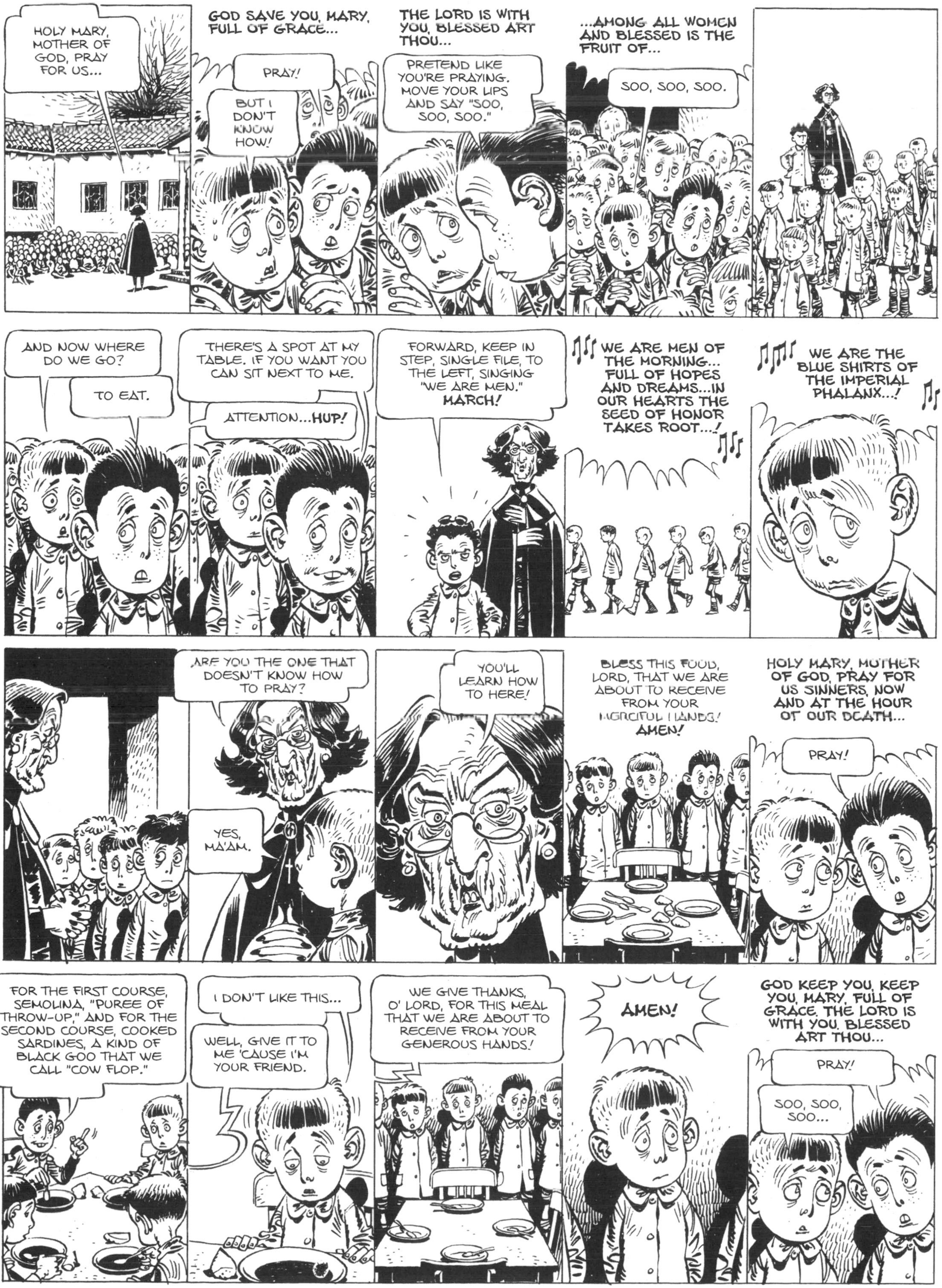

HOLY MARY, MOTHER OF GOD, PRAY FOR US...
GOD SAVE YOU, MARY, FULL OF GRACE...
PRAY!
BUT I DON'T KNOW HOW!
THE LORD IS WITH YOU, BLESSED ART THOU...
PRETEND LIKE YOU'RE PRAYING. MOVE YOUR LIPS AND SAY "SOO, SOO, SOO."
...AMONG ALL WOMEN AND BLESSED IS THE FRUIT OF...
SOO, SOO, SOO.
AND NOW WHERE DO WE GO?
TO EAT.
THERE'S A SPOT AT MY TABLE. IF YOU WANT YOU CAN SIT NEXT TO ME.
ATTENTION...HUP!
FORWARD, KEEP IN STEP, SINGLE FILE, TO THE LEFT, SINGING "WE ARE MEN." MARCH!
WE ARE MEN OF THE MORNING... FULL OF HOPES AND DREAMS...IN OUR HEARTS THE SEED OF HONOR TAKES ROOT...!
WE ARE THE BLUE SHIRTS OF THE IMPERIAL PHALANX...!
ARE YOU THE ONE THAT DOESN'T KNOW HOW TO PRAY?
YES, MA'AM.
YOU'LL LEARN HOW TO HERE!
BLESS THIS FOOD, LORD, THAT WE ARE ABOUT TO RECEIVE FROM YOUR MERCIFUL HANDS! AMEN!
HOLY MARY, MOTHER OF GOD, PRAY FOR US SINNERS, NOW AND AT THE HOUR OF OUR DEATH...
PRAY!
FOR THE FIRST COURSE, SEMOLINA, "PUREE OF THROW-UP," AND FOR THE SECOND COURSE, COOKED SARDINES, A KIND OF BLACK GOO THAT WE CALL "COW FLOP."
I DON'T LIKE THIS...
WELL, GIVE IT TO ME 'CAUSE I'M YOUR FRIEND.
WE GIVE THANKS, O' LORD, FOR THIS MEAL THAT WE ARE ABOUT TO RECEIVE FROM YOUR GENEROUS HANDS!
AMEN!
GOD KEEP YOU, KEEP YOU, MARY, FULL OF GRACE. THE LORD IS WITH YOU. BLESSED ART THOU...
PRAY!
SOO, SOO, SOO...

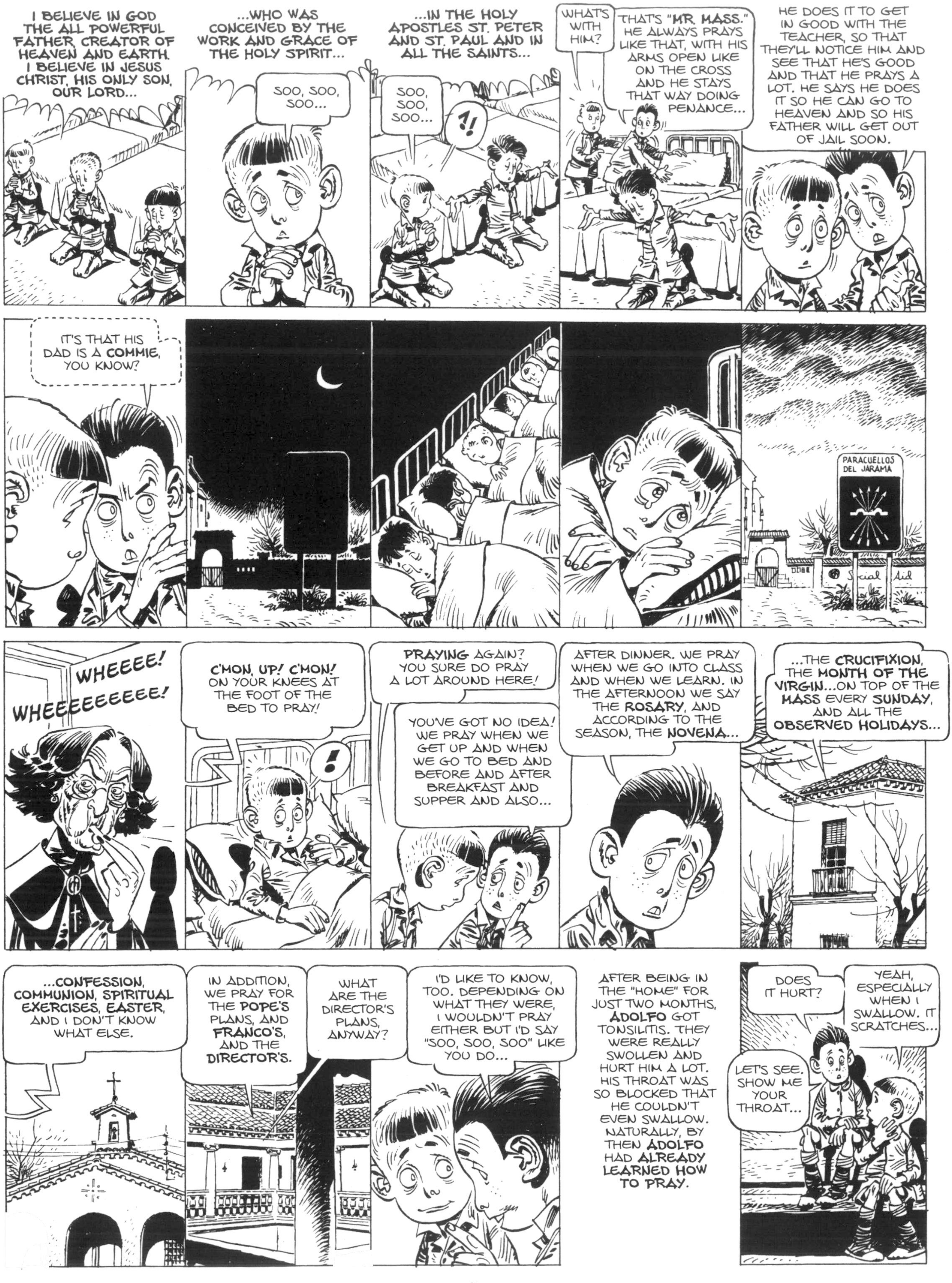

I BELIEVE IN GOD THE ALL POWERFUL FATHER, CREATOR OF HEAVEN AND EARTH. I BELIEVE IN JESUS CHRIST, HIS ONLY SON, OUR LORD...
...WHO WAS CONCEIVED BY THE WORK AND GRACE OF THE HOLY SPIRIT...
SOO, SOO, SOO...
...IN THE HOLY APOSTLES ST. PETER AND ST. PAUL AND IN ALL THE SAINTS...
SOO, SOO, SOO...
?!
WHAT'S WITH HIM?
THAT'S "MR. MASS." HE ALWAYS PRAYS LIKE THAT, WITH HIS ARMS OPEN LIKE ON THE CROSS AND HE STAYS THAT WAY DOING PENANCE...
HE DOES IT TO GET IN GOOD WITH THE TEACHER, SO THAT THEY'LL NOTICE HIM AND SEE THAT HE'S GOOD AND THAT HE PRAYS A LOT. HE SAYS HE DOES IT SO HE CAN GO TO HEAVEN AND SO HIS FATHER WILL GET OUT OF JAIL SOON.
IT'S THAT HIS DAD IS A COMMIE, YOU KNOW?
PARACUELLOS DEL JARAMA
Social Aid
WHEEEE!
WHEEEEEEEEE!
C'MON, UP! C'MON! ON YOUR KNEES AT THE FOOT OF THE BED TO PRAY!
!
PRAYING AGAIN? YOU SURE DO PRAY A LOT AROUND HERE!
YOU'VE GOT NO IDEA! WE PRAY WHEN WE GET UP AND WHEN WE GO TO BED AND BEFORE AND AFTER BREAKFAST AND SUPPER AND ALSO...
AFTER DINNER. WE PRAY WHEN WE GO INTO CLASS AND WHEN WE LEARN. IN THE AFTERNOON WE SAY THE ROSARY, AND ACCORDING TO THE SEASON, THE NOVENA...
...THE CRUCIFIXION, THE MONTH OF THE VIRGIN...ON TOP OF THE MASS EVERY SUNDAY, AND ALL THE OBSERVED HOLIDAYS...
...CONFESSION, COMMUNION, SPIRITUAL EXERCISES, EASTER, AND I DON'T KNOW WHAT ELSE.
IN ADDITION, WE PRAY FOR THE POPE'S PLANS, AND FRANCO'S, AND THE DIRECTOR'S.
WHAT ARE THE DIRECTOR'S PLANS, ANYWAY?
I'D LIKE TO KNOW, TOO. DEPENDING ON WHAT THEY WERE, I WOULDN'T PRAY EITHER BUT I'D SAY "SOO, SOO, SOO" LIKE YOU DO...
AFTER BEING IN THE "HOME" FOR JUST TWO MONTHS, ADOLFO GOT TONSILITIS. THEY WERE REALLY SWOLLEN AND HURT HIM A LOT. HIS THROAT WAS SO BLOCKED THAT HE COULDN'T EVEN SWALLOW. NATURALLY, BY THEN ADOLFO HAD ALREADY LEARNED HOW TO PRAY.
DOES IT HURT?
YEAH, ESPECIALLY WHEN I SWALLOW. IT SCRATCHES...
LET'S SEE. SHOW ME YOUR THROAT...

Panel 1: AAARRRGH! IT'S ALL STOPPED UP...AND PRETTY FULL UP PUS... IT SMELLS KIND OF BAD...

Panel 2: WHAT DID THE NURSE TELL YOU? — THAT I'VE GOT A FEVER AND I DON'T KNOW WHAT ELSE...AND THAT TOMORROW MORNING THEY'RE GONNA COME IN A CAR TO TAKE ME TO THE **INFIRMARY** FOR AN OPERATION...

Panel 3: BUT I DON'T WANT THEM TO OPERATE ON ME!

Panel 4: GLORY TO THE FATHER THE SON, AND THE HOLY GHOST... — I DON'T WANT THEM TO OPERATE ON ME ...I DON'T WANT THEM TO OPERATE ON ME...

Panel 5: I DON'T WANT AN OPERATION...PLEASE, DON'T LET THEM OPERATE ON ME, DEAR LORD, MAKE THE PAIN GO AWAY ...DON'T LET THEM OPERATE ON ME...

Panel 6: OUR FATHER WHO ART IN HEAVEN...PLEASE DON'T LET THEM OPERATE ON ME, DON'T LET THEM HURT ME, DON'T LET IT HURT... HOW COLD IT IS!

Panel 7: DON'T LET THEM OPERATE ON ME. YOU CAN PERFORM A MIRACLE TO HAVE THEM NOT OPERATE ON ME...IF YOU'LL JUST SAY, "DON'T OPERATE ON HIM," THAT'LL DO IT...C'MON GOD, SAY IT...

Panel 8: YOU SEE HOW COLD I AM?...I'M DOING ALL THIS SO THEY DON'T OPERATE ON ME. GO ON, JUST ONE MIRACLE, IT'LL BE SO EASY FOR YOU...DON'T LET THEM DO ANYTHING TO ME...DO YOU MIND IF I LAY DOWN FOR A WHILE AND KEEP PRAYING TO YOU IN BED?

Panel 9: LOOK, GOD, I'LL SPEND ALL NIGHT PRAYING TO YOU, AND YOU, IN EXCHANGE, WILL DO THE MIRACLE AND WHEN THEY COME FOR ME TOMORROW MORNING, ZAP! I'LL BE CURED. I'LL SAY THE ROSARY TO YOU, OKAY? I DON'T KNOW THE LITANY BY HEART...

Panel 10: OUR FATHER, WHO ART IN HEAVEN...HOW SLEEPY I AM! OUR FATHER WHO ART IN HEAVEN, HALLOWED BE...THY NAME...

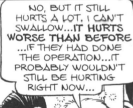

Panel 11: HAIL MARY, MOTHER OF GOD, PRAY FOR US...SINNERS...HOW MANY HAIL MARYS HAVE I SAID ALREADY? I LOST COUNT AGAIN! IF ONLY MY THROAT DIDN'T HURT SO MUCH!...LET'S SEE, I'LL START OVER -- HAIL MARY...MOTHER...OF... GOD...

Panel 12: *Z*

Panel 13: THE NEXT DAY, JUST AS HE HAD EXPECTED, A CAR CAME TO TAKE **ADOLFO** TO THE **INFIRMARY**. THE DOCTOR WHO WAS SUPPOSED TO OPERATE ON HIM DIDN'T SHOW UP AT THE CLINIC. **ADOLFO** WAITED ALL MORNING AND FINALLY THEY BROUGHT HIM BACK TO THE "HOME" WITH HIS TONSILS, HIS PUS, HIS PAINS, AND HIS FEVER.

Panel 14: THEY DIDN'T OPERATE ON YOU? — NO, BUT IT STILL HURTS A LOT. I CAN'T SWALLOW...**IT HURTS WORSE THAN BEFORE** ...IF THEY HAD DONE THE OPERATION...IT PROBABLY WOULDN'T STILL BE HURTING RIGHT NOW...

Panel 15: WHY DON'TCHA PRAY? MAYBE IF YOU PRAYED... — BUT THAT'S ALL I DO!

Panel 16: ...WHO ART IN HEAVEN... HALLOWED...BE THY NAME...

Panel 17: AARRRRGH...! — YOU DON'T HAVE ANYTHING. NO PUS OR ANYTHING...IT LOOKS NORMAL...IT SMELLS A LITTLE BAD, BUT NORMAL...

Panel 18: TWO DAYS LATER, **ADOLFO**'S TONSILITIS SUDDENLY DISAPPEARED... AND AS IF ALL THIS WEREN'T ENOUGH, THAT SAME DAY **ADOLFO**'S FATHER AND BROTHER CAME TO VISIT HIM FOR THE VERY FIRST TIME. HIS FATHER BROUGHT HIM A MINIATURE CAR AND HE GAVE HIM TWO PESETAS. THE MINIATURE CAR'S WIND-UP SPRING GOT BROKEN RIGHT AWAY, AND THE TWO PESETAS GOT LOST THAT SAME AFTERNOON.

Panel 19: OUR FATHER WHO ART IN HEAVEN...LET ME FIND THE TWO PESETAS... I DON'T MIND ABOUT THE CAR, BUT THE TWO PESETAS REALLY MATTER...HALLOWED BE THY NAME...DON'T FORGET, THE TWO PESETAS...

Panel 20: **ADOLFO** PRAYED UNTIL HE WAS SICK OF IT BUT THE TWO PESETAS NEVER TURNED UP. — WHY DON'T YOU PRAY FOR THE TWO PESETAS TO GET FOUND! — GO TO HELL!

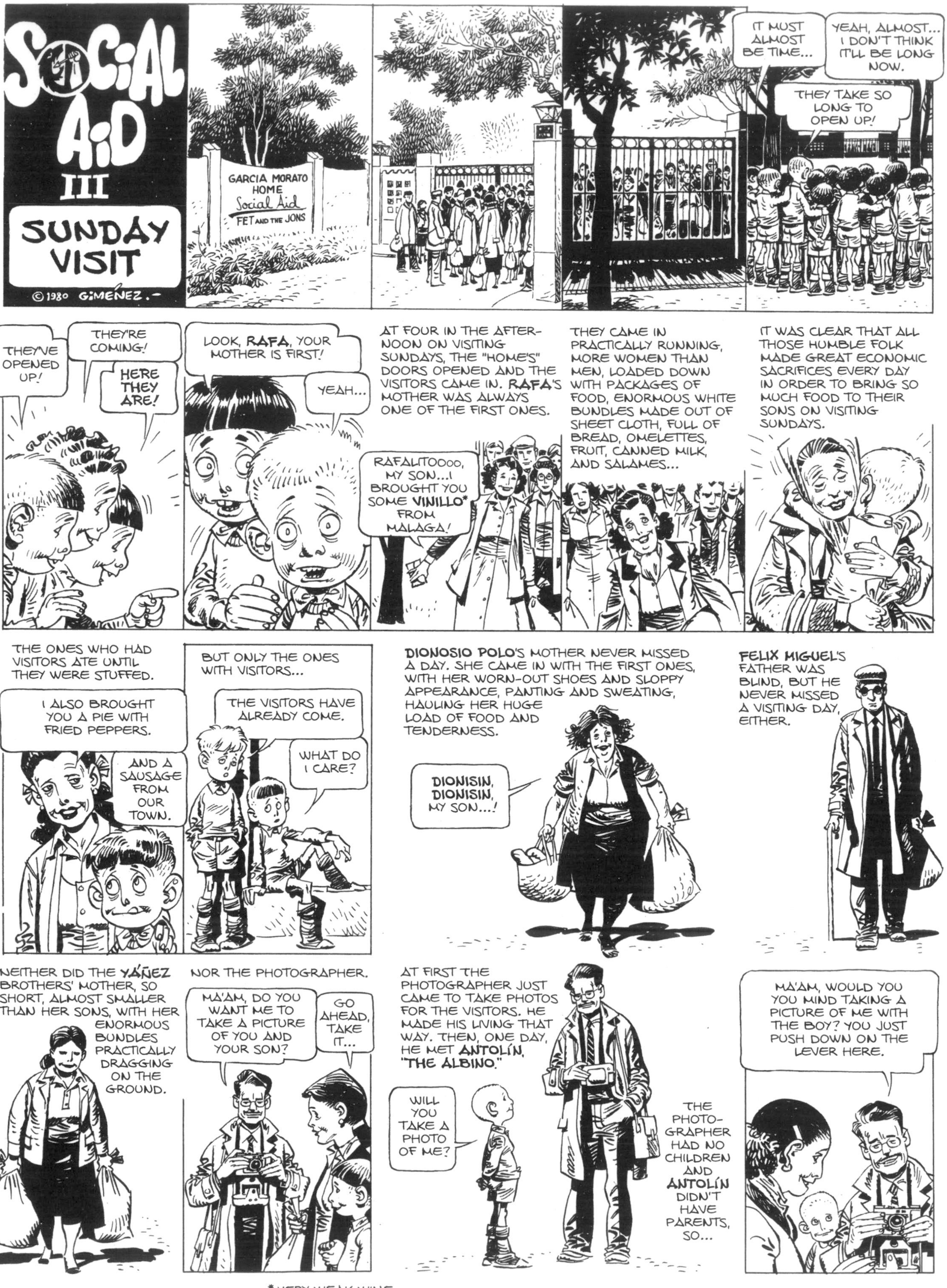
SOCIAL AID
III
SUNDAY VISIT
©1980 GIMENEZ.-
GARCIA MORATO HOME
Social Aid
FET AND THE JONS
IT MUST ALMOST BE TIME...
YEAH, ALMOST... I DON'T THINK IT'LL BE LONG NOW.
THEY TAKE SO LONG TO OPEN UP!
THEY'VE OPENED UP!
THEY'RE COMING!
HERE THEY ARE!
LOOK, RAFA, YOUR MOTHER IS FIRST!
YEAH...
AT FOUR IN THE AFTERNOON ON VISITING SUNDAYS, THE "HOME'S" DOORS OPENED AND THE VISITORS CAME IN. RAFA'S MOTHER WAS ALWAYS ONE OF THE FIRST ONES.
RAFALITOOOO, MY SON...I BROUGHT YOU SOME VINILLO* FROM MALAGA!
THEY CAME IN PRACTICALLY RUNNING, MORE WOMEN THAN MEN, LOADED DOWN WITH PACKAGES OF FOOD, ENORMOUS WHITE BUNDLES MADE OUT OF SHEET CLOTH, FULL OF BREAD, OMELETTES, FRUIT, CANNED MILK, AND SALAMES...
IT WAS CLEAR THAT ALL THOSE HUMBLE FOLK MADE GREAT ECONOMIC SACRIFICES EVERY DAY IN ORDER TO BRING SO MUCH FOOD TO THEIR SONS ON VISITING SUNDAYS.
THE ONES WHO HAD VISITORS ATE UNTIL THEY WERE STUFFED.
I ALSO BROUGHT YOU A PIE WITH FRIED PEPPERS.
AND A SAUSAGE FROM OUR TOWN.
BUT ONLY THE ONES WITH VISITORS...
THE VISITORS HAVE ALREADY COME.
WHAT DO I CARE?
DIONOSIO POLO'S MOTHER NEVER MISSED A DAY. SHE CAME IN WITH THE FIRST ONES, WITH HER WORN-OUT SHOES AND SLOPPY APPEARANCE, PANTING AND SWEATING, HAULING HER HUGE LOAD OF FOOD AND TENDERNESS.
DIONISIN, DIONISIN, MY SON...!
FELIX MIGUEL'S FATHER WAS BLIND, BUT HE NEVER MISSED A VISITING DAY, EITHER.
NEITHER DID THE YÁÑEZ BROTHERS' MOTHER, SO SHORT, ALMOST SMALLER THAN HER SONS, WITH HER ENORMOUS BUNDLES PRACTICALLY DRAGGING ON THE GROUND.
NOR THE PHOTOGRAPHER.
MA'AM, DO YOU WANT ME TO TAKE A PICTURE OF YOU AND YOUR SON?
GO AHEAD, TAKE IT...
AT FIRST THE PHOTOGRAPHER JUST CAME TO TAKE PHOTOS FOR THE VISITORS. HE MADE HIS LIVING THAT WAY. THEN, ONE DAY, HE MET ANTOLÍN, "THE ALBINO."
WILL YOU TAKE A PHOTO OF ME?
THE PHOTOGRAPHER HAD NO CHILDREN AND ANTOLÍN DIDN'T HAVE PARENTS, SO...
MA'AM, WOULD YOU YOU MIND TAKING A PICTURE OF ME WITH THE BOY? YOU JUST PUSH DOWN ON THE LEVER HERE.

* VERY WEAK WINE

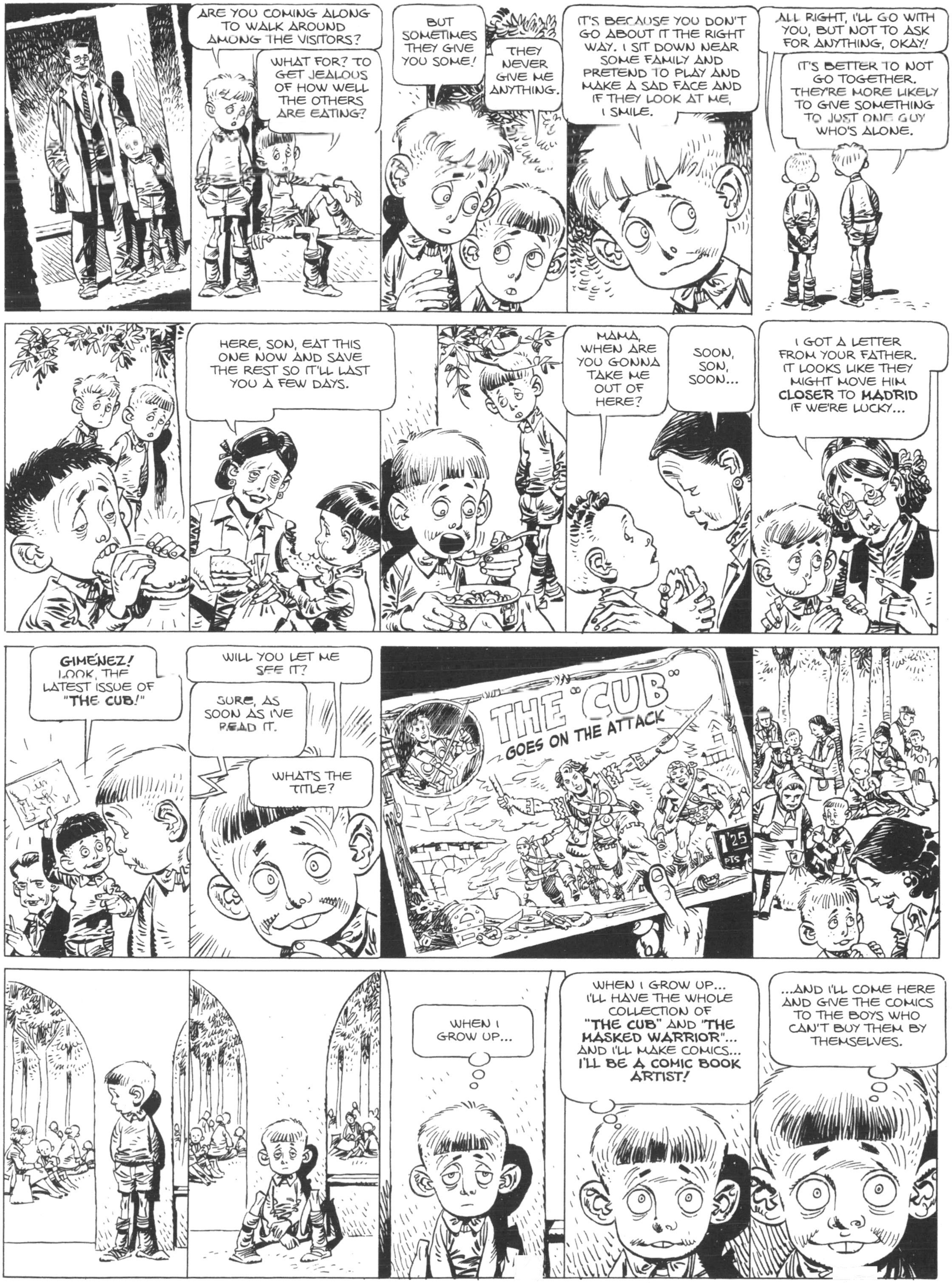

ARE YOU COMING ALONG TO WALK AROUND AMONG THE VISITORS?
WHAT FOR? TO GET JEALOUS OF HOW WELL THE OTHERS ARE EATING?
BUT SOMETIMES THEY GIVE YOU SOME!
THEY NEVER GIVE ME ANYTHING.
IT'S BECAUSE YOU DON'T GO ABOUT IT THE RIGHT WAY. I SIT DOWN NEAR SOME FAMILY AND PRETEND TO PLAY AND MAKE A SAD FACE AND IF THEY LOOK AT ME, I SMILE.
ALL RIGHT, I'LL GO WITH YOU, BUT NOT TO ASK FOR ANYTHING, OKAY!
IT'S BETTER TO NOT GO TOGETHER. THEY'RE MORE LIKELY TO GIVE SOMETHING TO JUST ONE GUY WHO'S ALONE.
HERE, SON, EAT THIS ONE NOW AND SAVE THE REST SO IT'LL LAST YOU A FEW DAYS.
MAMA, WHEN ARE YOU GONNA TAKE ME OUT OF HERE?
SOON, SON, SOON...
I GOT A LETTER FROM YOUR FATHER. IT LOOKS LIKE THEY MIGHT MOVE HIM CLOSER TO MADRID IF WE'RE LUCKY...
GIMÉNEZ! LOOK, THE LATEST ISSUE OF "THE CUB!"
WILL YOU LET ME SEE IT?
SURE, AS SOON AS I'VE READ IT.
WHAT'S THE TITLE?
THE "CUB"
GOES ON THE ATTACK
1'25 PTS
WHEN I GROW UP...
WHEN I GROW UP... I'LL HAVE THE WHOLE COLLECTION OF "THE CUB" AND "THE MASKED WARRIOR"... AND I'LL MAKE COMICS... I'LL BE A COMIC BOOK ARTIST!
...AND I'LL COME HERE AND GIVE THE COMICS TO THE BOYS WHO CAN'T BUY THEM BY THEMSELVES.

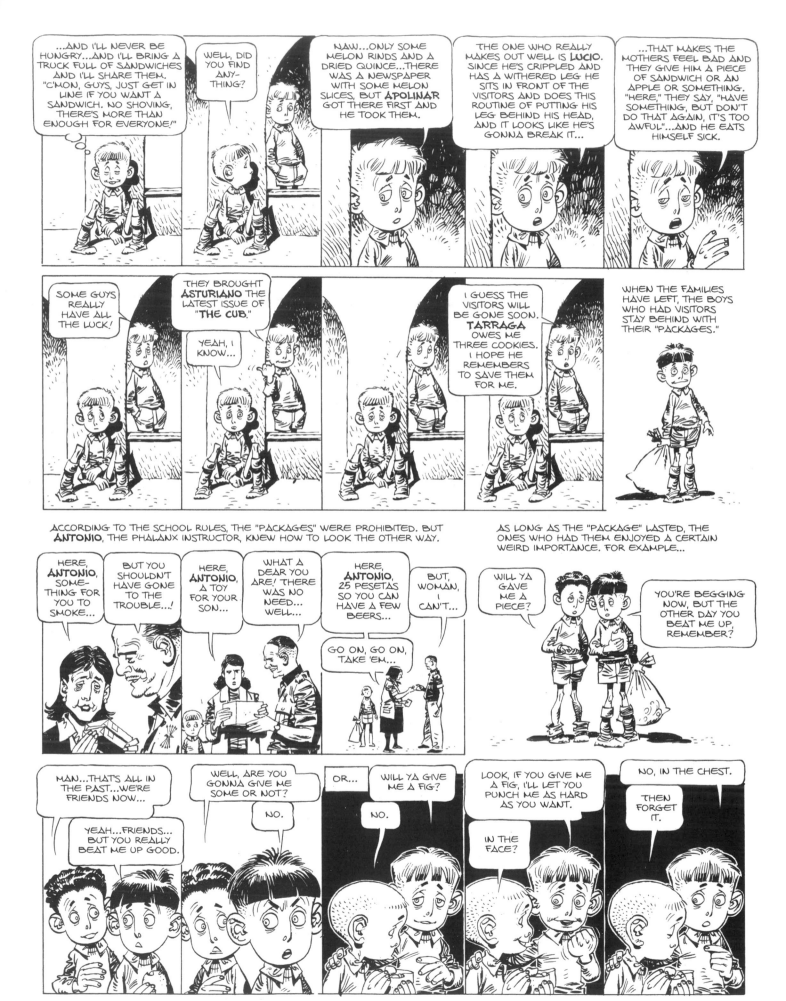

...AND I'LL NEVER BE HUNGRY...AND I'LL BRING A TRUCK FULL OF SANDWICHES AND I'LL SHARE THEM. "C'MON, GUYS, JUST GET IN LINE IF YOU WANT A SANDWICH. NO SHOVING, THERE'S MORE THAN ENOUGH FOR EVERYONE!"

WELL, DID YOU FIND ANYTHING?

NAW...ONLY SOME MELON RINDS AND A DRIED QUINCE...THERE WAS A NEWSPAPER WITH SOME MELON SLICES, BUT APOLINAR GOT THERE FIRST AND HE TOOK THEM.

THE ONE WHO REALLY MAKES OUT WELL IS LUCIO. SINCE HE'S CRIPPLED AND HAS A WITHERED LEG HE SITS IN FRONT OF THE VISITORS AND DOES THIS ROUTINE OF PUTTING HIS LEG BEHIND HIS HEAD, AND IT LOOKS LIKE HE'S GONNA BREAK IT...

...THAT MAKES THE MOTHERS FEEL BAD AND THEY GIVE HIM A PIECE OF SANDWICH OR AN APPLE OR SOMETHING. "HERE," THEY SAY, "HAVE SOMETHING, BUT DON'T DO THAT AGAIN, IT'S TOO AWFUL"...AND HE EATS HIMSELF SICK.

SOME GUYS REALLY HAVE ALL THE LUCK!

THEY BROUGHT ASTURIANO THE LATEST ISSUE OF "THE CUB."

YEAH, I KNOW...

I GUESS THE VISITORS WILL BE GONE SOON. TARRAGA OWES ME THREE COOKIES. I HOPE HE REMEMBERS TO SAVE THEM FOR ME.

WHEN THE FAMILIES HAVE LEFT, THE BOYS WHO HAD VISITORS STAY BEHIND WITH THEIR "PACKAGES."

ACCORDING TO THE SCHOOL RULES, THE "PACKAGES" WERE PROHIBITED. BUT ANTONIO, THE PHALANX INSTRUCTOR, KNEW HOW TO LOOK THE OTHER WAY.

AS LONG AS THE "PACKAGE" LASTED, THE ONES WHO HAD THEM ENJOYED A CERTAIN WEIRD IMPORTANCE. FOR EXAMPLE...

HERE, ANTONIO, SOMETHING FOR YOU TO SMOKE...

BUT YOU SHOULDN'T HAVE GONE TO THE TROUBLE...!

HERE, ANTONIO, A TOY FOR YOUR SON...

WHAT A DEAR YOU ARE! THERE WAS NO NEED... WELL...

HERE, ANTONIO, 25 PESETAS SO YOU CAN HAVE A FEW BEERS...

BUT, WOMAN, I CAN'T...

GO ON, GO ON, TAKE 'EM...

WILL YA GIVE ME A PIECE?

YOU'RE BEGGING NOW, BUT THE OTHER DAY YOU BEAT ME UP, REMEMBER?

MAN...THAT'S ALL IN THE PAST...WE'RE FRIENDS NOW...

YEAH...FRIENDS... BUT YOU REALLY BEAT ME UP GOOD.

WELL, ARE YOU GONNA GIVE ME SOME OR NOT?

NO.

OR...

WILL YA GIVE ME A FIG?

NO.

LOOK, IF YOU GIVE ME A FIG, I'LL LET YOU PUNCH ME AS HARD AS YOU WANT.

IN THE FACE?

NO, IN THE CHEST.

THEN FORGET IT.

72

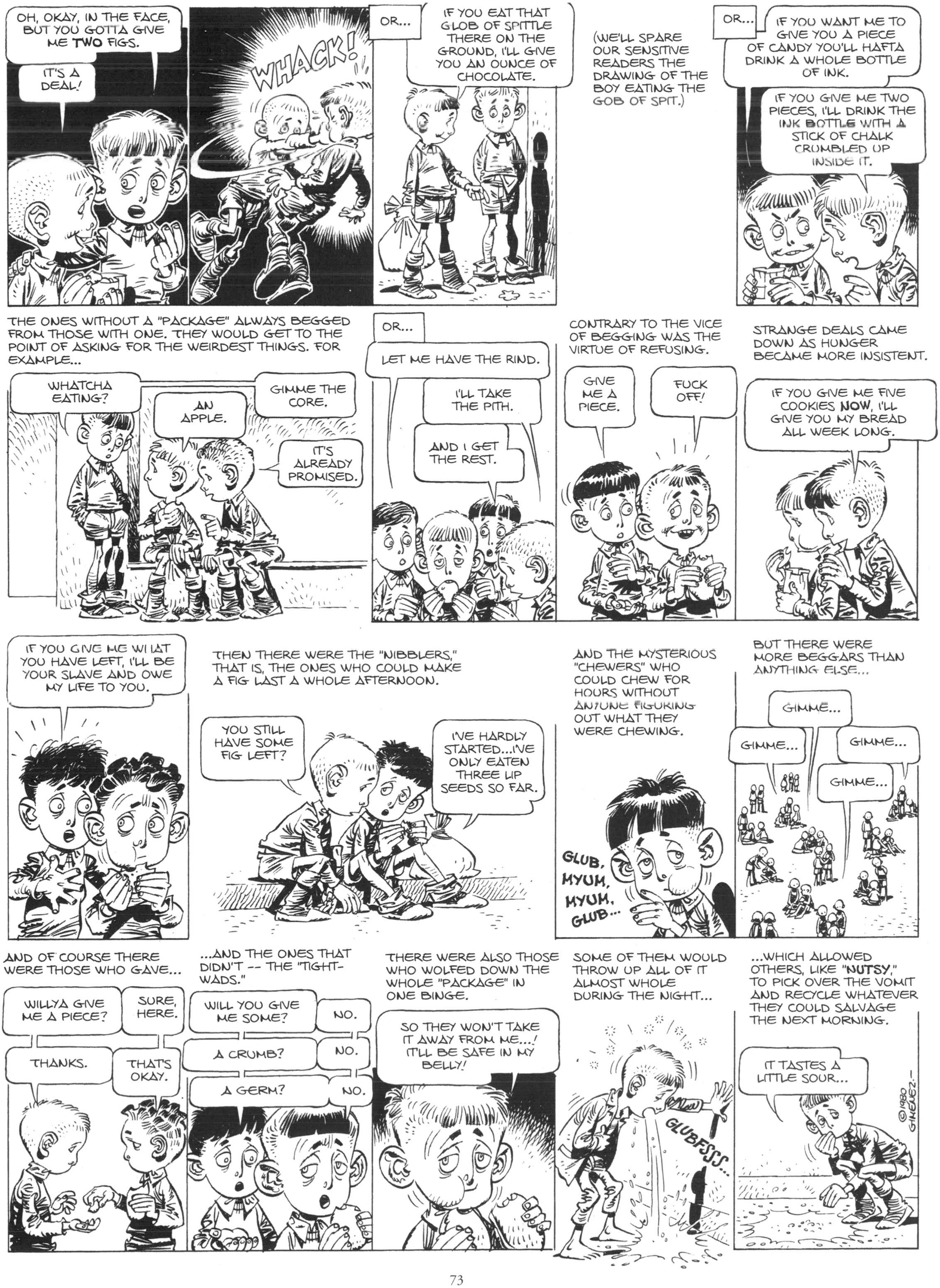

OH, OKAY, IN THE FACE, BUT YOU GOTTA GIVE ME TWO FIGS.
IT'S A DEAL!
WHACK!
OR...
IF YOU EAT THAT GLOB OF SPITTLE THERE ON THE GROUND, I'LL GIVE YOU AN OUNCE OF CHOCOLATE.
(WE'LL SPARE OUR SENSITIVE READERS THE DRAWING OF THE BOY EATING THE GOB OF SPIT.)
OR...
IF YOU WANT ME TO GIVE YOU A PIECE OF CANDY YOU'LL HAFTA DRINK A WHOLE BOTTLE OF INK.
IF YOU GIVE ME TWO PIECES, I'LL DRINK THE INK BOTTLE WITH A STICK OF CHALK CRUMBLED UP INSIDE IT.
THE ONES WITHOUT A "PACKAGE" ALWAYS BEGGED FROM THOSE WITH ONE. THEY WOULD GET TO THE POINT OF ASKING FOR THE WEIRDEST THINGS. FOR EXAMPLE...
WHATCHA EATING?
AN APPLE.
GIMME THE CORE.
IT'S ALREADY PROMISED.
OR...
LET ME HAVE THE RIND.
I'LL TAKE THE PITH.
AND I GET THE REST.
CONTRARY TO THE VICE OF BEGGING WAS THE VIRTUE OF REFUSING.
GIVE ME A PIECE.
FUCK OFF!
STRANGE DEALS CAME DOWN AS HUNGER BECAME MORE INSISTENT.
IF YOU GIVE ME FIVE COOKIES NOW, I'LL GIVE YOU MY BREAD ALL WEEK LONG.
IF YOU GIVE ME WHAT YOU HAVE LEFT, I'LL BE YOUR SLAVE AND OWE MY LIFE TO YOU.
THEN THERE WERE THE "NIBBLERS," THAT IS, THE ONES WHO COULD MAKE A FIG LAST A WHOLE AFTERNOON.
YOU STILL HAVE SOME FIG LEFT?
I'VE HARDLY STARTED...I'VE ONLY EATEN THREE LIP SEEDS SO FAR.
AND THE MYSTERIOUS "CHEWERS" WHO COULD CHEW FOR HOURS WITHOUT ANYONE FIGURING OUT WHAT THEY WERE CHEWING.
GLUB, MYUM, MYUM, GLUB...
BUT THERE WERE MORE BEGGARS THAN ANYTHING ELSE...
GIMME...
GIMME...
GIMME...
GIMME...
AND OF COURSE THERE WERE THOSE WHO GAVE...
WILLYA GIVE ME A PIECE?
SURE, HERE.
THANKS.
THAT'S OKAY.
...AND THE ONES THAT DIDN'T -- THE "TIGHT-WADS."
WILL YOU GIVE ME SOME?
NO.
A CRUMB?
NO.
A GERM?
NO.
THERE WERE ALSO THOSE WHO WOLFED DOWN THE WHOLE "PACKAGE" IN ONE BINGE.
SO THEY WON'T TAKE IT AWAY FROM ME...! IT'LL BE SAFE IN MY BELLY!
SOME OF THEM WOULD THROW UP ALL OF IT ALMOST WHOLE DURING THE NIGHT...
GLUBFSSS...
...WHICH ALLOWED OTHERS, LIKE "NUTSY," TO PICK OVER THE VOMIT AND RECYCLE WHATEVER THEY COULD SALVAGE THE NEXT MORNING.
IT TASTES A LITTLE SOUR...
©1980 GIMENEZ.-

SOCiAL AiD
IV
BRUISED FRUIT
© 1980 GIMENEZ.-

GARCIA MORATO
HOME
Social Aid
FET AND THE JONS

THE FRUIT SELLER WOULD COME TO THE SCHOOL A COUPLE OF TIMES A WEEK DURING MORNING RECESS. HE WAS A SAD OLD GEEZER WITH A BEAT-UP CART PULLED BY A MELANCHOLY DONKEY.

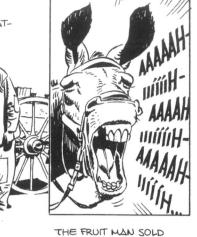

AAAAAH-iiiiiiH-AAAAAH-iiiiiiH-AAAAAH-iiiiiiH...

AT THE **GARCIA MORATO** "HOME," THE FRUIT MAN'S DONKEY FASCINATED ALL THE BOYS.

SOME OF THEM -- GO FIGURE OUT WHY -- INEXPLICABLY INSISTED ON SWITCHING THE POOR DONKEY'S GENDER.

THE FACT THAT THE DONKEY WAS A **MALE** WAS OBVIOUS, AND ON SOME DAYS **MUCH MORE** OBVIOUS THAN ON OTHERS!

THE FRUIT MAN SOLD BRUISED FRUIT TO THE BOYS, MERCHANDISE THAT DIDN'T MOVE FAST OUTSIDE THE SCHOOL. THEREFORE, HE SOLD IT VERY CHEAP.

THE FRUIT MAN!

THE FRUIT MAN'S DONKEY IS HERE!

SHE'S HERE...THE FRUIT MAN'S DONKEY.

AAAAAH-iiiiiiH-AAAAAAH...-iiiiiiH-AAAAAH....!

GIVE ME TWO ORANGES AND TWO APPLES.

QUALITY DIDN'T MATTER TO THE BOYS -- JUST QUANTITY.

HE ALSO SOLD BREAD, BIG HUNKS OF WHITE BREAD CALLED "COLONES."

WHEN THE BOYS' FAMILIES CAME TO VISIT, THEY USED TO LET THEM HAVE A LITTLE MONEY.

ADOLFO -- AS WE RECOUNTED IN ANOTHER CHAPTER -- WAS GIVEN TWO SHINY PESETAS WHEN HIS FATHER HAD COME TO SEE HIM AND **ADOLFO** LOST THEM PLAYING COIN TOSS.

LEMME HAVE THE CORE.

I ALREADY HAVE DIBS ON IT.

I WANT TWO "COLONES."

CAN I HAVE SOME?

WE'LL SEE...

TAKE THESE THREE PESETAS SO YOU CAN BUY SOMETHING FROM THE FRUIT MAN. DON'T LOSE THEM NOW.

DON'TCHA KNOW HOW TO DO THIS? YOU TAKE A COIN AND...

POP!

ZAP!

LOOK, NOW. I'LL DO IT AGAIN, BUT I'LL THROW IT A LOT HIGHER.

POP!

WHERE DID IT FALL?

I DUNNO, I DIDN'T SEE IT...

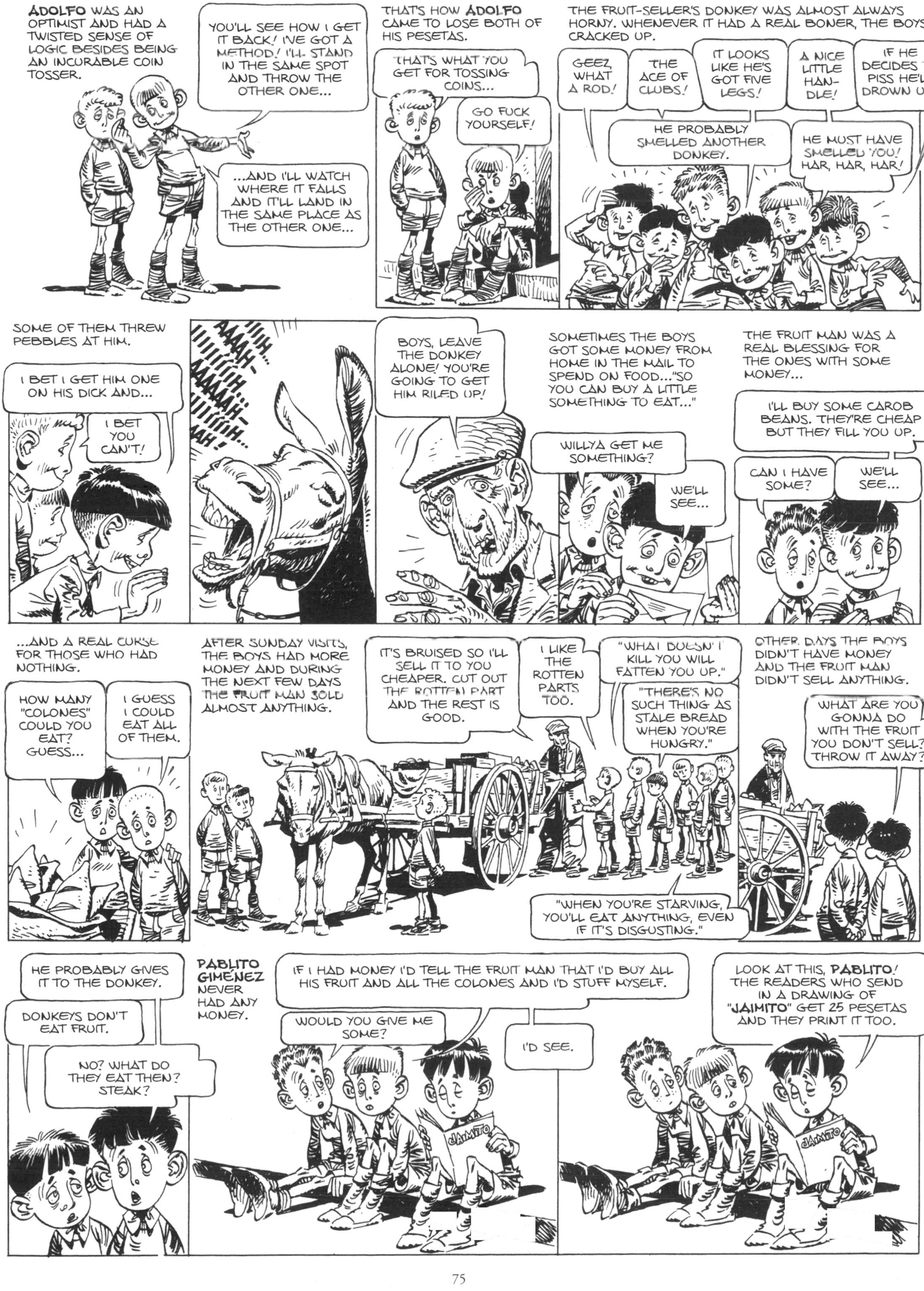
ADOLFO WAS AN OPTIMIST AND HAD A TWISTED SENSE OF LOGIC BESIDES BEING AN INCURABLE COIN TOSSER.
YOU'LL SEE HOW I GET IT BACK! I'VE GOT A METHOD! I'LL STAND IN THE SAME SPOT AND THROW THE OTHER ONE...
...AND I'LL WATCH WHERE IT FALLS AND IT'LL LAND IN THE SAME PLACE AS THE OTHER ONE...
THAT'S HOW ADOLFO CAME TO LOSE BOTH OF HIS PESETAS.
THAT'S WHAT YOU GET FOR TOSSING COINS...
GO FUCK YOURSELF!
THE FRUIT-SELLER'S DONKEY WAS ALMOST ALWAYS HORNY. WHENEVER IT HAD A REAL BONER, THE BOYS CRACKED UP.
GEEZ, WHAT A ROD!
THE ACE OF CLUBS!
IT LOOKS LIKE HE'S GOT FIVE LEGS!
A NICE LITTLE HAN-DLE!
IF HE DECIDES TO PISS HE'LL DROWN US!
HE PROBABLY SMELLED ANOTHER DONKEY.
HE MUST HAVE SMELLED YOU! HAR, HAR, HAR!
SOME OF THEM THREW PEBBLES AT HIM.
I BET I GET HIM ONE ON HIS DICK AND...
I BET YOU CAN'T!
AAAAH-HHH!
BOYS, LEAVE THE DONKEY ALONE! YOU'RE GOING TO GET HIM RILED UP!
SOMETIMES THE BOYS GOT SOME MONEY FROM HOME IN THE MAIL TO SPEND ON FOOD..."SO YOU CAN BUY A LITTLE SOMETHING TO EAT..."
WILLYA GET ME SOMETHING?
WE'LL SEE...
THE FRUIT MAN WAS A REAL BLESSING FOR THE ONES WITH SOME MONEY...
I'LL BUY SOME CAROB BEANS. THEY'RE CHEAP BUT THEY FILL YOU UP.
CAN I HAVE SOME?
WE'LL SEE...
...AND A REAL CURSE FOR THOSE WHO HAD NOTHING.
HOW MANY "COLONES" COULD YOU EAT? GUESS...
I GUESS I COULD EAT ALL OF THEM.
AFTER SUNDAY VISITS, THE BOYS HAD MORE MONEY AND DURING THE NEXT FEW DAYS THE FRUIT MAN SOLD ALMOST ANYTHING.
IT'S BRUISED SO I'LL SELL IT TO YOU CHEAPER. CUT OUT THE ROTTEN PART AND THE REST IS GOOD.
I LIKE THE ROTTEN PARTS TOO.
"WHAT DOESN'T KILL YOU WILL FATTEN YOU UP."
"THERE'S NO SUCH THING AS STALE BREAD WHEN YOU'RE HUNGRY."
"WHEN YOU'RE STARVING, YOU'LL EAT ANYTHING, EVEN IF IT'S DISGUSTING."
OTHER DAYS THE BOYS DIDN'T HAVE MONEY AND THE FRUIT MAN DIDN'T SELL ANYTHING.
WHAT ARE YOU GONNA DO WITH THE FRUIT YOU DON'T SELL? THROW IT AWAY?
HE PROBABLY GIVES IT TO THE DONKEY.
DONKEYS DON'T EAT FRUIT.
NO? WHAT DO THEY EAT THEN? STEAK?
PABLITO GIMÉNEZ NEVER HAD ANY MONEY.
IF I HAD MONEY I'D TELL THE FRUIT MAN THAT I'D BUY ALL HIS FRUIT AND ALL THE COLONES AND I'D STUFF MYSELF.
WOULD YOU GIVE ME SOME?
I'D SEE.
JAIMITO
LOOK AT THIS, PABLITO! THE READERS WHO SEND IN A DRAWING OF "JAIMITO" GET 25 PESETAS AND THEY PRINT IT TOO.
JAIMITO

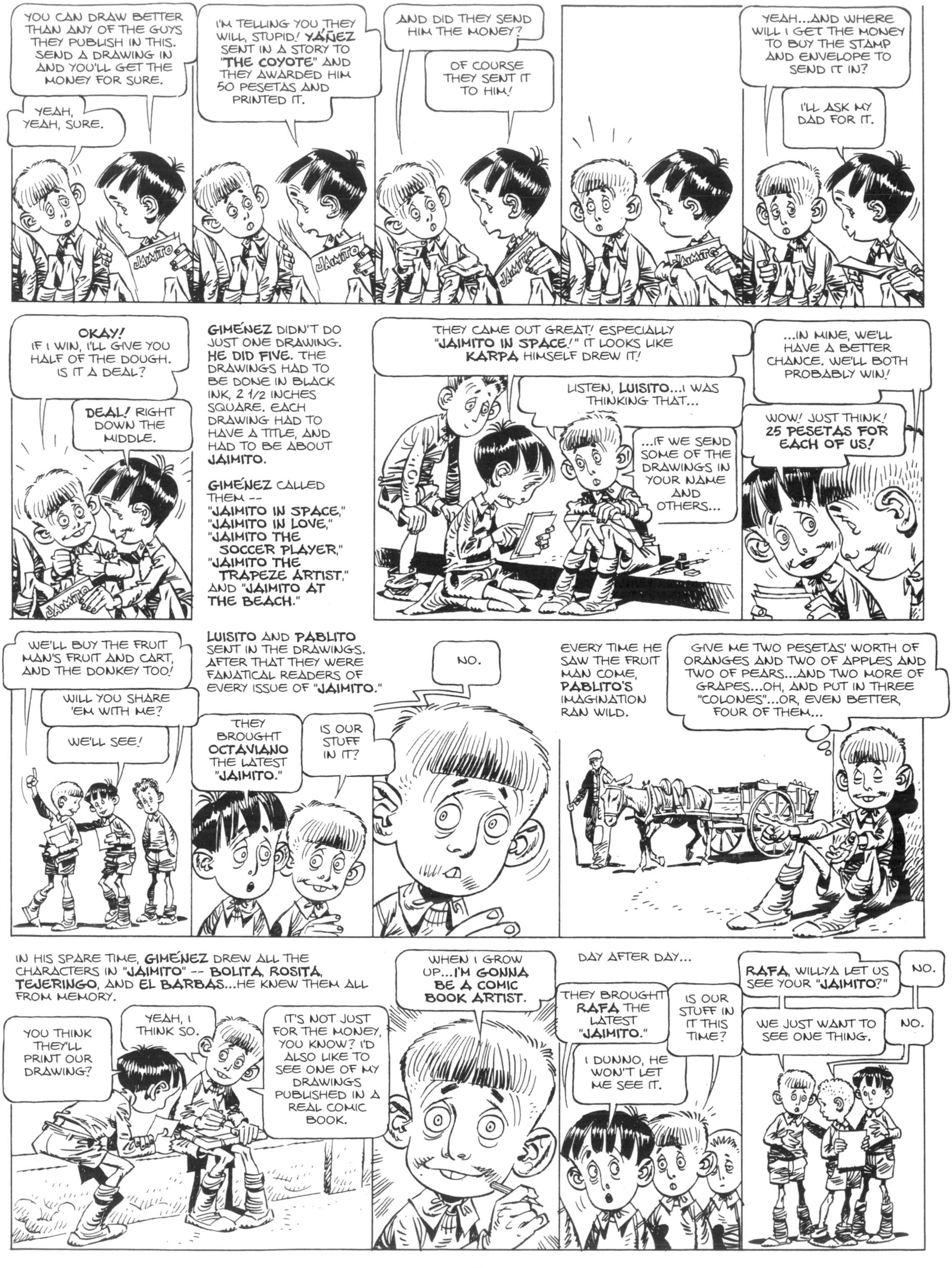
YOU CAN DRAW BETTER THAN ANY OF THE GUYS THEY PUBLISH IN THIS. SEND A DRAWING IN AND YOU'LL GET THE MONEY FOR SURE.
YEAH, YEAH, SURE.
I'M TELLING YOU THEY WILL, STUPID! YÁÑEZ SENT IN A STORY TO "THE COYOTE" AND THEY AWARDED HIM 50 PESETAS AND PRINTED IT.
AND DID THEY SEND HIM THE MONEY?
OF COURSE THEY SENT IT TO HIM!
YEAH...AND WHERE WILL I GET THE MONEY TO BUY THE STAMP AND ENVELOPE TO SEND IT IN?
I'LL ASK MY DAD FOR IT.
OKAY! IF I WIN, I'LL GIVE YOU HALF OF THE DOUGH. IS IT A DEAL?
DEAL! RIGHT DOWN THE MIDDLE.
GIMÉNEZ DIDN'T DO JUST ONE DRAWING. HE DID FIVE. THE DRAWINGS HAD TO BE DONE IN BLACK INK, 2 1/2 INCHES SQUARE. EACH DRAWING HAD TO HAVE A TITLE, AND HAD TO BE ABOUT JAIMITO.
GIMÉNEZ CALLED THEM -- "JAIMITO IN SPACE," "JAIMITO IN LOVE," "JAIMITO THE SOCCER PLAYER," "JAIMITO THE TRAPEZE ARTIST," AND "JAIMITO AT THE BEACH."
THEY CAME OUT GREAT! ESPECIALLY "JAIMITO IN SPACE!" IT LOOKS LIKE KARPA HIMSELF DREW IT!
LISTEN, LUISITO...I WAS THINKING THAT...
...IF WE SEND SOME OF THE DRAWINGS IN YOUR NAME AND OTHERS...
...IN MINE, WE'LL HAVE A BETTER CHANCE. WE'LL BOTH PROBABLY WIN!
WOW! JUST THINK! 25 PESETAS FOR EACH OF US!
WE'LL BUY THE FRUIT MAN'S FRUIT AND CART, AND THE DONKEY TOO!
WILL YOU SHARE 'EM WITH ME?
WE'LL SEE!
LUISITO AND PABLITO SENT IN THE DRAWINGS. AFTER THAT THEY WERE FANATICAL READERS OF EVERY ISSUE OF "JAIMITO."
THEY BROUGHT OCTAVIANO THE LATEST "JAIMITO."
IS OUR STUFF IN IT?
NO.
EVERY TIME HE SAW THE FRUIT MAN COME, PABLITO'S IMAGINATION RAN WILD.
GIVE ME TWO PESETAS' WORTH OF ORANGES AND TWO OF APPLES AND TWO OF PEARS...AND TWO MORE OF GRAPES...OH, AND PUT IN THREE "COLONES"...OR, EVEN BETTER, FOUR OF THEM...
IN HIS SPARE TIME, GIMÉNEZ DREW ALL THE CHARACTERS IN "JAIMITO" -- BOLITA, ROSITA, TEJERINGO, AND EL BARBAS...HE KNEW THEM ALL FROM MEMORY.
YOU THINK THEY'LL PRINT OUR DRAWING?
YEAH, I THINK SO.
IT'S NOT JUST FOR THE MONEY, YOU KNOW? I'D ALSO LIKE TO SEE ONE OF MY DRAWINGS PUBLISHED IN A REAL COMIC BOOK.
WHEN I GROW UP...I'M GONNA BE A COMIC BOOK ARTIST.
DAY AFTER DAY...
THEY BROUGHT RAFA THE LATEST "JAIMITO."
IS OUR STUFF IN IT THIS TIME?
I DUNNO, HE WON'T LET ME SEE IT.
RAFA, WILLYA LET US SEE YOUR "JAIMITO?"
NO.
WE JUST WANT TO SEE ONE THING.
NO.

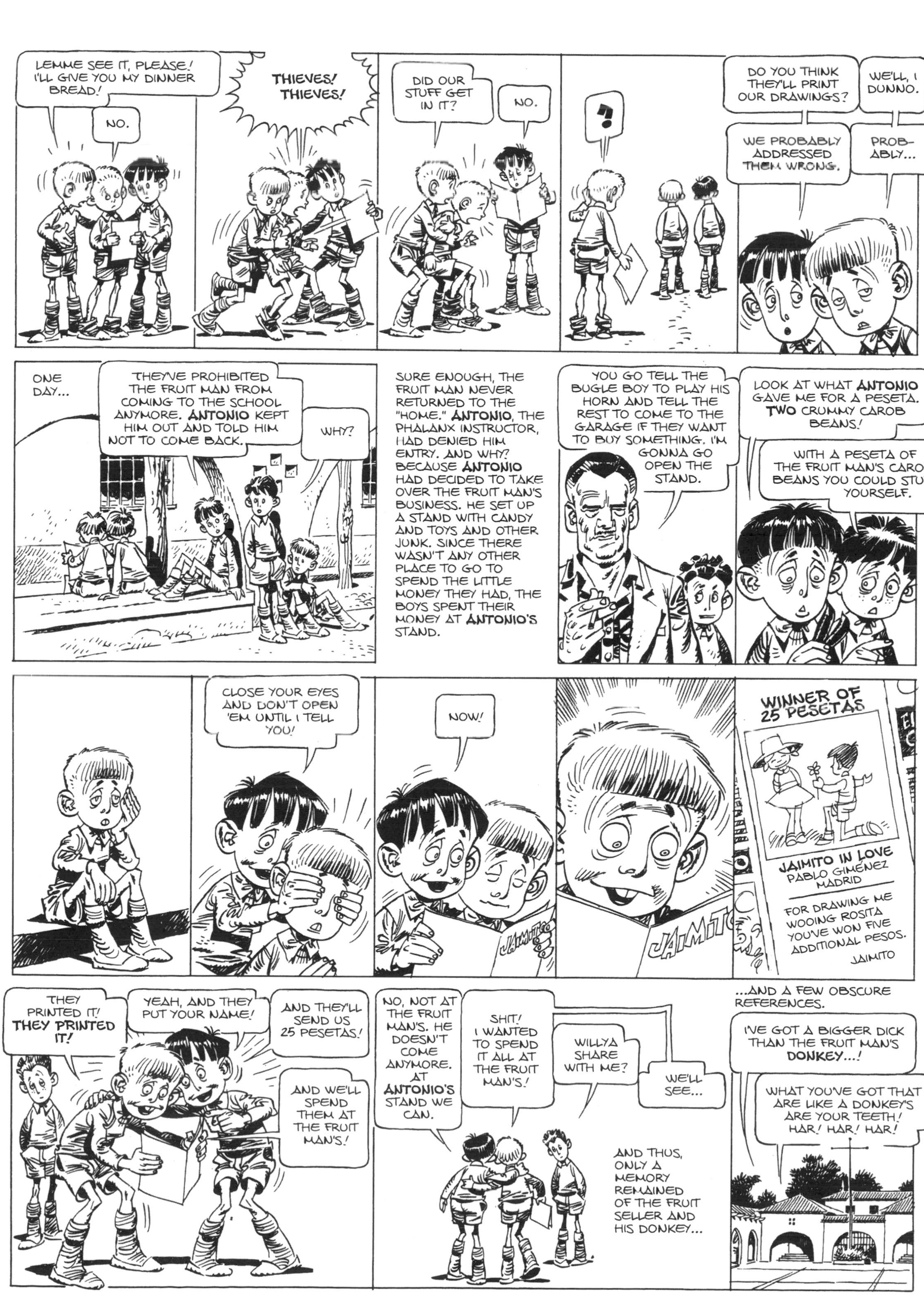
LEMME SEE IT, PLEASE! I'LL GIVE YOU MY DINNER BREAD!
NO.
THIEVES! THIEVES!
DID OUR STUFF GET IN IT?
NO.
DO YOU THINK THEY'LL PRINT OUR DRAWINGS?
WE'LL, I DUNNO.
WE PROBABLY ADDRESSED THEM WRONG.
PROB-ABLY...
ONE DAY...
THEY'VE PROHIBITED THE FRUIT MAN FROM COMING TO THE SCHOOL ANYMORE. ANTONIO KEPT HIM OUT AND TOLD HIM NOT TO COME BACK.
WHY?
SURE ENOUGH, THE FRUIT MAN NEVER RETURNED TO THE "HOME." ANTONIO, THE PHALANX INSTRUCTOR, HAD DENIED HIM ENTRY. AND WHY? BECAUSE ANTONIO HAD DECIDED TO TAKE OVER THE FRUIT MAN'S BUSINESS. HE SET UP A STAND WITH CANDY AND TOYS AND OTHER JUNK. SINCE THERE WASN'T ANY OTHER PLACE TO GO TO SPEND THE LITTLE MONEY THEY HAD, THE BOYS SPENT THEIR MONEY AT ANTONIO'S STAND.
YOU GO TELL THE BUGLE BOY TO PLAY HIS HORN AND TELL THE REST TO COME TO THE GARAGE IF THEY WANT TO BUY SOMETHING. I'M GONNA GO OPEN THE STAND.
LOOK AT WHAT ANTONIO GAVE ME FOR A PESETA. TWO CRUMMY CAROB BEANS!
WITH A PESETA OF THE FRUIT MAN'S CAROB BEANS YOU COULD STUFF YOURSELF.
CLOSE YOUR EYES AND DON'T OPEN 'EM UNTIL I TELL YOU!
NOW!
JAIMITO
JAIMITO
WINNER OF 25 PESETAS
JAIMITO IN LOVE
PABLO GIMÉNEZ
MADRID
FOR DRAWING ME WOOING ROSITA YOU'VE WON FIVE ADDITIONAL PESOS.
JAIMITO
THEY PRINTED IT! THEY PRINTED IT!
YEAH, AND THEY PUT YOUR NAME!
AND THEY'LL SEND US 25 PESETAS!
AND WE'LL SPEND THEM AT THE FRUIT MAN'S!
NO, NOT AT THE FRUIT MAN'S. HE DOESN'T COME ANYMORE. AT ANTONIO'S STAND WE CAN.
SHIT! I WANTED TO SPEND IT ALL AT THE FRUIT MAN'S!
WILLYA SHARE WITH ME?
WE'LL SEE...
AND THUS, ONLY A MEMORY REMAINED OF THE FRUIT SELLER AND HIS DONKEY...
...AND A FEW OBSCURE REFERENCES.
I'VE GOT A BIGGER DICK THAN THE FRUIT MAN'S DONKEY...!
WHAT YOU'VE GOT THAT ARE LIKE A DONKEY'S ARE YOUR TEETH! HAR! HAR! HAR!

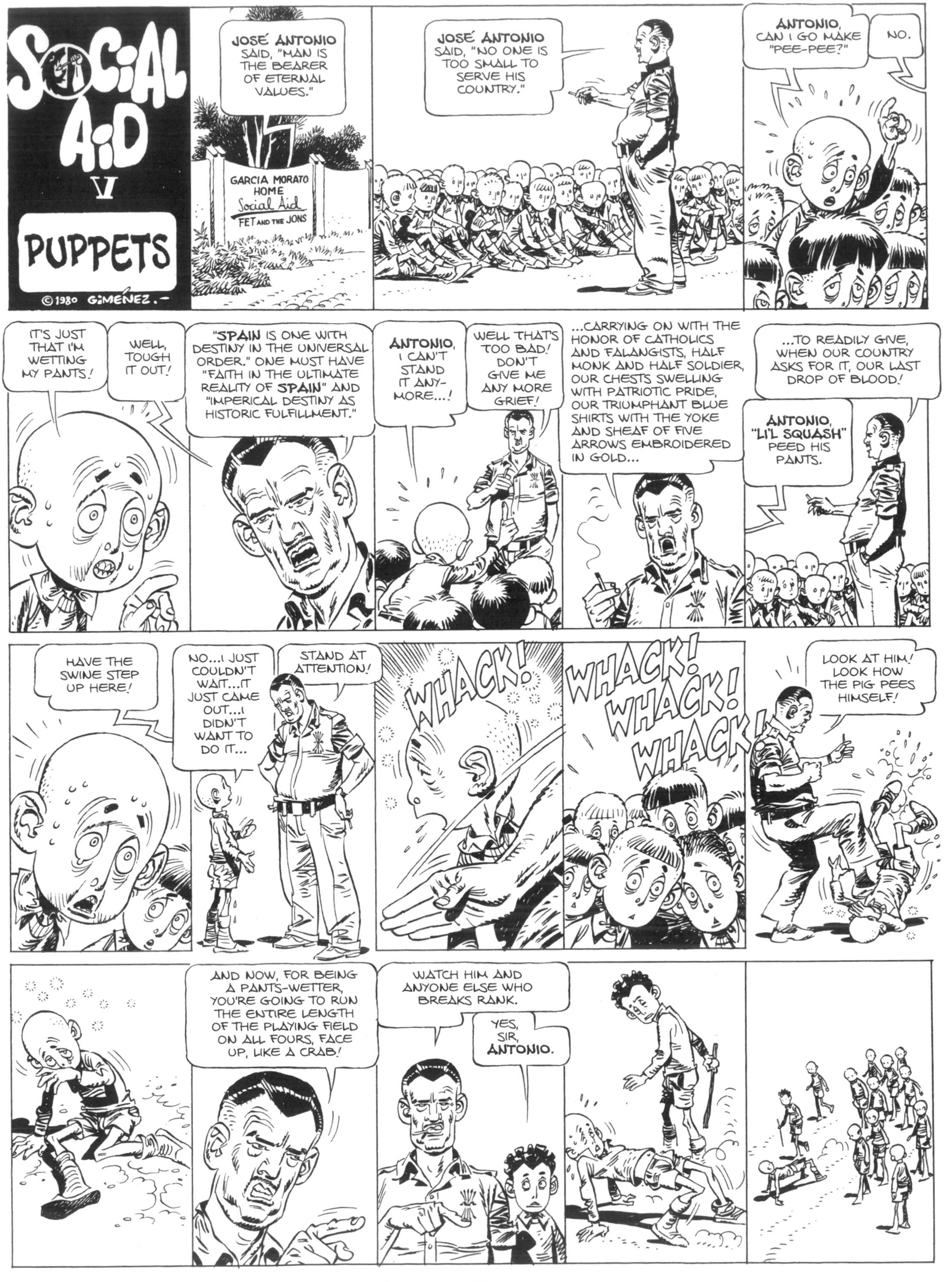
SOCIAL AID
V
PUPPETS
©1980 GIMÉNEZ.-
JOSÉ ANTONIO SAID, "MAN IS THE BEARER OF ETERNAL VALUES."
GARCIA MORATO HOME
Social Aid
FET AND THE JONS
JOSÉ ANTONIO SAID, "NO ONE IS TOO SMALL TO SERVE HIS COUNTRY."
ANTONIO, CAN I GO MAKE "PEE-PEE?"
NO.
IT'S JUST THAT I'M WETTING MY PANTS!
WELL, TOUGH IT OUT!
"SPAIN IS ONE WITH DESTINY IN THE UNIVERSAL ORDER." ONE MUST HAVE "FAITH IN THE ULTIMATE REALITY OF SPAIN" AND "IMPERICAL DESTINY AS HISTORIC FULFILLMENT."
ANTONIO, I CAN'T STAND IT ANYMORE...!
WELL THAT'S TOO BAD! DON'T GIVE ME ANY MORE GRIEF!
...CARRYING ON WITH THE HONOR OF CATHOLICS AND FALANGISTS, HALF MONK AND HALF SOLDIER, OUR CHESTS SWELLING WITH PATRIOTIC PRIDE, OUR TRIUMPHANT BLUE SHIRTS WITH THE YOKE AND SHEAF OF FIVE ARROWS EMBROIDERED IN GOLD...
...TO READILY GIVE, WHEN OUR COUNTRY ASKS FOR IT, OUR LAST DROP OF BLOOD!
ANTONIO, "LI'L SQUASH" PEED HIS PANTS.
HAVE THE SWINE STEP UP HERE!
NO...I JUST COULDN'T WAIT...IT JUST CAME OUT...I DIDN'T WANT TO DO IT...
STAND AT ATTENTION!
WHACK!
WHACK! WHACK! WHACK!
LOOK AT HIM! LOOK HOW THE PIG PEES HIMSELF!
AND NOW, FOR BEING A PANTS-WETTER, YOU'RE GOING TO RUN THE ENTIRE LENGTH OF THE PLAYING FIELD ON ALL FOURS, FACE UP, LIKE A CRAB!
WATCH HIM AND ANYONE ELSE WHO BREAKS RANK.
YES, SIR, ANTONIO.

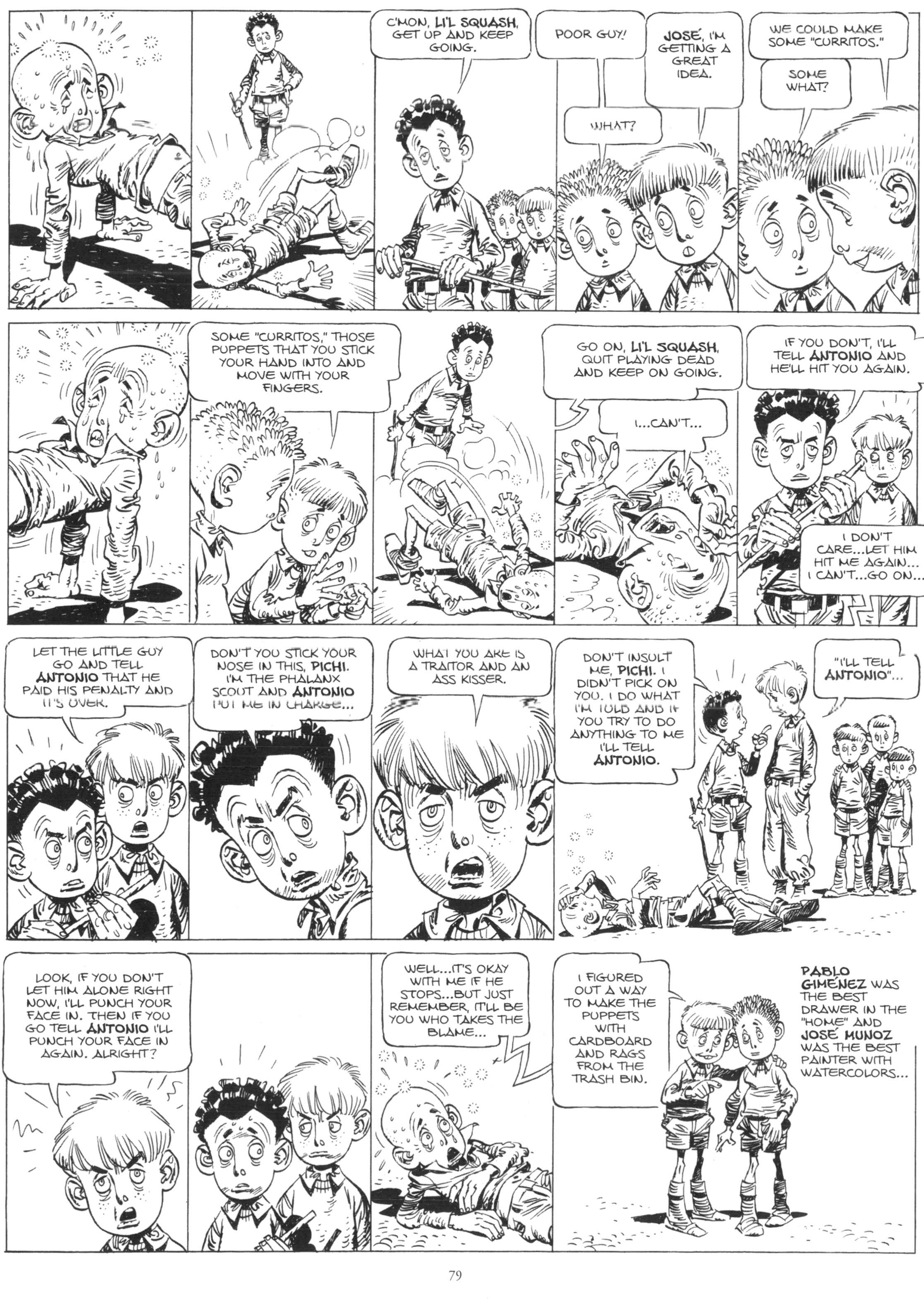

C'MON, LI'L SQUASH, GET UP AND KEEP GOING.
POOR GUY!
WHAT?
JOSÉ, I'M GETTING A GREAT IDEA.
WE COULD MAKE SOME "CURRITOS."
SOME WHAT?
SOME "CURRITOS," THOSE PUPPETS THAT YOU STICK YOUR HAND INTO AND MOVE WITH YOUR FINGERS.
GO ON, LI'L SQUASH, QUIT PLAYING DEAD AND KEEP ON GOING.
I...CAN'T...
IF YOU DON'T, I'LL TELL ANTONIO AND HE'LL HIT YOU AGAIN.
I DON'T CARE...LET HIM HIT ME AGAIN... I CAN'T...GO ON...
LET THE LITTLE GUY GO AND TELL ANTONIO THAT HE PAID HIS PENALTY AND IT'S OVER.
DON'T YOU STICK YOUR NOSE IN THIS, PICHI. I'M THE PHALANX SCOUT AND ANTONIO PUT ME IN CHARGE...
WHAT YOU ARE IS A TRAITOR AND AN ASS KISSER.
DON'T INSULT ME, PICHI. I DIDN'T PICK ON YOU. I DO WHAT I'M TOLD AND IF YOU TRY TO DO ANYTHING TO ME I'LL TELL ANTONIO.
"I'LL TELL ANTONIO"...
LOOK, IF YOU DON'T LET HIM ALONE RIGHT NOW, I'LL PUNCH YOUR FACE IN. THEN IF YOU GO TELL ANTONIO I'LL PUNCH YOUR FACE IN AGAIN. ALRIGHT?
WELL...IT'S OKAY WITH ME IF HE STOPS...BUT JUST REMEMBER, IT'LL BE YOU WHO TAKES THE BLAME...
I FIGURED OUT A WAY TO MAKE THE PUPPETS WITH CARDBOARD AND RAGS FROM THE TRASH BIN.
PABLO GIMÉNEZ WAS THE BEST DRAWER IN THE "HOME" AND JOSÉ MUNOZ WAS THE BEST PAINTER WITH WATERCOLORS...

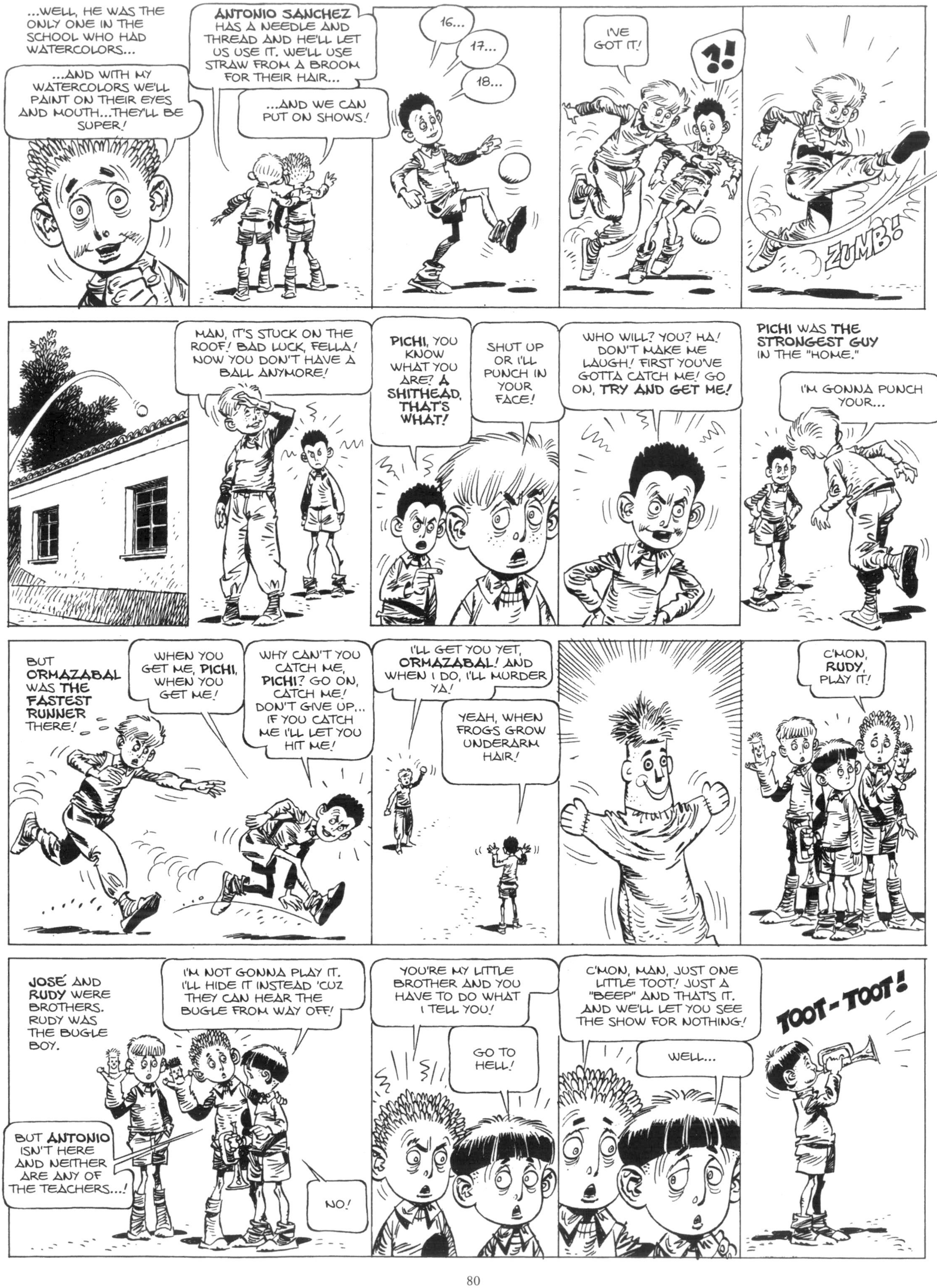
...WELL, HE WAS THE ONLY ONE IN THE SCHOOL WHO HAD WATERCOLORS...
...AND WITH MY WATERCOLORS WE'LL PAINT ON THEIR EYES AND MOUTH...THEY'LL BE SUPER!
ANTONIO SANCHEZ HAS A NEEDLE AND THREAD AND HE'LL LET US USE IT. WE'LL USE STRAW FROM A BROOM FOR THEIR HAIR...
...AND WE CAN PUT ON SHOWS!
16...
17...
18...
I'VE GOT IT!
?!
ZUMB!
MAN, IT'S STUCK ON THE ROOF! BAD LUCK, FELLA! NOW YOU DON'T HAVE A BALL ANYMORE!
PICHI, YOU KNOW WHAT YOU ARE? A SHITHEAD, THAT'S WHAT!
SHUT UP OR I'LL PUNCH IN YOUR FACE!
WHO WILL? YOU? HA! DON'T MAKE ME LAUGH! FIRST YOU'VE GOTTA CATCH ME! GO ON, TRY AND GET ME!
PICHI WAS THE STRONGEST GUY IN THE "HOME."
I'M GONNA PUNCH YOUR...
BUT ORMAZABAL WAS THE FASTEST RUNNER THERE!
WHEN YOU GET ME, PICHI, WHEN YOU GET ME!
WHY CAN'T YOU CATCH ME, PICHI? GO ON, CATCH ME! DON'T GIVE UP... IF YOU CATCH ME I'LL LET YOU HIT ME!
I'LL GET YOU YET, ORMAZABAL! AND WHEN I DO, I'LL MURDER YA!
YEAH, WHEN FROGS GROW UNDERARM HAIR!
C'MON, RUDY, PLAY IT!
JOSÉ AND RUDY WERE BROTHERS. RUDY WAS THE BUGLE BOY.
I'M NOT GONNA PLAY IT. I'LL HIDE IT INSTEAD 'CUZ THEY CAN HEAR THE BUGLE FROM WAY OFF!
BUT ANTONIO ISN'T HERE AND NEITHER ARE ANY OF THE TEACHERS...!
NO!
YOU'RE MY LITTLE BROTHER AND YOU HAVE TO DO WHAT I TELL YOU!
GO TO HELL!
C'MON, MAN, JUST ONE LITTLE TOOT! JUST A "BEEP" AND THAT'S IT. AND WE'LL LET YOU SEE THE SHOW FOR NOTHING!
WELL...
TOOT-TOOT!

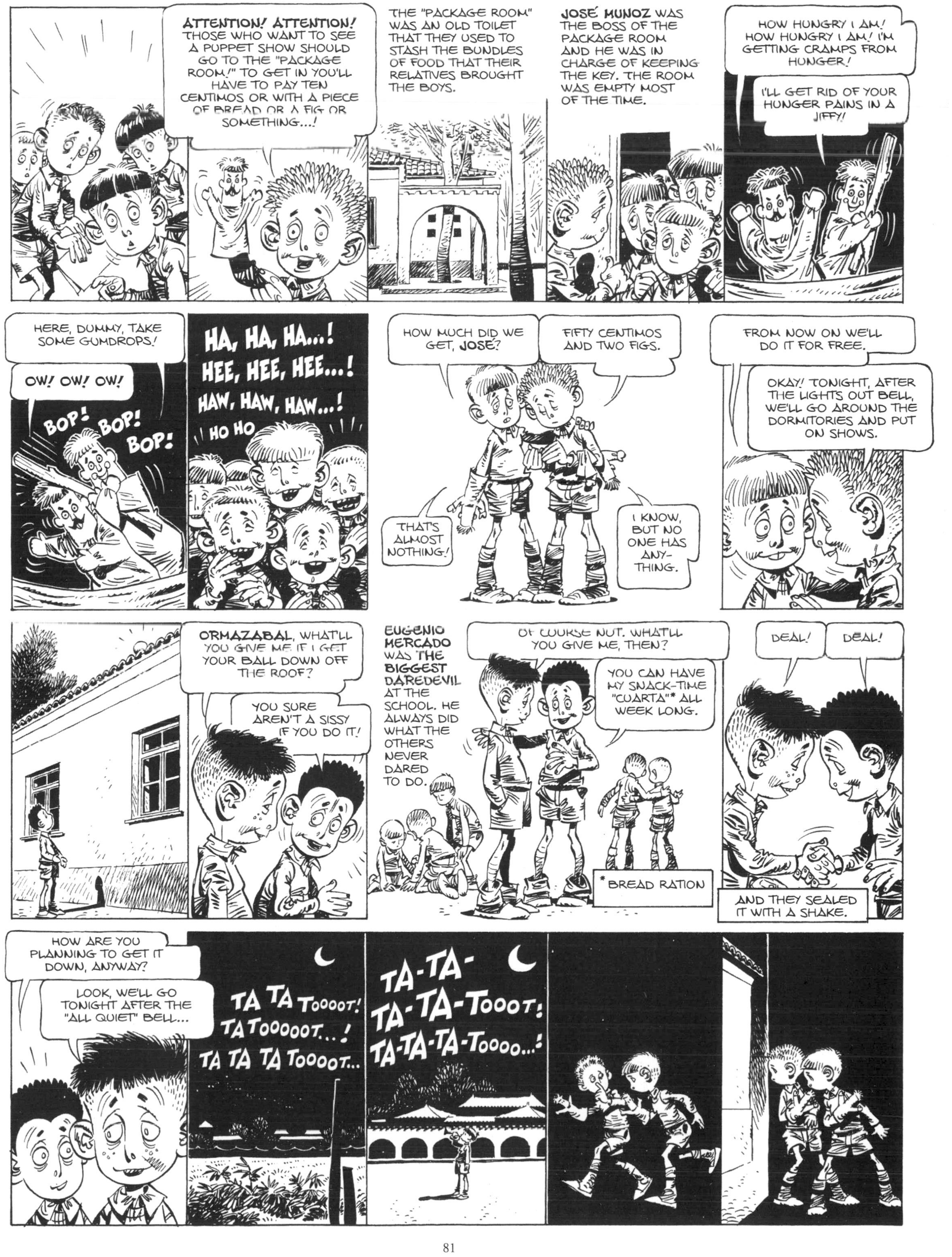
ATTENTION! ATTENTION! THOSE WHO WANT TO SEE A PUPPET SHOW SHOULD GO TO THE "PACKAGE ROOM!" TO GET IN YOU'LL HAVE TO PAY TEN CENTIMOS OR WITH A PIECE OF BREAD OR A FIG OR SOMETHING...!
THE "PACKAGE ROOM" WAS AN OLD TOILET THAT THEY USED TO STASH THE BUNDLES OF FOOD THAT THEIR RELATIVES BROUGHT THE BOYS.
JOSÉ MUNOZ WAS THE BOSS OF THE PACKAGE ROOM AND HE WAS IN CHARGE OF KEEPING THE KEY. THE ROOM WAS EMPTY MOST OF THE TIME.
HOW HUNGRY I AM! HOW HUNGRY I AM! I'M GETTING CRAMPS FROM HUNGER!
I'LL GET RID OF YOUR HUNGER PAINS IN A JIFFY!
HERE, DUMMY, TAKE SOME GUMDROPS!
OW! OW! OW!
BOP! BOP! BOP!
HA, HA, HA...! HEE, HEE, HEE...! HAW, HAW, HAW...! HO HO
HOW MUCH DID WE GET, JOSE?
FIFTY CENTIMOS AND TWO FIGS.
THAT'S ALMOST NOTHING!
I KNOW, BUT NO ONE HAS ANYTHING.
FROM NOW ON WE'LL DO IT FOR FREE.
OKAY! TONIGHT, AFTER THE LIGHTS OUT BELL, WE'LL GO AROUND THE DORMITORIES AND PUT ON SHOWS.
ORMAZABAL, WHAT'LL YOU GIVE ME IF I GET YOUR BALL DOWN OFF THE ROOF?
YOU SURE AREN'T A SISSY IF YOU DO IT!
EUGENIO MERCADO WAS THE BIGGEST DAREDEVIL AT THE SCHOOL. HE ALWAYS DID WHAT THE OTHERS NEVER DARED TO DO.
OF COURSE NOT. WHAT'LL YOU GIVE ME, THEN?
YOU CAN HAVE MY SNACK-TIME "CUARTA"* ALL WEEK LONG.
*BREAD RATION
DEAL!
DEAL!
AND THEY SEALED IT WITH A SHAKE.
HOW ARE YOU PLANNING TO GET IT DOWN, ANYWAY?
LOOK, WE'LL GO TONIGHT AFTER THE "ALL QUIET" BELL...
TA TA TOOOOT! TA TOOOOOT...! TA TA TA TOOOOT...
TA-TA-TA-TA-TOOOT! TA-TA-TA-TOOOO...!

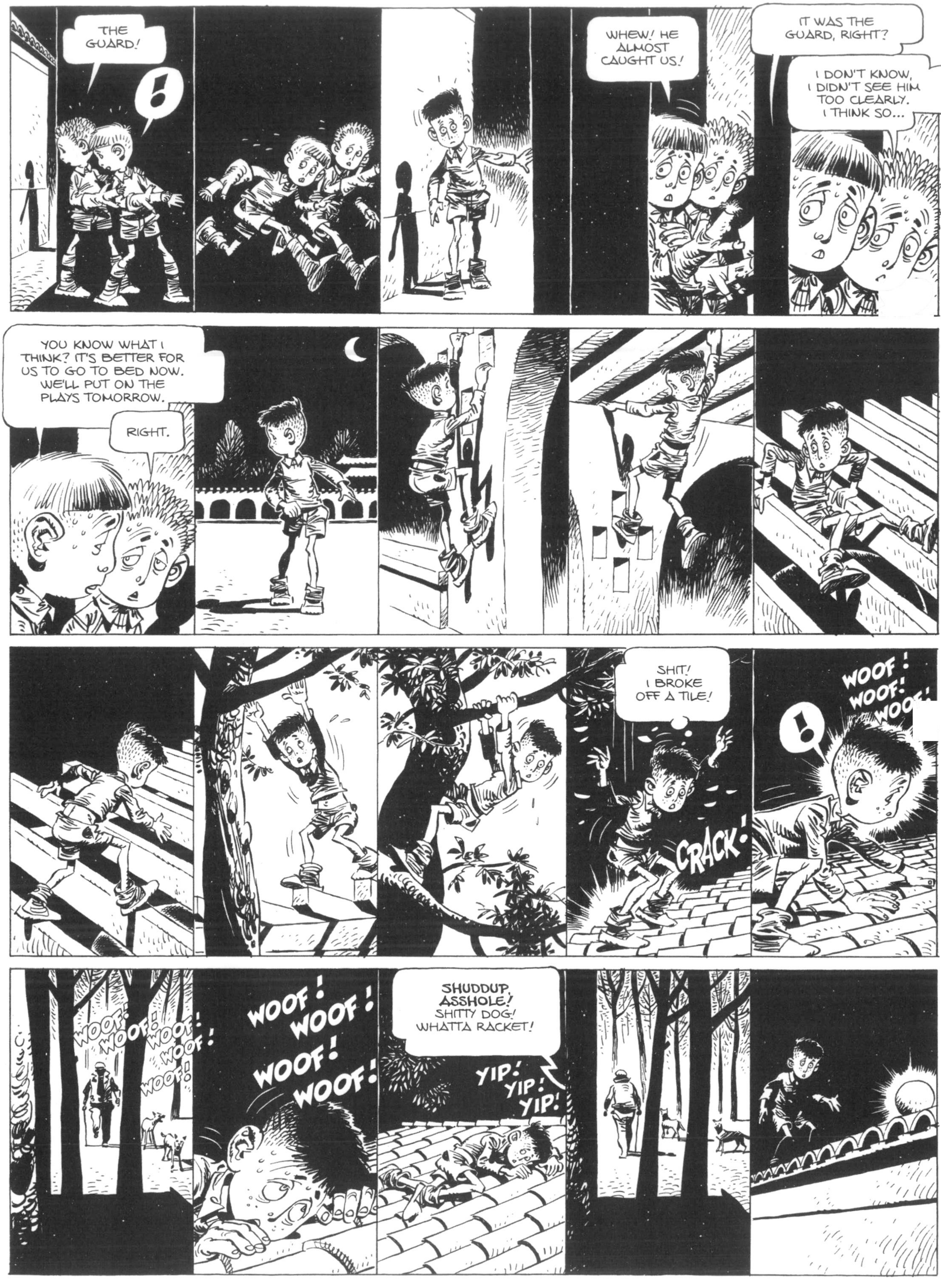
THE GUARD!
!
WHEW! HE ALMOST CAUGHT US!
IT WAS THE GUARD, RIGHT?
I DON'T KNOW, I DIDN'T SEE HIM TOO CLEARLY. I THINK SO...
YOU KNOW WHAT I THINK? IT'S BETTER FOR US TO GO TO BED NOW. WE'LL PUT ON THE PLAYS TOMORROW.
RIGHT.
SHIT! I BROKE OFF A TILE!
CRACK!
!
WOOF! WOOF! WOOF!
WOOF! WOOF! WOOF! WOOF! WOOF!
WOOF! WOOF! WOOF! WOOF!
SHUDDUP, ASSHOLE! SHITTY DOG! WHATTA RACKET!
YIP! YIP! YIP!

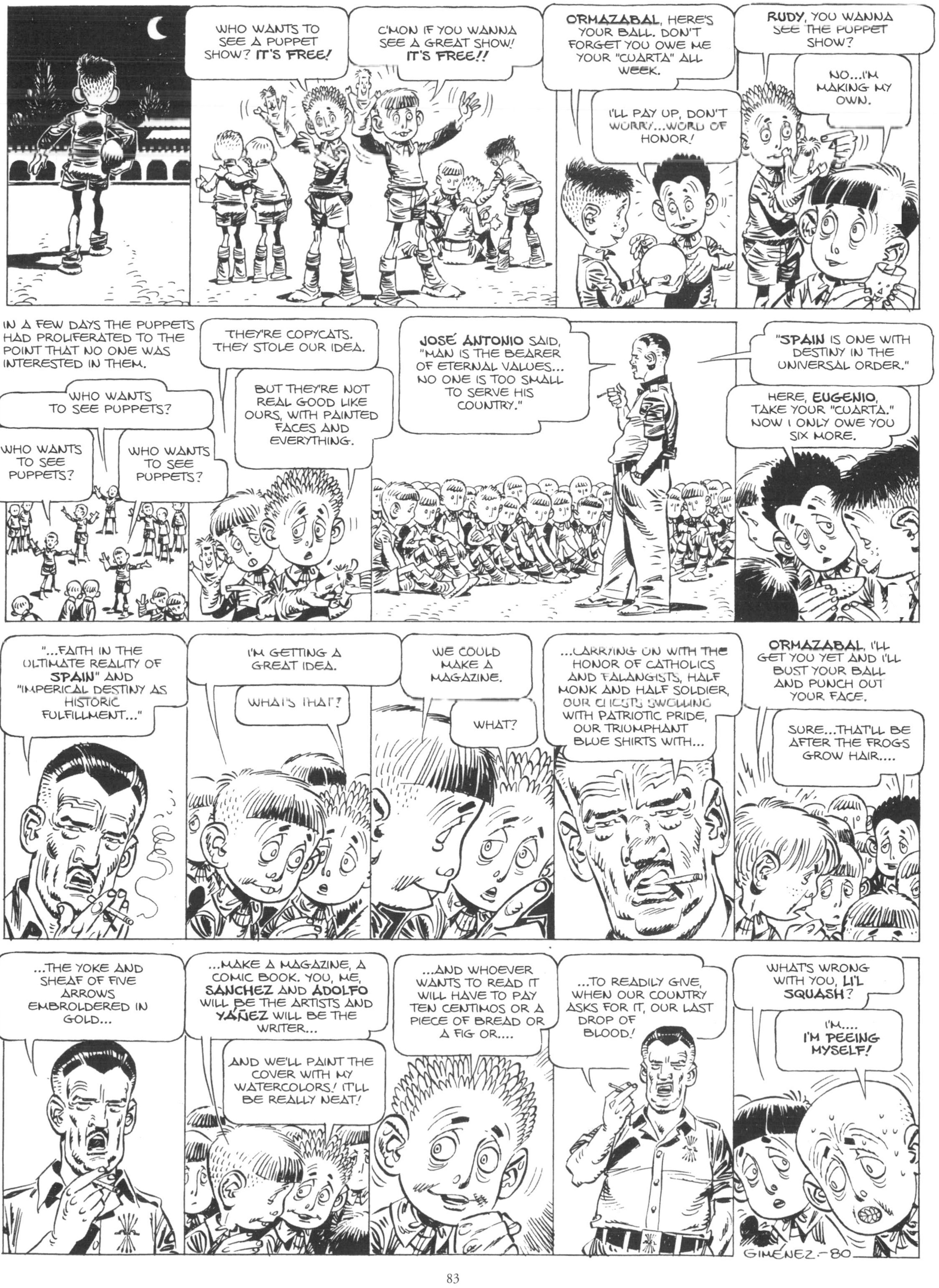

WHO WANTS TO SEE A PUPPET SHOW? IT'S FREE!
C'MON IF YOU WANNA SEE A GREAT SHOW! IT'S FREE!!
ORMAZABAL, HERE'S YOUR BALL. DON'T FORGET YOU OWE ME YOUR "CUARTA" ALL WEEK.
I'LL PAY UP, DON'T WORRY...WORD OF HONOR!
RUDY, YOU WANNA SEE THE PUPPET SHOW?
NO...I'M MAKING MY OWN.
IN A FEW DAYS THE PUPPETS HAD PROLIFERATED TO THE POINT THAT NO ONE WAS INTERESTED IN THEM.
WHO WANTS TO SEE PUPPETS?
WHO WANTS TO SEE PUPPETS?
WHO WANTS TO SEE PUPPETS?
THEY'RE COPYCATS. THEY STOLE OUR IDEA.
BUT THEY'RE NOT REAL GOOD LIKE OURS, WITH PAINTED FACES AND EVERYTHING.
JOSÉ ANTONIO SAID, "MAN IS THE BEARER OF ETERNAL VALUES... NO ONE IS TOO SMALL TO SERVE HIS COUNTRY."
"SPAIN IS ONE WITH DESTINY IN THE UNIVERSAL ORDER."
HERE, EUGENIO, TAKE YOUR "CUARTA." NOW I ONLY OWE YOU SIX MORE.
"...FAITH IN THE ULTIMATE REALITY OF SPAIN" AND "IMPERICAL DESTINY AS HISTORIC FULFILLMENT..."
I'M GETTING A GREAT IDEA.
WHAT'S THAT?
WE COULD MAKE A MAGAZINE.
WHAT?
...CARRYING ON WITH THE HONOR OF CATHOLICS AND FALANGISTS, HALF MONK AND HALF SOLDIER, OUR CHESTS SWELLING WITH PATRIOTIC PRIDE, OUR TRIUMPHANT BLUE SHIRTS WITH...
ORMAZABAL, I'LL GET YOU YET AND I'LL BUST YOUR BALL AND PUNCH OUT YOUR FACE.
SURE...THAT'LL BE AFTER THE FROGS GROW HAIR....
...THE YOKE AND SHEAF OF FIVE ARROWS EMBROIDERED IN GOLD...
...MAKE A MAGAZINE, A COMIC BOOK. YOU, ME, SANCHEZ AND ADOLFO WILL BE THE ARTISTS AND YÁÑEZ WILL BE THE WRITER...
AND WE'LL PAINT THE COVER WITH MY WATERCOLORS! IT'LL BE REALLY NEAT!
...AND WHOEVER WANTS TO READ IT WILL HAVE TO PAY TEN CENTIMOS OR A PIECE OF BREAD OR A FIG OR....
...TO READILY GIVE, WHEN OUR COUNTRY ASKS FOR IT, OUR LAST DROP OF BLOOD!
WHAT'S WRONG WITH YOU, LI'L SQUASH?
I'M.... I'M PEEING MYSELF!
GIMENEZ -80

SOCIAL AID VI
GOODBYE, SANCHA!
© 1980 GIMÉNEZ.

SANCHA HAD MIGUEL DÍAZ COMPLETELY UNDER HIS THUMB.

MIGUEL, PUNCH YOURSELF HARD IN THE FACE.

WHACK!

YOU DIDN'T HIT YOURSELF HARD ENOUGH! DO IT AGAIN, BUT HARDER!

WHACK!

THAT'S GOOD. YOU CAN GO PLAY FOR AWHILE.

MIGUEL "OWED HIS LIFE" TO SANCHA. HE'D TRADED IT TO HIM FOR HALF A LOAF OF BREAD. THIS IS HOW IT CAME ABOUT, PURE AND SIMPLE.

IF YOU GIVE ME HALF YOUR LOAF, I'LL OWE YOU MY LIFE.

IT'S A DEAL, MIGUEL...BUT FIRST YOU GOTTA SWEAR IT.

I SWEAR BY GOD, WORD OF HONOR, MAY I DROP DEAD, THAT I OWE YOU MY LIFE.

VERY GOOD. HERE, EAT YOUR BREAD AND THEN COME BACK HERE SO I CAN ORDER YOU TO DO SOMETHING.

REMEMBER THAT YOU'VE SWORN AND YOU CAN'T GO BACK ON YOUR WORD!

YES, YES...

...AND IF YOU DON'T REPORT BACK HERE TO ME, I'LL COME FIND YOU AND IT'LL BE WORSE FOR YOU!

GLUB, HMMH, YEAH...

SANCHA HAD A BOX WITH PATCHES AND GLUE FOR FIXING PUNCTURES IN RUBBER BALLS. EVERYBODY WITH A BALL DEPENDED ON HIM, WHICH MADE HIM FEEL IMPORTANT AND GAVE HIM SOME POWER OVER THEM.

SANCHA, MY BALL'S GOT A HOLE IN IT. CAN YOU PATCH IT FOR ME?

WE'LL SEE!

SANCHA WOULD PATCH BALLS FOR MONEY, BREAD RATIONS, AND OTHER STUFF...

WHAT'LL YA GIMME IF I FIX IT FOR YOU?

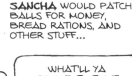

I DUNNO...ALL I'VE GOT IS A "FLORITA" COMIC BOOK...

YUCK, "FLORITA"...! THAT'S A COMIC FOR GIRLS!...WILL YOU GIMME YOUR BREAD ALL WEEK?

SOMETIMES HE'D PUT ON A PATCH IN EXCHANGE FOR A FEW PUNCHES...

I'LL PUT ON A PATCH AND THEN I'LL PUNCH YOU TWENTY TIMES WHEREVER I WANT.

WELL, OKAY...

SANCHA KEPT THE PATCHES IN AN OLD LAXATIVE BOX. A FEW PATCHES, A TUBE OF GLUE, A PIECE OF SANDPAPER, AND A SYRINGE ATTACHED TO A RUBBER TUBE TO INFLATE THE BALLS WERE WHAT HE USED TO FIX THE OTHERS' BALLS AND MAKE A PROFIT.

SANCHA'S CHEST WAS FLAT AND SHAPELESS, DISFIGURED WITH TIGHT, GLOSSY SKIN LIKE GLASS, THE RESULT OF A BAD BURN THAT HE GOT WHEN HE WAS LITTLE. THAT'S WHY THEY CALLED HIM SANCHA, THE "PLANCHA" ("CLOTHES IRON"), A NICKNAME THAT BUGGED THE HELL OUT OF HIM.

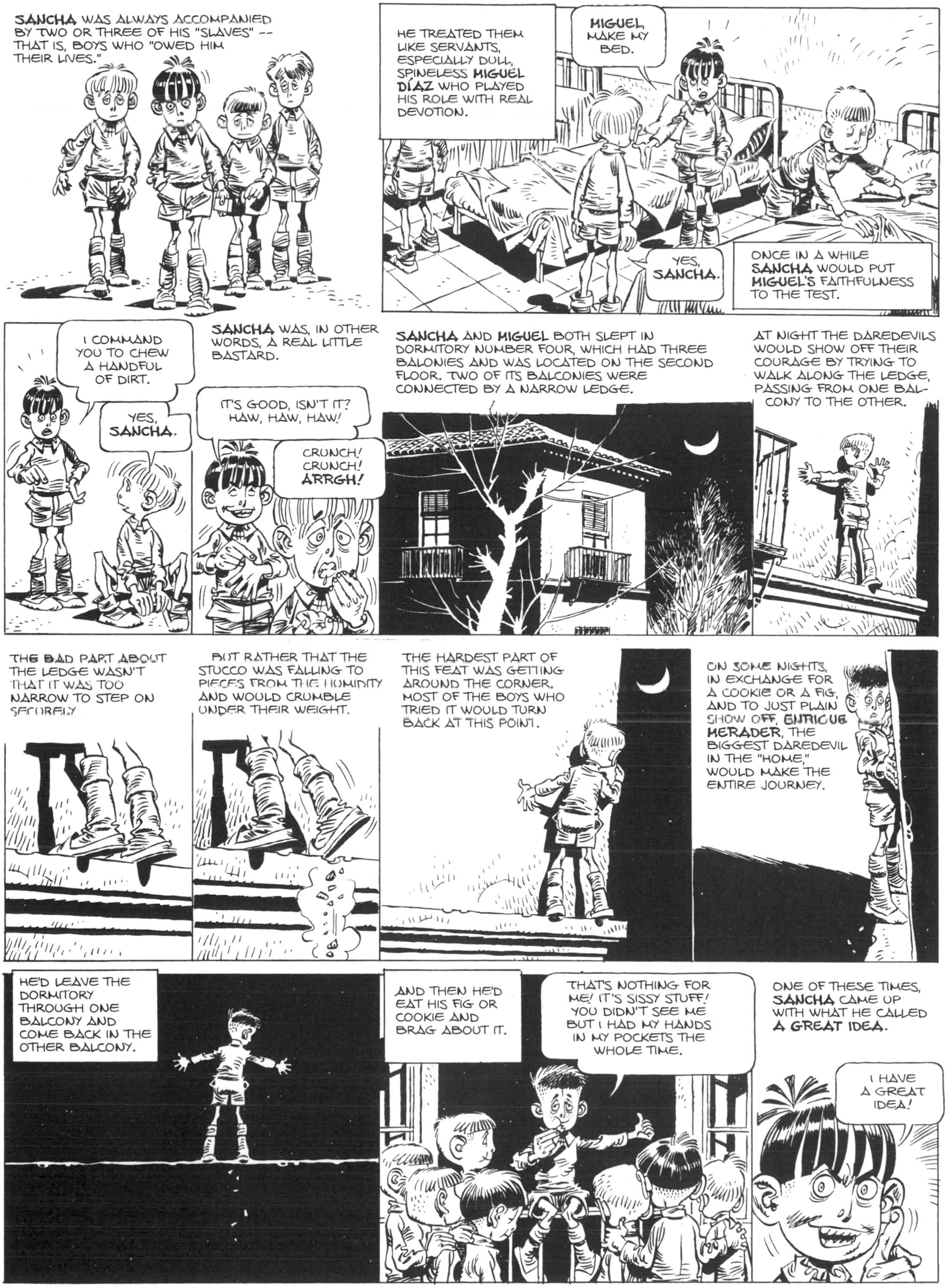
SANCHA WAS ALWAYS ACCOMPANIED BY TWO OR THREE OF HIS "SLAVES" -- THAT IS, BOYS WHO "OWED HIM THEIR LIVES."
HE TREATED THEM LIKE SERVANTS, ESPECIALLY DULL, SPINELESS MIGUEL DÍAZ WHO PLAYED HIS ROLE WITH REAL DEVOTION.
MIGUEL, MAKE MY BED.
YES, SANCHA.
ONCE IN A WHILE SANCHA WOULD PUT MIGUEL'S FAITHFULNESS TO THE TEST.
I COMMAND YOU TO CHEW A HANDFUL OF DIRT.
YES, SANCHA.
SANCHA WAS, IN OTHER WORDS, A REAL LITTLE BASTARD.
IT'S GOOD, ISN'T IT? HAW, HAW, HAW!
CRUNCH! CRUNCH! ARRGH!
SANCHA AND MIGUEL BOTH SLEPT IN DORMITORY NUMBER FOUR, WHICH HAD THREE BALONIES AND WAS LOCATED ON THE SECOND FLOOR. TWO OF ITS BALCONIES WERE CONNECTED BY A NARROW LEDGE.
AT NIGHT THE DAREDEVILS WOULD SHOW OFF THEIR COURAGE BY TRYING TO WALK ALONG THE LEDGE, PASSING FROM ONE BALCONY TO THE OTHER.
THE BAD PART ABOUT THE LEDGE WASN'T THAT IT WAS TOO NARROW TO STEP ON SECURELY
BUT RATHER THAT THE STUCCO WAS FALLING TO PIECES FROM THE HUMIDITY AND WOULD CRUMBLE UNDER THEIR WEIGHT.
THE HARDEST PART OF THIS FEAT WAS GETTING AROUND THE CORNER. MOST OF THE BOYS WHO TRIED IT WOULD TURN BACK AT THIS POINT.
ON SOME NIGHTS, IN EXCHANGE FOR A COOKIE OR A FIG, AND TO JUST PLAIN SHOW OFF, ENRIQUE MERADER, THE BIGGEST DAREDEVIL IN THE "HOME," WOULD MAKE THE ENTIRE JOURNEY.
HE'D LEAVE THE DORMITORY THROUGH ONE BALCONY AND COME BACK IN THE OTHER BALCONY.
AND THEN HE'D EAT HIS FIG OR COOKIE AND BRAG ABOUT IT.
THAT'S NOTHING FOR ME! IT'S SISSY STUFF! YOU DIDN'T SEE ME BUT I HAD MY HANDS IN MY POCKETS THE WHOLE TIME.
ONE OF THESE TIMES, SANCHA CAME UP WITH WHAT HE CALLED A GREAT IDEA.
I HAVE A GREAT IDEA!

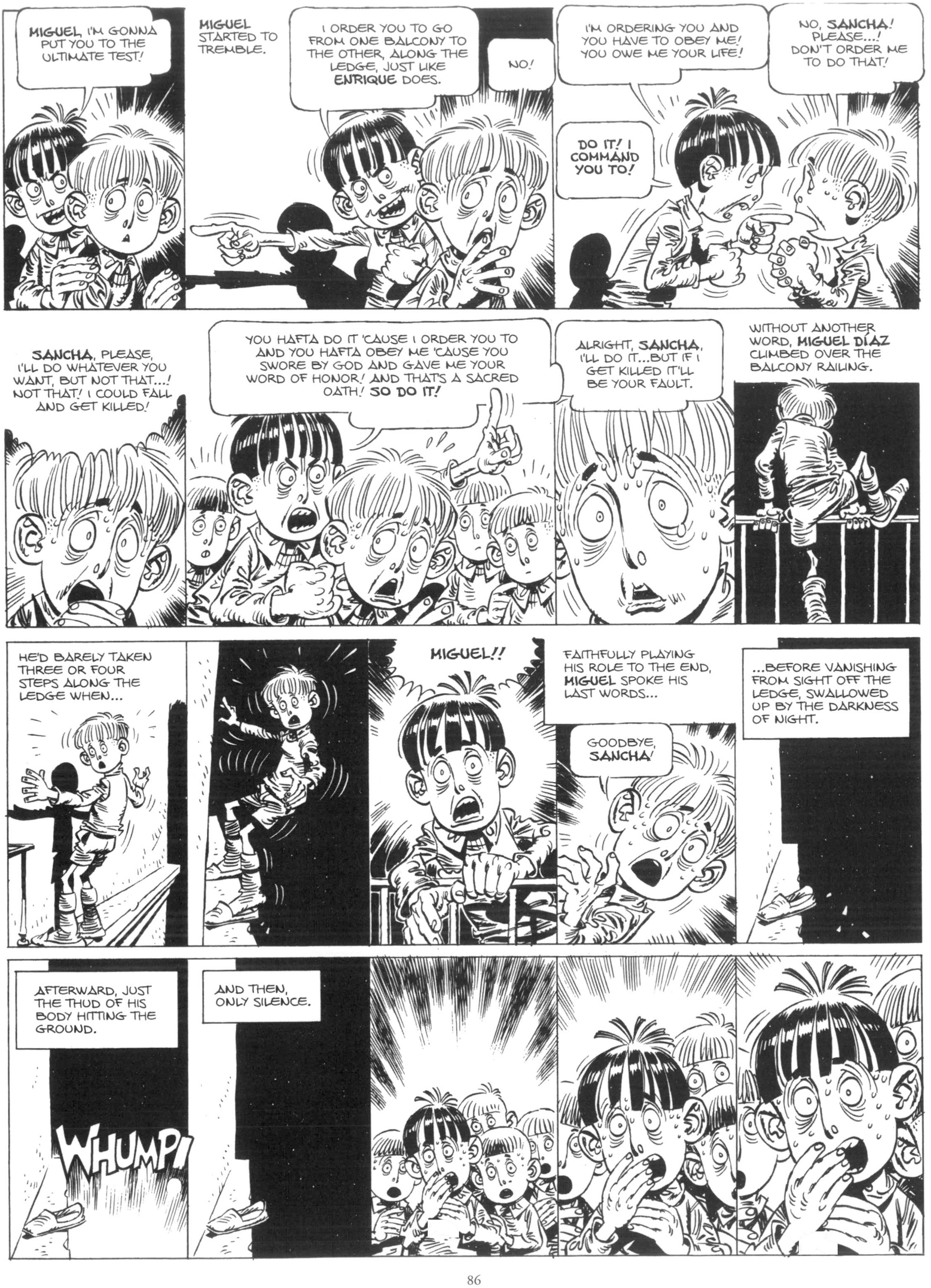

MIGUEL, I'M GONNA PUT YOU TO THE ULTIMATE TEST!
MIGUEL STARTED TO TREMBLE.
I ORDER YOU TO GO FROM ONE BALCONY TO THE OTHER, ALONG THE LEDGE, JUST LIKE ENRIQUE DOES.
NO!
I'M ORDERING YOU AND YOU HAVE TO OBEY ME! YOU OWE ME YOUR LIFE!
NO, SANCHA! PLEASE...! DON'T ORDER ME TO DO THAT!
DO IT! I COMMAND YOU TO!
SANCHA, PLEASE, I'LL DO WHATEVER YOU WANT, BUT NOT THAT...! NOT THAT! I COULD FALL AND GET KILLED!
YOU HAFTA DO IT 'CAUSE I ORDER YOU TO AND YOU HAFTA OBEY ME 'CAUSE YOU SWORE BY GOD AND GAVE ME YOUR WORD OF HONOR! AND THAT'S A SACRED OATH! SO DO IT!
ALRIGHT, SANCHA, I'LL DO IT...BUT IF I GET KILLED IT'LL BE YOUR FAULT.
WITHOUT ANOTHER WORD, MIGUEL DÍAZ CLIMBED OVER THE BALCONY RAILING.
HE'D BARELY TAKEN THREE OR FOUR STEPS ALONG THE LEDGE WHEN...
MIGUEL!!
FAITHFULLY PLAYING HIS ROLE TO THE END, MIGUEL SPOKE HIS LAST WORDS...
GOODBYE, SANCHA!
...BEFORE VANISHING FROM SIGHT OFF THE LEDGE, SWALLOWED UP BY THE DARKNESS OF NIGHT.
AFTERWARD, JUST THE THUD OF HIS BODY HITTING THE GROUND.
WHUMP!
AND THEN, ONLY SILENCE.

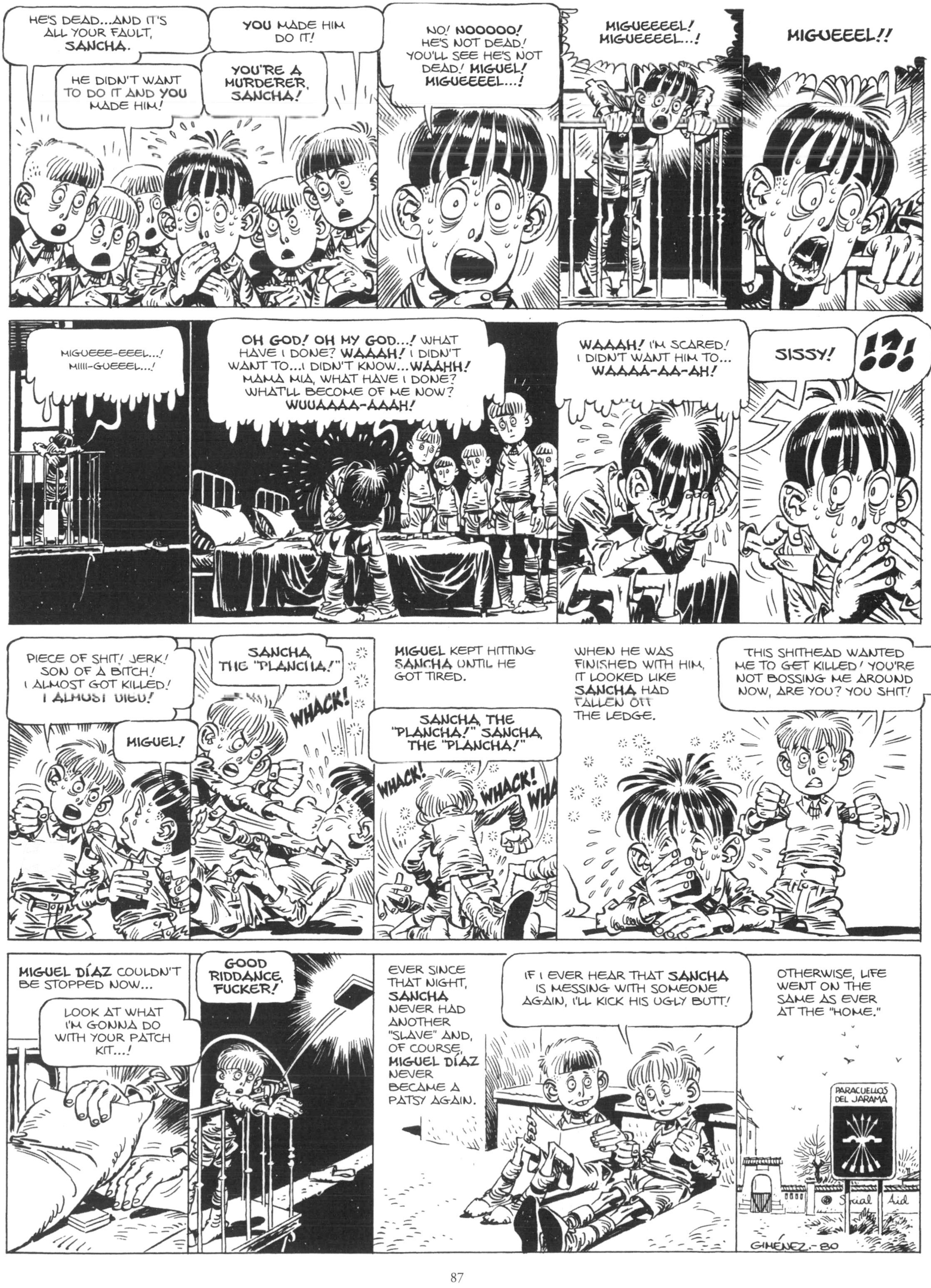

HE'S DEAD...AND IT'S ALL YOUR FAULT, SANCHA.
HE DIDN'T WANT TO DO IT AND YOU MADE HIM!
YOU MADE HIM DO IT!
YOU'RE A MURDERER, SANCHA!
NO! NOOOOO! HE'S NOT DEAD! YOU'LL SEE HE'S NOT DEAD! MIGUEL! MIGUEEEEL...!
MIGUEEEEL! MIGUEEEEL...!
MIGUEEEL!!
MIGUEEE-EEEL...! MIIII-GUEEEL...!
OH GOD! OH MY GOD...! WHAT HAVE I DONE? WAAAH! I DIDN'T WANT TO...I DIDN'T KNOW...WAAHH! MAMA MIA, WHAT HAVE I DONE? WHAT'LL BECOME OF ME NOW? WUUAAAA-AAAH!
WAAAH! I'M SCARED! I DIDN'T WANT HIM TO... WAAAA-AA-AH!
SISSY!
!?!
PIECE OF SHIT! JERK! SON OF A BITCH! I ALMOST GOT KILLED! I ALMOST DIED!
MIGUEL!
SANCHA, THE "PLANCHA!"
WHACK!
MIGUEL KEPT HITTING SANCHA UNTIL HE GOT TIRED.
SANCHA, THE "PLANCHA!" SANCHA, THE "PLANCHA!"
WHACK!
WHACK!
WHACK!
WHEN HE WAS FINISHED WITH HIM, IT LOOKED LIKE SANCHA HAD FALLEN OFF THE LEDGE.
THIS SHITHEAD WANTED ME TO GET KILLED! YOU'RE NOT BOSSING ME AROUND NOW, ARE YOU? YOU SHIT!
MIGUEL DÍAZ COULDN'T BE STOPPED NOW...
LOOK AT WHAT I'M GONNA DO WITH YOUR PATCH KIT...!
GOOD RIDDANCE, FUCKER!
EVER SINCE THAT NIGHT, SANCHA NEVER HAD ANOTHER "SLAVE" AND, OF COURSE, MIGUEL DÍAZ NEVER BECAME A PATSY AGAIN.
IF I EVER HEAR THAT SANCHA IS MESSING WITH SOMEONE AGAIN, I'LL KICK HIS UGLY BUTT!
OTHERWISE, LIFE WENT ON THE SAME AS EVER AT THE "HOME."
PARACUELLOS DEL JARAMA
Social Aid
GIMÉNEZ.-80

Vallecano's "Egg"

Giménez had broken his arm in a fight; it got bent backwards -- behind him, as if he had his elbow in front rather than in back. Did he ever scream!

They took him to the infirmary and kept him in the Bone Ward for forty days.

Vallecano was in the Bone Ward too. He had a cyst on his forehead that was the size of a large egg. The doctors didn't dare lance it; it looked like a difficult and risky job. Difficult for the doctors and risky for Vallecano, that is.

The boy's bathroom in the bone ward was connected to the girl's bathroom by a common roof and a narrow ventilation opening. On some nights there were social gatherings of sorts in the toilets; naturally, these were strictly forbidden. One night, during one of these get-togethers, Vallecano stayed behind in the dormitory to give everyone a warning whistle if one of the nurses came around.

Instead of keeping watch, Vallecano fell asleep, and since he always slept with his eyes wide open, everybody just figured that he was on the lookout.

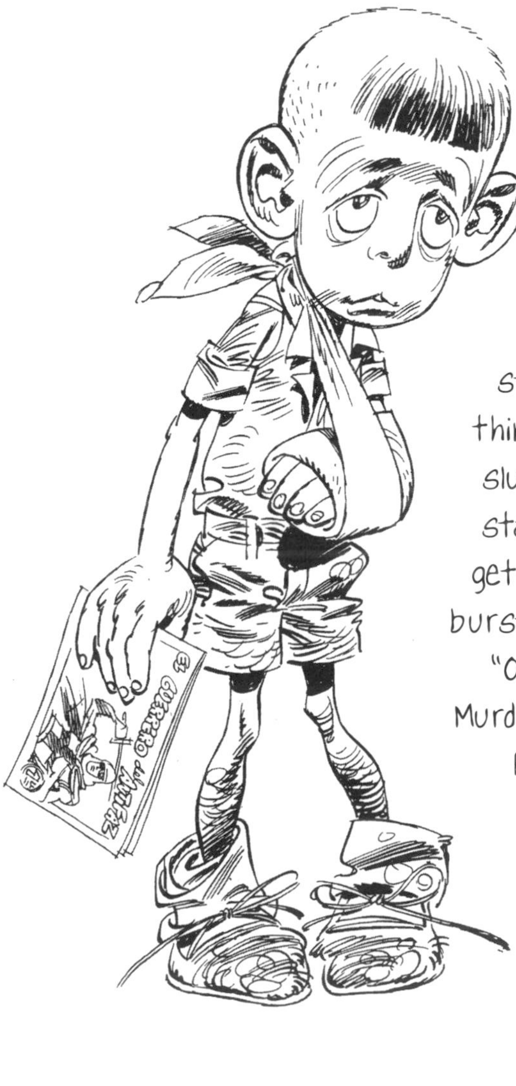

Well, it turned out that the nurse did come around that night and she caught them all red-handed at the get-together. And Vallecano didn't even know it because he slept right through the whole thing.

When the nurse had gone, Giménez confronted Vallecano, thinking that he was awake.

"Why didn't you warn us, you asshole?" Vallecano was still sound asleep and didn't answer. "You're right on top of things, Huh?" Giménez jumped on top of him like a monkey, slugged him hard and popped open his cyst. Vallecano woke up startled, with no idea of what was going on or why he was getting beaten up. And when he realized that his cyst had burst, he thought he was going to die and began screaming: "Oh! I want my mommy!...you busted my 'Egg' You killer! Murderer!"

Everything squirted out of the cyst. Was it ever gross! The very next day the doctors released Vallecano, saying that his cyst was "cured." That afternoon, Giménez bragged, "I cured you, huh!?! And with this!" and he raised his hand in its plaster cast.

The Fistful of Prunes

Adolfo was one of the tallest boys in the "Home".

His father was a tuberculosis patient in the Valdelatas Sanitorium. He also had a brother and various step-brothers and sisters. The brother was in another state school, like him. The others...he didn't really know. He also had more relatives: aunts and uncles, cousins... no one ever came to see him.

It was St. Joseph's Day, actually. Father's Day, too: life's little ironies.

The boys were standing in line on the playing field. They had already had their daily snack, which consisted that day of dried plums, three prunes apiece. Before breaking ranks, Antonio, the Phalanx instructor, called Adolfo over:

"So...did you get something to eat?" -- "Yes, Antonio."

"You like prunes?" -- "Yes, Antonio." -- "Well, here...have some..."

Antonio stuck his hand in the sack of prunes and pulled out a fistful.

"Take some, sit down over here when you break ranks and eat them --"

It seemed like Antonio was going to say something else, but instead he put his hand on Adolfo's shoulder and went back with him to where the boys stood in formation.

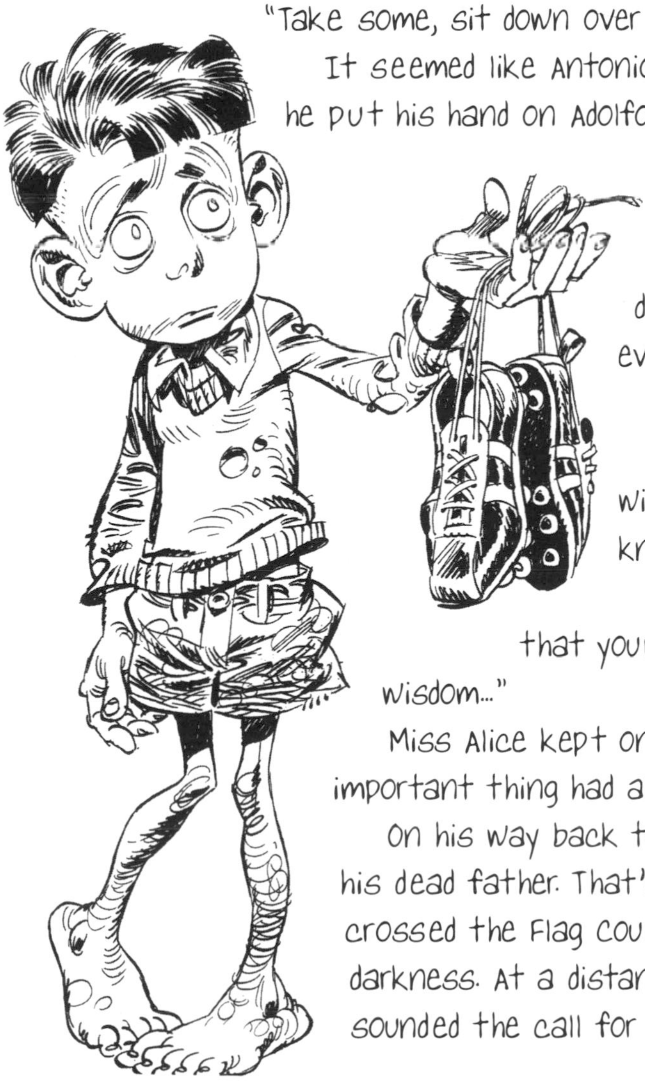

Adolfo was stunned. Stupefied.

That same night, as he was leaving the dining hall, Miss Alicia, the teacher on duty that evening, stopped him.

"Adolfo, you stay here; I want to talk to you."

From the door Rudi, the bugler, looked at him with friendly eyes; it seemed as if he already knew what he was going to be told.

"Look, Adolfo, you're already a man...you know that your father was very sick. God, in his infinite wisdom..."

Miss Alice kept on talking for a long time, but for Adolfo the important thing had already been said.

On his way back to the dormitory, Adolfo cried. He thought about his dead father. That's why Antonio had given him the prunes. He crossed the Flag Courtyard. The whole school was submerged in darkness. At a distance, like on any other night, Rudi, the bugle boy, sounded the call for all quiet.

The Mouthful of Mortadella

García García had a brother who was three or four years older than him named Antonio. They called him Toñin at home. Toñin was also at a Social Aid school, in a "home" for older boys.

The two boys hadn't seen each other for a long time, several years, ever since they were sent to the "homes."

One day, García García's school held a gymnastic exhibition and boys representing each of the Social Aid "homes" came.

And by pure chance one of the boys who came to do gymnastics was Toñin.

The exhibition consisted of doing a series of gymnastic moves in front of the Social Aid delegates and other personages, primarily priests and Falangists.

After the gymnastics, the boys, who were all dressed in white gym pants, shirts, shoes and socks, and red berets, paraded to the beat of drums and trumpets and sang patriotic anthems:

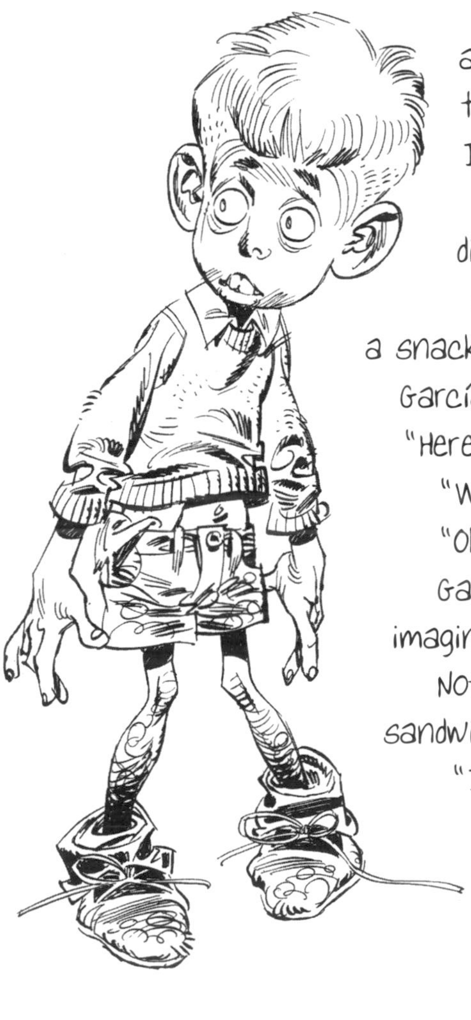

"I'm a National-Unionist, I believe in the rules of honor and an end to workers' bitterness and to the bosses who exploit them. I'm Labor's Phalanx so that good may triumph over evil. I'm happiness and justice, I'm Imperial Spain!"

Later that afternoon, after the parading and gymnastic displays, the two brothers were finally able to get together.

As a treat on this special day, they had given the gymnasts a snack: a tiny bread roll with mortadella.

García García's brother had his treat in his hand.

"Here, little guy; a present from your big brother!"

"What about you? Aren't you hungry?"

"Oh, man...I...it's that...I...I don't like mortadella."

García García knew full well that this was a lie. He couldn't imagine anyone in the world not liking mortadella.

Not meeting his brother's eye, García García wolfed down the sandwich. His brother watched him.

"Is it good?" -- "Yeah..."

"Yeah..." -- "Well, enjoy it."

Later that night, alone in bed, before going to sleep, García García thought about his brother Toñin and the mortadella sandwich. And he felt bad.

Like the Baby Jesus

Before Matias was called Matias he was named Jesusin, like the Baby Jesus.

It seems that a few months after he was born they found him abandoned in the middle of the street.

It was a night watchman that found him.

They put him in a Social Aid "Home" for infants and since he didn't have a name, they called him Jesus, like the Baby Jesus.

Then one day, many years later, a mother showed up to claim him and said that he wasn't named Jesus, but rather Matias.

She went to see him two or three times at the "Home" and then she didn't come anymore. In other words, she abandoned him for the second time.

During one of her visits, Matias asked his mother:

"When you left me, why didn't you leave a piece of paper that said 'this boy is named Matias?'"

"Son," his mother answered, "It was because I don't know how to write and I wasn't about to ask the neighbor lady -- 'Listen, write me a note because I want to abandon my little boy.'"

The Bully

"Goalie" was a bully. He liked to be mean, the same way that others like to sing.

He hit the rest of the boys just for the hell of it, because he felt like it, because that's how he was.

Anyone who was undersized or sickly pissed him off.

It was raining hard the day he first came to the school and he arrived completely soaked. He was real scared and didn't say a word. He stayed in a corner of the courtyard, sitting curled up on the ground, with blank staring eyes and a frightened face.

And that's how he spent the whole first week, curled up in his corner. The other boys felt bad for him. Above all -- Moratalla.

Moratalla sat with him and let him read his comics. Little by little "Goalie" mellowed out.

Then it turned out that he played soccer really well, especially the goalkeeper position. No one got a goal past him; he leaped like a frog in all directions and always caught the ball. He was great at stopping the ball and that's how he got his nickname.

After a while he started to beat up on everybody. He wet their ears. That is, he would challenge them by spitting on their ear lobes. If they accepted the challenge, he would fight them and he usually won.

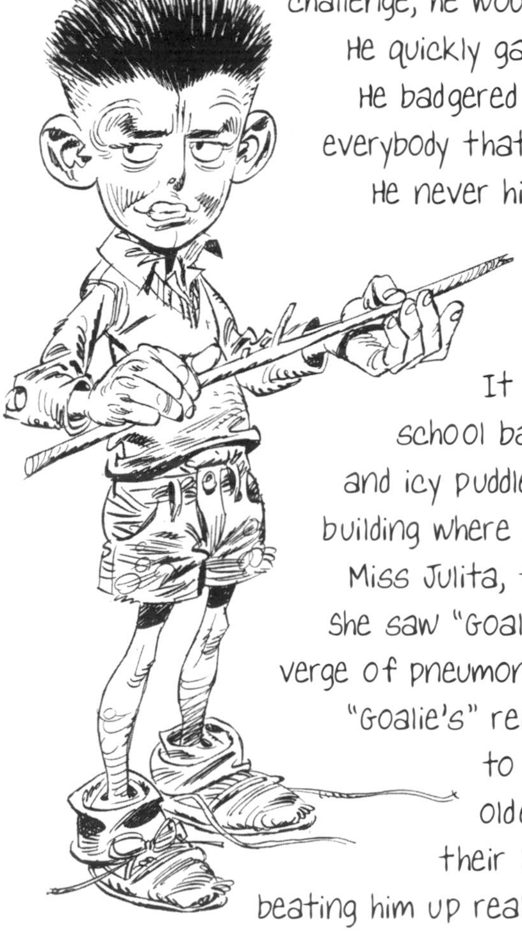

He quickly gained fame as a fighter. He hit everyone. He was a bully.

He badgered Gálvez and "Jam-pot" and Domiciano and Morcis...almost everybody that seemed weaker than him.

He never hit Moratalla, maybe out of gratitude for those first days, but he took away his comics and ripped them up. Moratalla was terrified of him.

One night, "Goalie" got up and started to sleepwalk. It was in the winter and terribly cold. He crossed the entire school barefoot, just wearing his pajamas, walking on the frost and icy puddles. He got as far as the well-house, an out-of-the-way building where some of the teachers slept, and knocked on the door. Miss Julita, the oldest of all the teachers, opened the door. She saw "Goalie," barefoot and blue with cold, shivering and on the verge of pneumonia. He said to her: "Mother! Mother! It's me!"

"Goalie's" reign lasted almost four years. When they transferred him to another school, he got paid back and then some. The older brothers of all the boys he'd hit held him down while their little brothers, now free of fear, got even with him by beating him up real good. They even made up a game with the refrain: "Whoever doesn't hit 'Goalie' is a sissy."

Mr. Evelio's Water Jug

One was always thirsty in the Paracuellos "Home," above all in the summer. There were days, even weeks, when there wasn't any water in the faucets; not in the showers or in the sinks or in the toilets or in the kitchen or in the laundry room. Nowhere. There wasn't any water whatsoever.

They had water brought in from somewhere else, in a tanker-truck.

They had all the boys stand in line and gave each one a glass of water. That was their treat at snack-time.

Moratalla had cried from thirst many times. Also from cold. Not from hunger, though. One doesn't cry from hunger; it's as if being hungry was more logical and one gets used to it. But one cries from thirst with rage, with fury, with impotence, and, naturally, one tries to drink up one's own tears.

On one of those thirsty days, Moratalla and "Wasp" had slipped away at nap time and were wandering around behind the chapel, near the pool, which was empty and bone-dry, its bottom covered with dirt. They were looking for vines and tendrils and other more or less edible weeds and wild roots to suck on when suddenly, in the shade of a giant toadstool, half hidden, they found a water jug.

"It's the gardener's, Mr. Evelio's, water jug!"

It was a pretty red jar, cool, clean, shiny, and full. About two liters of water.

They drank it all up, down to the last drop.

"When Mr. Evelio comes and sees that there isn't any more water in the jar..."

"He'll tell the head-mistress."

"They'll punish everybody."

"What shall we do?"

"We can pee in the jug; that way it'll look like there's water in it."

"And if Mr. Evelio drinks it and dies?"

"Enrique Mercader drinks piss and it hasn't killed him."

"But when he drinks it...he'll realize that it's piss..."

"He'll just think that it's water that's gotten salty."

"Sure, he will, man! Do you think he's stupid?"

"You'll see...you'll see...here, let me..."

And so "Wasp" pissed in the jug. Well, partly inside and

Mr. Evelio's Water Jug (cont.d)

partly outside it. And part went on his pants and part on his shoes.

He still had the jug in his hand when Mr. Evelio showed up.

Moratalla and "Wasp" wished that the earth would open up and swallow them. "Wasp" was paralyzed with fear, the jug in one hand and his dick in the other. Moratalla began to whimper.

Mr. Evelio, dead serious, stared at them. He carried a hoe on his shoulder, his hands, face, and clothes covered with dust and dirt. It was obvious that he'd been working hard, digging.

He was tall, thin, and old with several days' growth of white beard.

The two kids were pale, sweaty, on the point of tears, with their legs trembling.

"And now, what do I do with you? Do you think it's nice to pee in a working man's jug? Huh?"

"No, sir."

"No, sir."

Moratalla started to cry big fat tears like fists.

"Good grief! So why did you pee in my jug?"

"It was so you wouldn't notice that we'd drunk all your water…!"

"Damn it, that's even worse! And you've ruined my jug, too!"

"We didn't mean to…"

"Didn't mean to, huh? Does one kill a donkey without meaning to? Come over here, come on…"

Moratalla, shaking all over, went to him.

"Don't be scared, son, I'm not going to do anything to you. What's your name?"

"Pablo Moratalla…"

"Do you have a father?"

"No, sir."

"And a mother?"

"Yes, sir."

"Does she come to visit you?"

"No, she can't…she's in a tuberculosis sanitorium."

"So…"

The next day, Mr. Evelio brought a new water jug, a much bigger one, filled it to the top with water, and put it in the same spot. He also put in two fat slices of white bread.

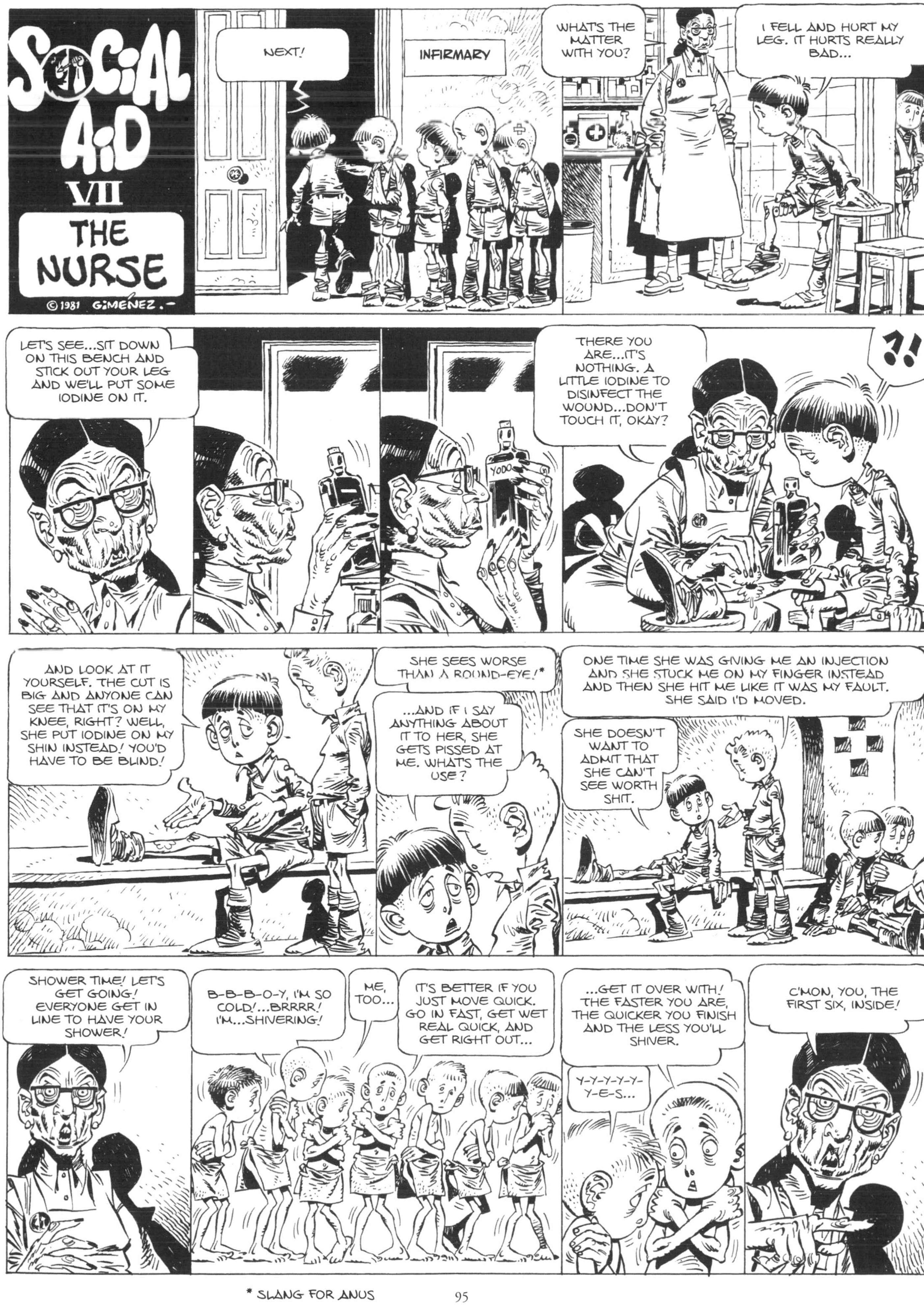
SOCIAL AID
VII
THE NURSE
©1981 GIMÉNEZ.-
NEXT!
INFIRMARY
WHAT'S THE MATTER WITH YOU?
I FELL AND HURT MY LEG. IT HURTS REALLY BAD...
LET'S SEE...SIT DOWN ON THIS BENCH AND STICK OUT YOUR LEG AND WE'LL PUT SOME IODINE ON IT.
YODO
THERE YOU ARE...IT'S NOTHING. A LITTLE IODINE TO DISINFECT THE WOUND...DON'T TOUCH IT, OKAY?
?!
AND LOOK AT IT YOURSELF. THE CUT IS BIG AND ANYONE CAN SEE THAT IT'S ON MY KNEE, RIGHT? WELL, SHE PUT IODINE ON MY SHIN INSTEAD! YOU'D HAVE TO BE BLIND!
SHE SEES WORSE THAN A ROUND-EYE!*
...AND IF I SAY ANYTHING ABOUT IT TO HER, SHE GETS PISSED AT ME. WHAT'S THE USE?
ONE TIME SHE WAS GIVING ME AN INJECTION AND SHE STUCK ME ON MY FINGER INSTEAD AND THEN SHE HIT ME LIKE IT WAS MY FAULT. SHE SAID I'D MOVED.
SHE DOESN'T WANT TO ADMIT THAT SHE CAN'T SEE WORTH SHIT.
SHOWER TIME! LET'S GET GOING! EVERYONE GET IN LINE TO HAVE YOUR SHOWER!
B-B-B-O-Y, I'M SO COLD!...BRRRR! I'M...SHIVERING!
ME, TOO...
IT'S BETTER IF YOU JUST MOVE QUICK. GO IN FAST, GET WET REAL QUICK, AND GET RIGHT OUT...
...GET IT OVER WITH! THE FASTER YOU ARE, THE QUICKER YOU FINISH AND THE LESS YOU'LL SHIVER.
Y-Y-Y-Y-Y-Y-E-S...
C'MON, YOU, THE FIRST SIX, INSIDE!

* SLANG FOR ANUS

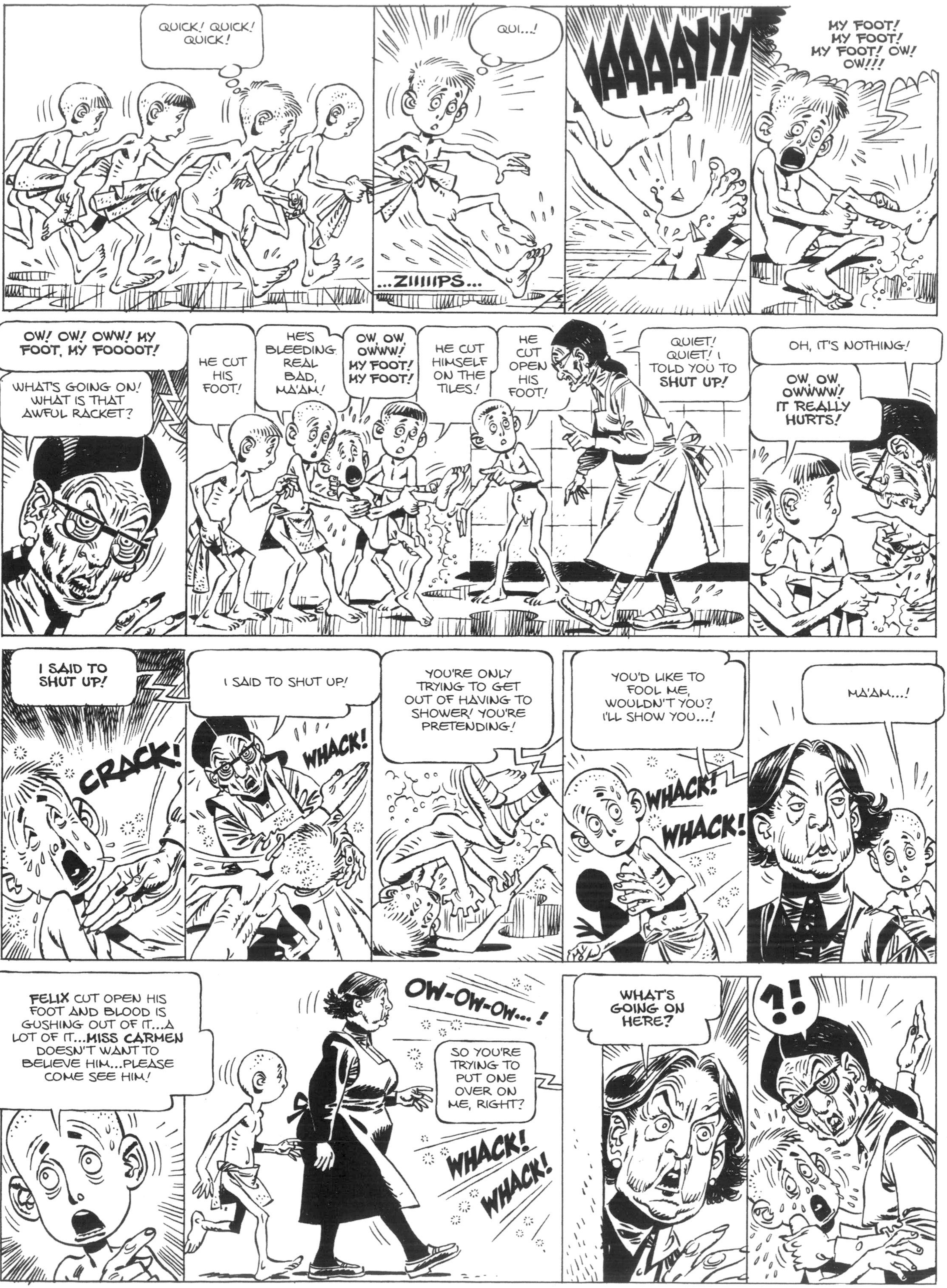
QUICK! QUICK! QUICK!
QUI...!
...ZIIIIPS...
AAAAAYYY
MY FOOT! MY FOOT! MY FOOT! OW! OW!!!
OW! OW! OWW! MY FOOT, MY FOOOOT!
WHAT'S GOING ON! WHAT IS THAT AWFUL RACKET?
HE CUT HIS FOOT!
HE'S BLEEDING REAL BAD, MA'AM!
OW, OW, OWWW! MY FOOT! MY FOOT!
HE CUT HIMSELF ON THE TILES!
HE CUT OPEN HIS FOOT!
QUIET! QUIET! I TOLD YOU TO SHUT UP!
OH, IT'S NOTHING!
OW, OW, OWWWW! IT REALLY HURTS!
I SAID TO SHUT UP!
CRACK!
I SAID TO SHUT UP!
WHACK!
YOU'RE ONLY TRYING TO GET OUT OF HAVING TO SHOWER! YOU'RE PRETENDING!
YOU'D LIKE TO FOOL ME, WOULDN'T YOU? I'LL SHOW YOU...!
WHACK! WHACK!
MA'AM...!
FELIX CUT OPEN HIS FOOT AND BLOOD IS GUSHING OUT OF IT...A LOT OF IT...MISS CARMEN DOESN'T WANT TO BELIEVE HIM...PLEASE COME SEE HIM!
OW-OW-OW...!
SO YOU'RE TRYING TO PUT ONE OVER ON ME, RIGHT?
WHACK! WHACK!
WHAT'S GOING ON HERE?
?!

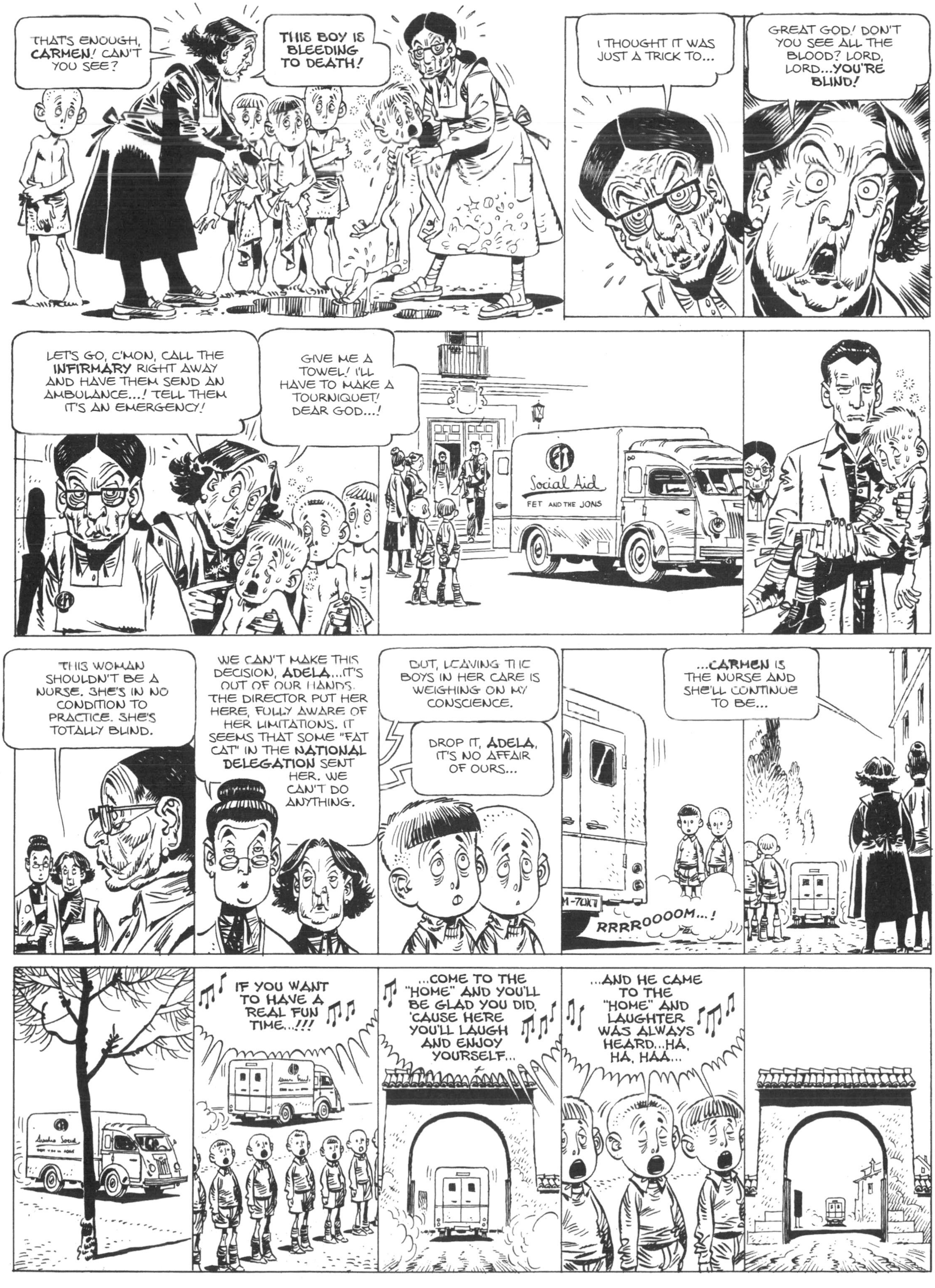

THAT'S ENOUGH, CARMEN! CAN'T YOU SEE?
THIS BOY IS BLEEDING TO DEATH!
I THOUGHT IT WAS JUST A TRICK TO...
GREAT GOD! DON'T YOU SEE ALL THE BLOOD? LORD, LORD...YOU'RE BLIND!
LET'S GO, C'MON, CALL THE INFIRMARY RIGHT AWAY AND HAVE THEM SEND AN AMBULANCE...! TELL THEM IT'S AN EMERGENCY!
GIVE ME A TOWEL! I'LL HAVE TO MAKE A TOURNIQUET! DEAR GOD...!
Social Aid
FET AND THE JONS
THIS WOMAN SHOULDN'T BE A NURSE. SHE'S IN NO CONDITION TO PRACTICE. SHE'S TOTALLY BLIND.
WE CAN'T MAKE THIS DECISION, ADELA...IT'S OUT OF OUR HANDS. THE DIRECTOR PUT HER HERE, FULLY AWARE OF HER LIMITATIONS. IT SEEMS THAT SOME "FAT CAT" IN THE NATIONAL DELEGATION SENT HER. WE CAN'T DO ANYTHING.
BUT, LEAVING THE BOYS IN HER CARE IS WEIGHING ON MY CONSCIENCE.
DROP IT, ADELA, IT'S NO AFFAIR OF OURS...
RRRROOOOM...!
...CARMEN IS THE NURSE AND SHE'LL CONTINUE TO BE...
IF YOU WANT TO HAVE A REAL FUN TIME...!!!
...COME TO THE "HOME" AND YOU'LL BE GLAD YOU DID, 'CAUSE HERE YOU'LL LAUGH AND ENJOY YOURSELF...
...AND HE CAME TO THE "HOME" AND LAUGHTER WAS ALWAYS HEARD...HA, HA, HAA...

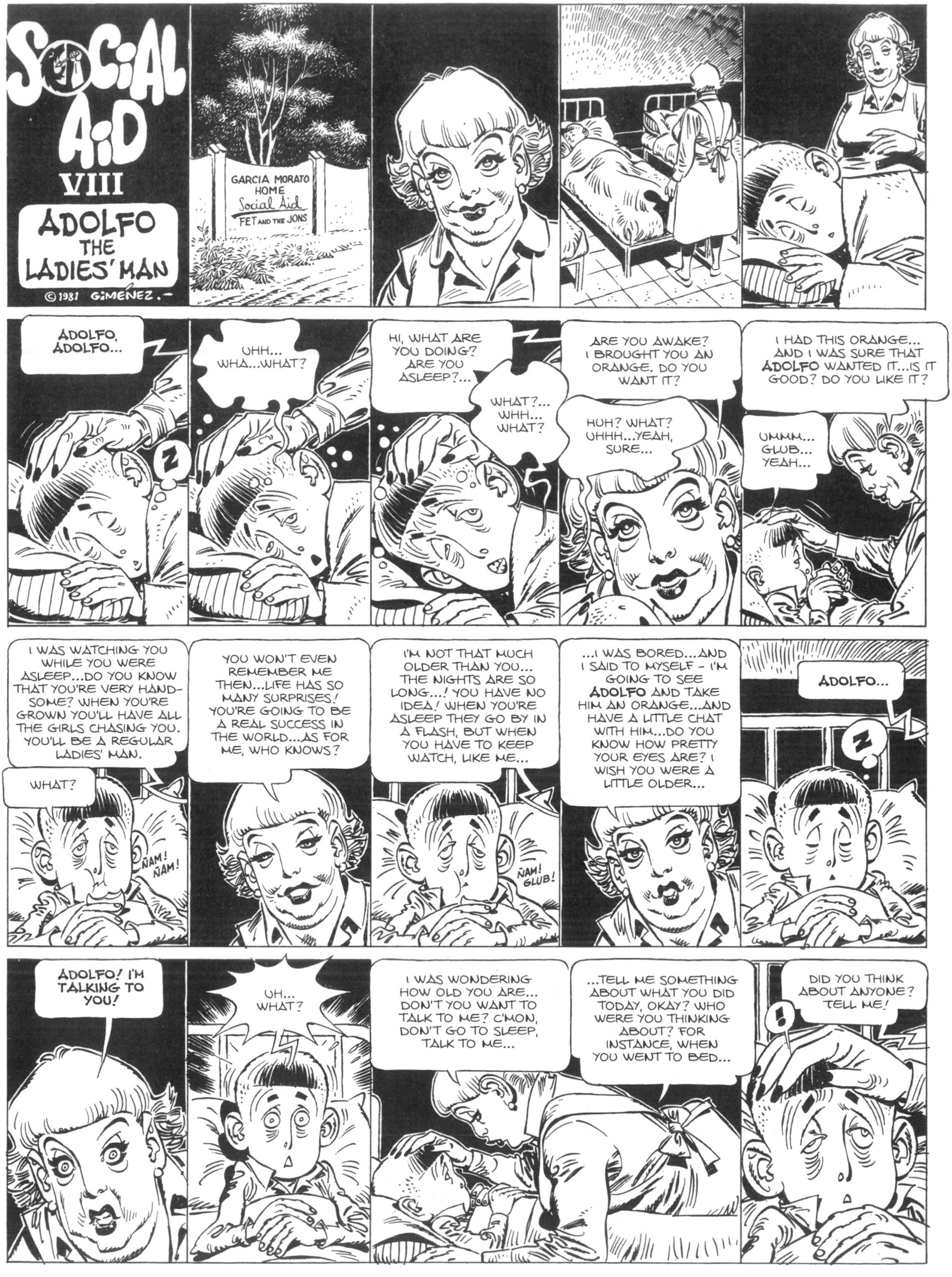
SOCIAL AID
VIII
ADOLFO THE LADIES' MAN
©1981 GIMENEZ.-
GARCIA MORATO HOME
Social Aid
FET AND THE JONS
ADOLFO, ADOLFO...
Z
UHH... WHA...WHAT?
HI, WHAT ARE YOU DOING? ARE YOU ASLEEP?...
WHAT?... WHH... WHAT?
ARE YOU AWAKE? I BROUGHT YOU AN ORANGE. DO YOU WANT IT?
HUH? WHAT? UHHH...YEAH, SURE...
I HAD THIS ORANGE... AND I WAS SURE THAT ADOLFO WANTED IT...IS IT GOOD? DO YOU LIKE IT?
UMMM... GLUB... YEAH...
I WAS WATCHING YOU WHILE YOU WERE ASLEEP...DO YOU KNOW THAT YOU'RE VERY HANDSOME? WHEN YOU'RE GROWN YOU'LL HAVE ALL THE GIRLS CHASING YOU. YOU'LL BE A REGULAR LADIES' MAN.
WHAT?
ÑAM! ÑAM!
YOU WON'T EVEN REMEMBER ME THEN...LIFE HAS SO MANY SURPRISES! YOU'RE GOING TO BE A REAL SUCCESS IN THE WORLD...AS FOR ME, WHO KNOWS?
I'M NOT THAT MUCH OLDER THAN YOU... THE NIGHTS ARE SO LONG...! YOU HAVE NO IDEA! WHEN YOU'RE ASLEEP THEY GO BY IN A FLASH, BUT WHEN YOU HAVE TO KEEP WATCH, LIKE ME...
ÑAM! GLUB!
...I WAS BORED...AND I SAID TO MYSELF - I'M GOING TO SEE ADOLFO AND TAKE HIM AN ORANGE...AND HAVE A LITTLE CHAT WITH HIM...DO YOU KNOW HOW PRETTY YOUR EYES ARE? I WISH YOU WERE A LITTLE OLDER...
ADOLFO...
Z
ADOLFO! I'M TALKING TO YOU!
UH... WHAT?
I WAS WONDERING HOW OLD YOU ARE... DON'T YOU WANT TO TALK TO ME? C'MON, DON'T GO TO SLEEP, TALK TO ME...
...TELL ME SOMETHING ABOUT WHAT YOU DID TODAY, OKAY? WHO WERE YOU THINKING ABOUT? FOR INSTANCE, WHEN YOU WENT TO BED...
!
DID YOU THINK ABOUT ANYONE? TELL ME!

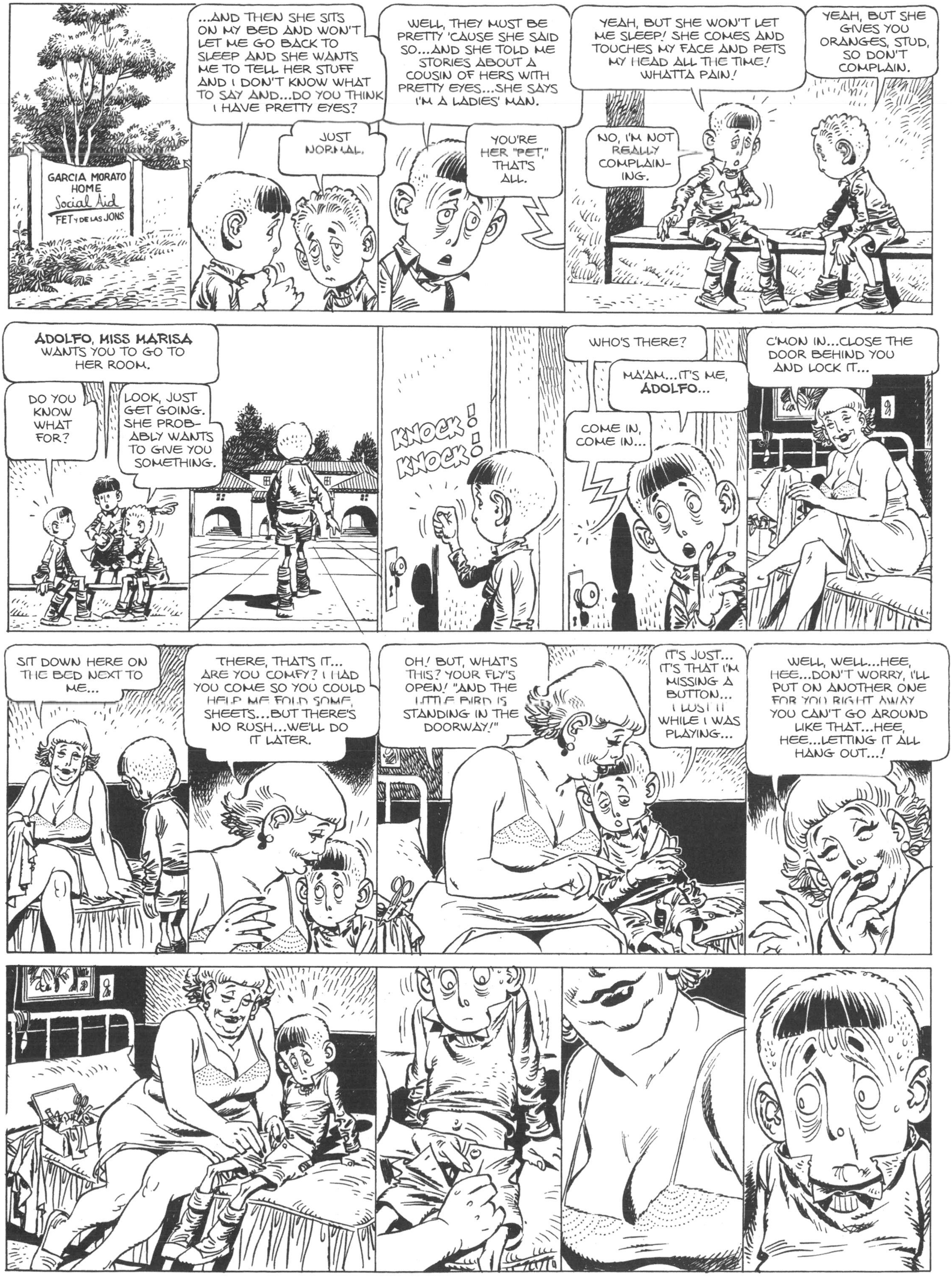

GARCIA MORATO HOME
Social Aid
FET y DE LAS JONS
...AND THEN SHE SITS ON MY BED AND WON'T LET ME GO BACK TO SLEEP AND SHE WANTS ME TO TELL HER STUFF AND I DON'T KNOW WHAT TO SAY AND...DO YOU THINK I HAVE PRETTY EYES?
JUST NORMAL.
WELL, THEY MUST BE PRETTY 'CAUSE SHE SAID SO...AND SHE TOLD ME STORIES ABOUT A COUSIN OF HERS WITH PRETTY EYES...SHE SAYS I'M A LADIES' MAN.
YOU'RE HER "PET," THAT'S ALL.
YEAH, BUT SHE WON'T LET ME SLEEP! SHE COMES AND TOUCHES MY FACE AND PETS MY HEAD ALL THE TIME! WHATTA PAIN!
YEAH, BUT SHE GIVES YOU ORANGES, STUD, SO DON'T COMPLAIN.
NO, I'M NOT REALLY COMPLAINING.
ADOLFO, MISS MARISA WANTS YOU TO GO TO HER ROOM.
DO YOU KNOW WHAT FOR?
LOOK, JUST GET GOING. SHE PROBABLY WANTS TO GIVE YOU SOMETHING.
KNOCK! KNOCK!
WHO'S THERE?
MA'AM...IT'S ME, ADOLFO...
COME IN, COME IN...
C'MON IN...CLOSE THE DOOR BEHIND YOU AND LOCK IT...
SIT DOWN HERE ON THE BED NEXT TO ME...
THERE, THAT'S IT... ARE YOU COMFY? I HAD YOU COME SO YOU COULD HELP ME FOLD SOME SHEETS...BUT THERE'S NO RUSH...WE'LL DO IT LATER.
OH! BUT, WHAT'S THIS? YOUR FLY'S OPEN! "AND THE LITTLE BIRD IS STANDING IN THE DOORWAY!"
IT'S JUST... IT'S THAT I'M MISSING A BUTTON... I LOST IT WHILE I WAS PLAYING...
WELL, WELL...HEE, HEE...DON'T WORRY, I'LL PUT ON ANOTHER ONE FOR YOU RIGHT AWAY YOU CAN'T GO AROUND LIKE THAT...HEE, HEE...LETTING IT ALL HANG OUT...!

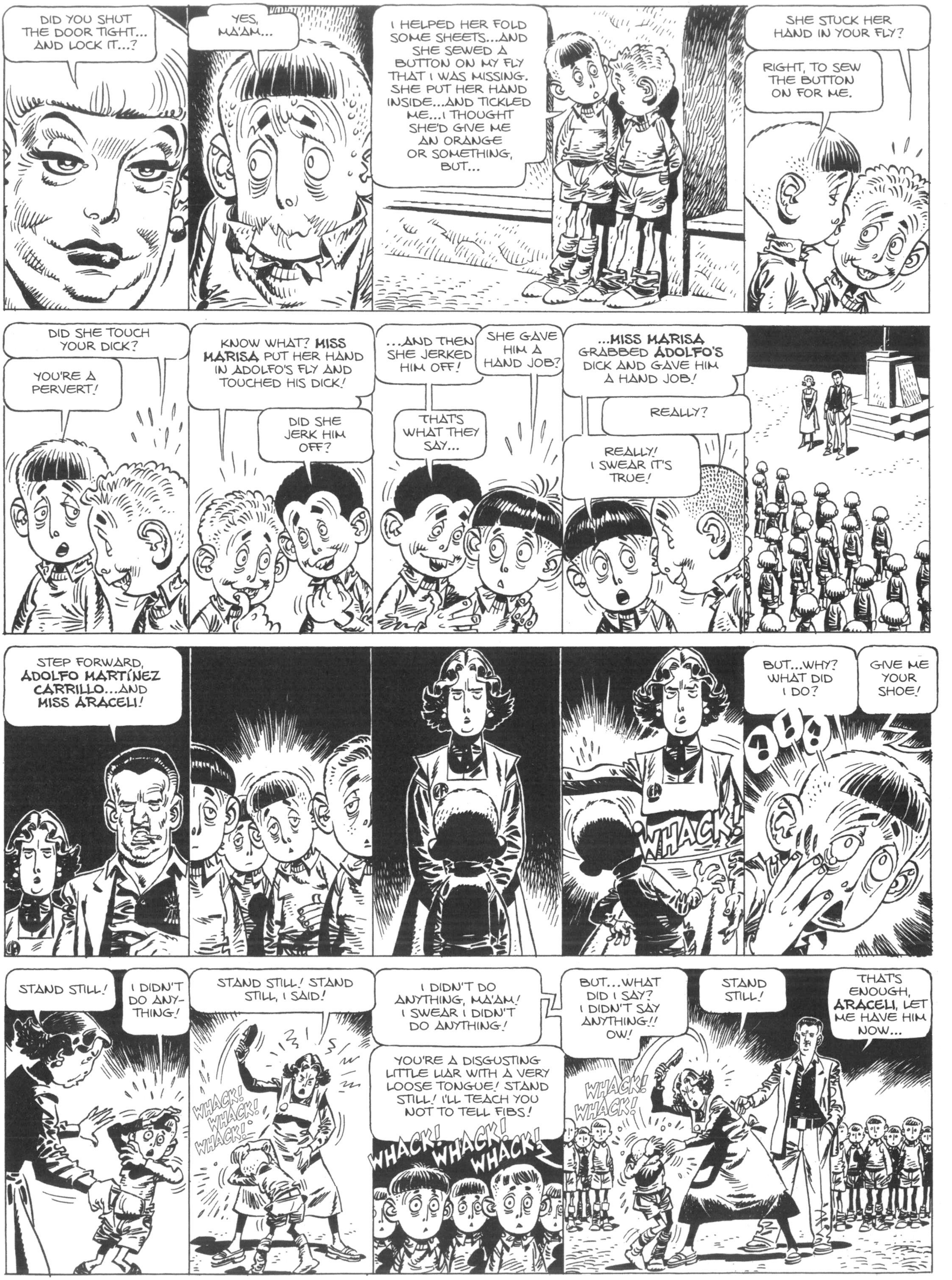
DID YOU SHUT THE DOOR TIGHT... AND LOCK IT...?
YES, MA'AM...
I HELPED HER FOLD SOME SHEETS...AND SHE SEWED A BUTTON ON MY FLY THAT I WAS MISSING. SHE PUT HER HAND INSIDE...AND TICKLED ME...I THOUGHT SHE'D GIVE ME AN ORANGE OR SOMETHING, BUT...
SHE STUCK HER HAND IN YOUR FLY?
RIGHT, TO SEW THE BUTTON ON FOR ME.
DID SHE TOUCH YOUR DICK?
YOU'RE A PERVERT!
KNOW WHAT? MISS MARISA PUT HER HAND IN ADOLFO'S FLY AND TOUCHED HIS DICK!
DID SHE JERK HIM OFF?
...AND THEN SHE JERKED HIM OFF!
SHE GAVE HIM A HAND JOB?
THAT'S WHAT THEY SAY...
...MISS MARISA GRABBED ADOLFO'S DICK AND GAVE HIM A HAND JOB!
REALLY?
REALLY! I SWEAR IT'S TRUE!
STEP FORWARD, ADOLFO MARTÍNEZ CARRILLO...AND MISS ARACELI!
WHACK!
BUT...WHY? WHAT DID I DO?
GIVE ME YOUR SHOE!
?!?
STAND STILL!
I DIDN'T DO ANY-THING!
STAND STILL! STAND STILL, I SAID!
WHACK! WHACK! WHACK!
I DIDN'T DO ANYTHING, MA'AM! I SWEAR I DIDN'T DO ANYTHING!
YOU'RE A DISGUSTING LITTLE LIAR WITH A VERY LOOSE TONGUE! STAND STILL! I'LL TEACH YOU NOT TO TELL FIBS!
WHACK! WHACK! WHACK!
BUT...WHAT DID I SAY? I DIDN'T SAY ANYTHING!! OW!
WHACK! WHACK!
STAND STILL!
THAT'S ENOUGH, ARACELI, LET ME HAVE HIM NOW...

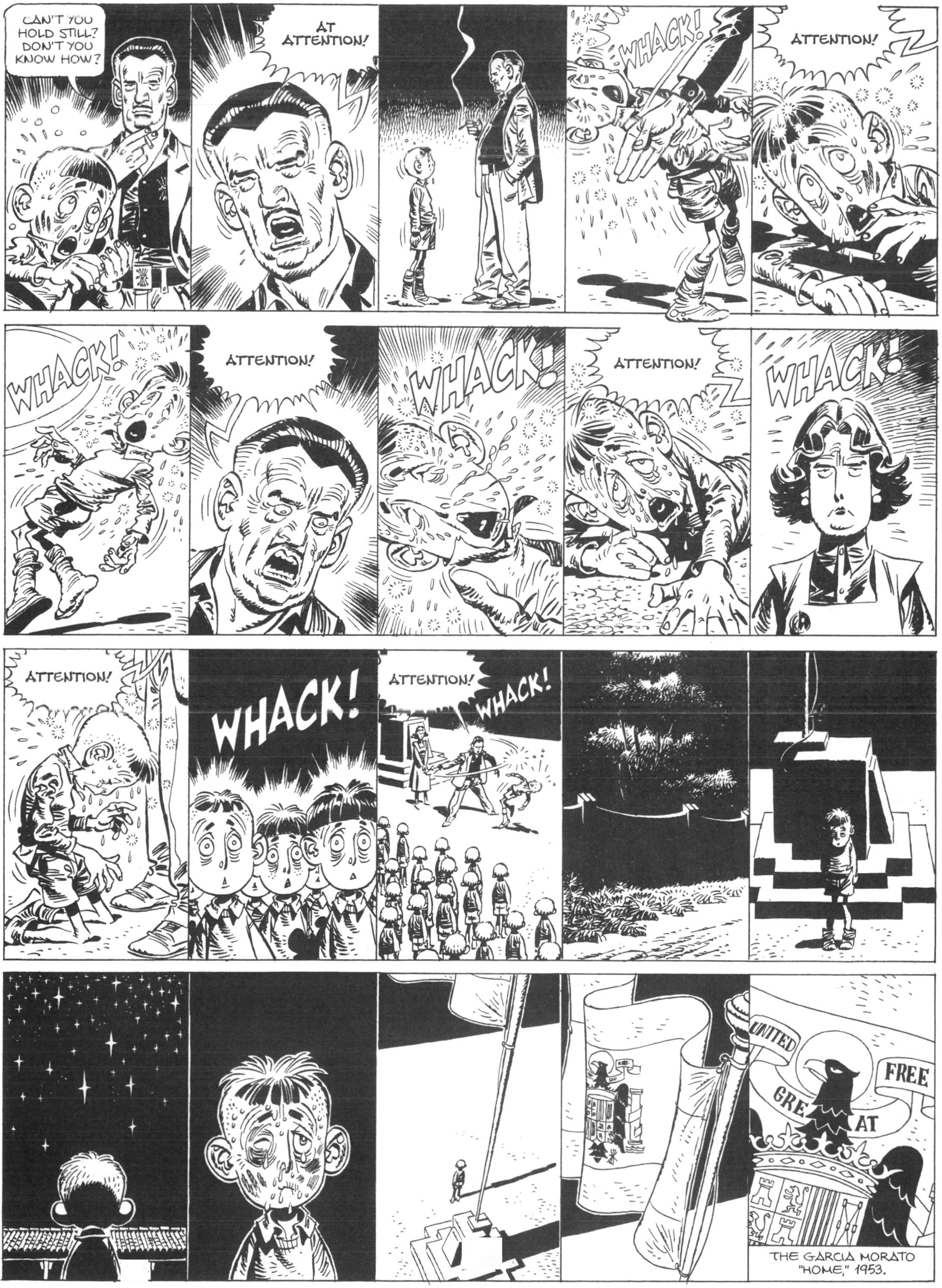
CAN'T YOU HOLD STILL? DON'T YOU KNOW HOW?
AT ATTENTION!
WHACK!
ATTENTION!
WHACK!
ATTENTION!
WHACK!
ATTENTION!
WHACK!
ATTENTION!
WHACK!
ATTENTION!
WHACK!
UNITED
GRE
AT
FREE
THE GARCIA MORATO "HOME," 1953.

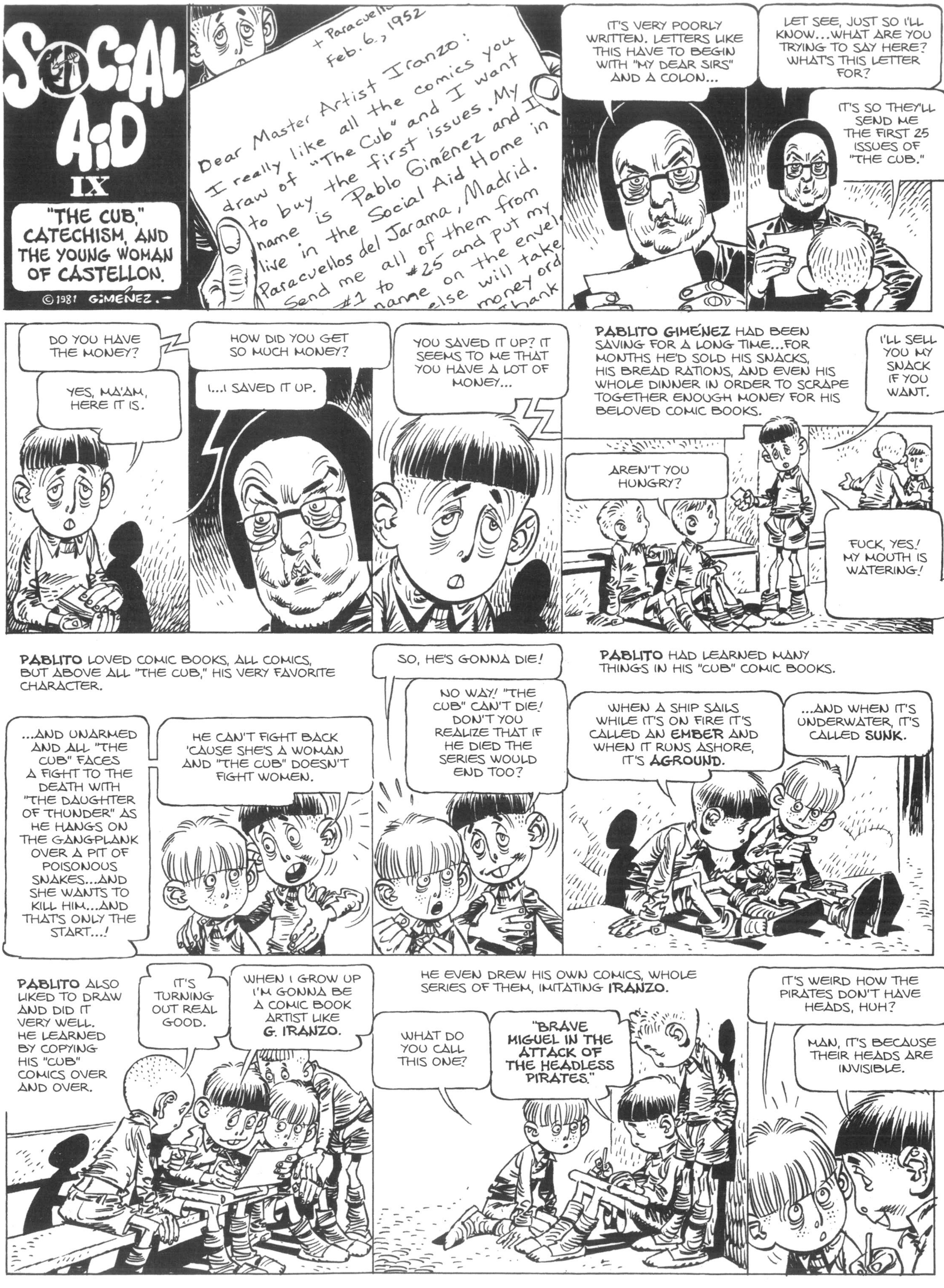
SOCIAL AID
IX
"THE CUB," CATECHISM, AND THE YOUNG WOMAN OF CASTELLON.
©1981 GIMÉNEZ.-
+ Paracuellos Feb. 6, 1952
Dear Master Artist Iranzo: I really like all the comics you draw of "The Cub" and I want to buy the first issues. My name is Pablo Giménez and I live in the Social Aid Home in Paracuellos del Jarama, Madrid. Send me all of them from #1 to #25 and put my name on the envel... else will take... money ord... Thank
IT'S VERY POORLY WRITTEN. LETTERS LIKE THIS HAVE TO BEGIN WITH "MY DEAR SIRS" AND A COLON...
LET SEE, JUST SO I'LL KNOW... WHAT ARE YOU TRYING TO SAY HERE? WHAT'S THIS LETTER FOR?
IT'S SO THEY'LL SEND ME THE FIRST 25 ISSUES OF "THE CUB."
DO YOU HAVE THE MONEY?
YES, MA'AM, HERE IT IS.
HOW DID YOU GET SO MUCH MONEY?
I... I SAVED IT UP.
YOU SAVED IT UP? IT SEEMS TO ME THAT YOU HAVE A LOT OF MONEY...
PABLITO GIMÉNEZ HAD BEEN SAVING FOR A LONG TIME... FOR MONTHS HE'D SOLD HIS SNACKS, HIS BREAD RATIONS, AND EVEN HIS WHOLE DINNER IN ORDER TO SCRAPE TOGETHER ENOUGH MONEY FOR HIS BELOVED COMIC BOOKS.
I'LL SELL YOU MY SNACK IF YOU WANT.
AREN'T YOU HUNGRY?
FUCK, YES! MY MOUTH IS WATERING!
PABLITO LOVED COMIC BOOKS, ALL COMICS, BUT ABOVE ALL "THE CUB," HIS VERY FAVORITE CHARACTER.
...AND UNARMED AND ALL "THE CUB" FACES A FIGHT TO THE DEATH WITH "THE DAUGHTER OF THUNDER" AS HE HANGS ON THE GANGPLANK OVER A PIT OF POISONOUS SNAKES...AND SHE WANTS TO KILL HIM...AND THAT'S ONLY THE START...!
HE CAN'T FIGHT BACK 'CAUSE SHE'S A WOMAN AND "THE CUB" DOESN'T FIGHT WOMEN.
SO, HE'S GONNA DIE!
NO WAY! "THE CUB" CAN'T DIE! DON'T YOU REALIZE THAT IF HE DIED THE SERIES WOULD END TOO?
PABLITO HAD LEARNED MANY THINGS IN HIS "CUB" COMIC BOOKS.
WHEN A SHIP SAILS WHILE IT'S ON FIRE IT'S CALLED AN EMBER AND WHEN IT RUNS ASHORE, IT'S AGROUND.
...AND WHEN IT'S UNDERWATER, IT'S CALLED SUNK.
PABLITO ALSO LIKED TO DRAW AND DID IT VERY WELL. HE LEARNED BY COPYING HIS "CUB" COMICS OVER AND OVER.
IT'S TURNING OUT REAL GOOD.
WHEN I GROW UP I'M GONNA BE A COMIC BOOK ARTIST LIKE G. IRANZO.
HE EVEN DREW HIS OWN COMICS, WHOLE SERIES OF THEM, IMITATING IRANZO.
WHAT DO YOU CALL THIS ONE?
"BRAVE MIGUEL IN THE ATTACK OF THE HEADLESS PIRATES."
IT'S WEIRD HOW THE PIRATES DON'T HAVE HEADS, HUH?
MAN, IT'S BECAUSE THEIR HEADS ARE INVISIBLE.

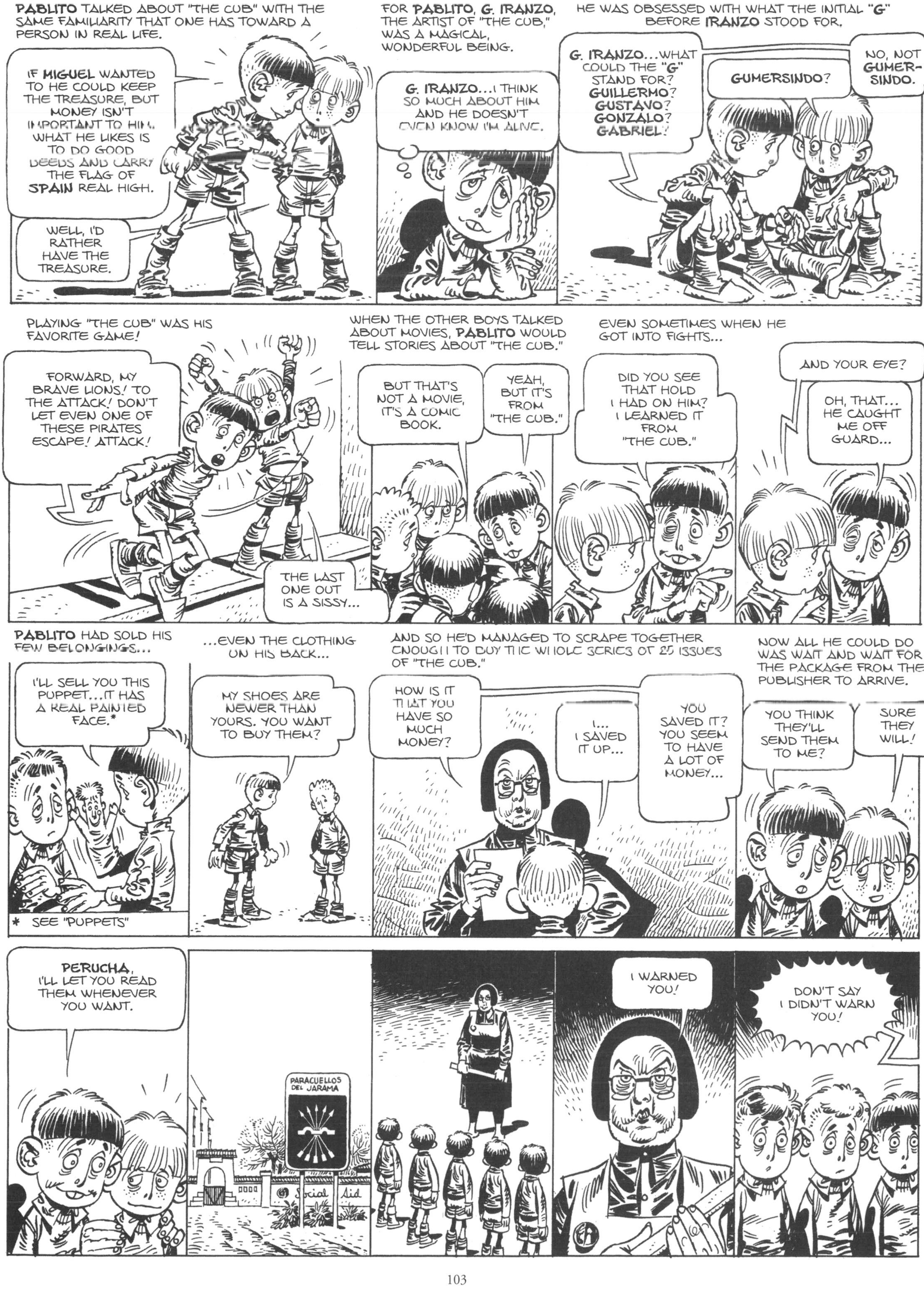
PABLITO TALKED ABOUT "THE CUB" WITH THE SAME FAMILIARITY THAT ONE HAS TOWARD A PERSON IN REAL LIFE.
IF MIGUEL WANTED TO HE COULD KEEP THE TREASURE, BUT MONEY ISN'T IMPORTANT TO HIM. WHAT HE LIKES IS TO DO GOOD DEEDS AND CARRY THE FLAG OF SPAIN REAL HIGH.
WELL, I'D RATHER HAVE THE TREASURE.
FOR PABLITO, G. IRANZO, THE ARTIST OF "THE CUB," WAS A MAGICAL, WONDERFUL BEING.
G. IRANZO... I THINK SO MUCH ABOUT HIM AND HE DOESN'T EVEN KNOW I'M ALIVE.
HE WAS OBSESSED WITH WHAT THE INITIAL "G" BEFORE IRANZO STOOD FOR.
G. IRANZO... WHAT COULD THE "G" STAND FOR? GUILLERMO? GUSTAVO? GONZALO? GABRIEL?
GUMERSINDO?
NO, NOT GUMERSINDO.
PLAYING "THE CUB" WAS HIS FAVORITE GAME!
FORWARD, MY BRAVE LIONS! TO THE ATTACK! DON'T LET EVEN ONE OF THESE PIRATES ESCAPE! ATTACK!
THE LAST ONE OUT IS A SISSY...
WHEN THE OTHER BOYS TALKED ABOUT MOVIES, PABLITO WOULD TELL STORIES ABOUT "THE CUB."
BUT THAT'S NOT A MOVIE, IT'S A COMIC BOOK.
YEAH, BUT IT'S FROM "THE CUB."
EVEN SOMETIMES WHEN HE GOT INTO FIGHTS...
DID YOU SEE THAT HOLD I HAD ON HIM? I LEARNED IT FROM "THE CUB."
AND YOUR EYE?
OH, THAT... HE CAUGHT ME OFF GUARD...
PABLITO HAD SOLD HIS FEW BELONGINGS...
I'LL SELL YOU THIS PUPPET... IT HAS A REAL PAINTED FACE.*
* SEE "PUPPETS"
...EVEN THE CLOTHING ON HIS BACK...
MY SHOES ARE NEWER THAN YOURS. YOU WANT TO BUY THEM?
AND SO HE'D MANAGED TO SCRAPE TOGETHER ENOUGH TO BUY THE WHOLE SERIES OF 25 ISSUES OF "THE CUB."
HOW IS IT THAT YOU HAVE SO MUCH MONEY?
I... I SAVED IT UP...
YOU SAVED IT? YOU SEEM TO HAVE A LOT OF MONEY...
NOW ALL HE COULD DO WAS WAIT AND WAIT FOR THE PACKAGE FROM THE PUBLISHER TO ARRIVE.
YOU THINK THEY'LL SEND THEM TO ME?
SURE THEY WILL!
PERUCHA, I'LL LET YOU READ THEM WHENEVER YOU WANT.
PARACUELLOS DEL JARAMA
Social Aid
I WARNED YOU!
DON'T SAY I DIDN'T WARN YOU!

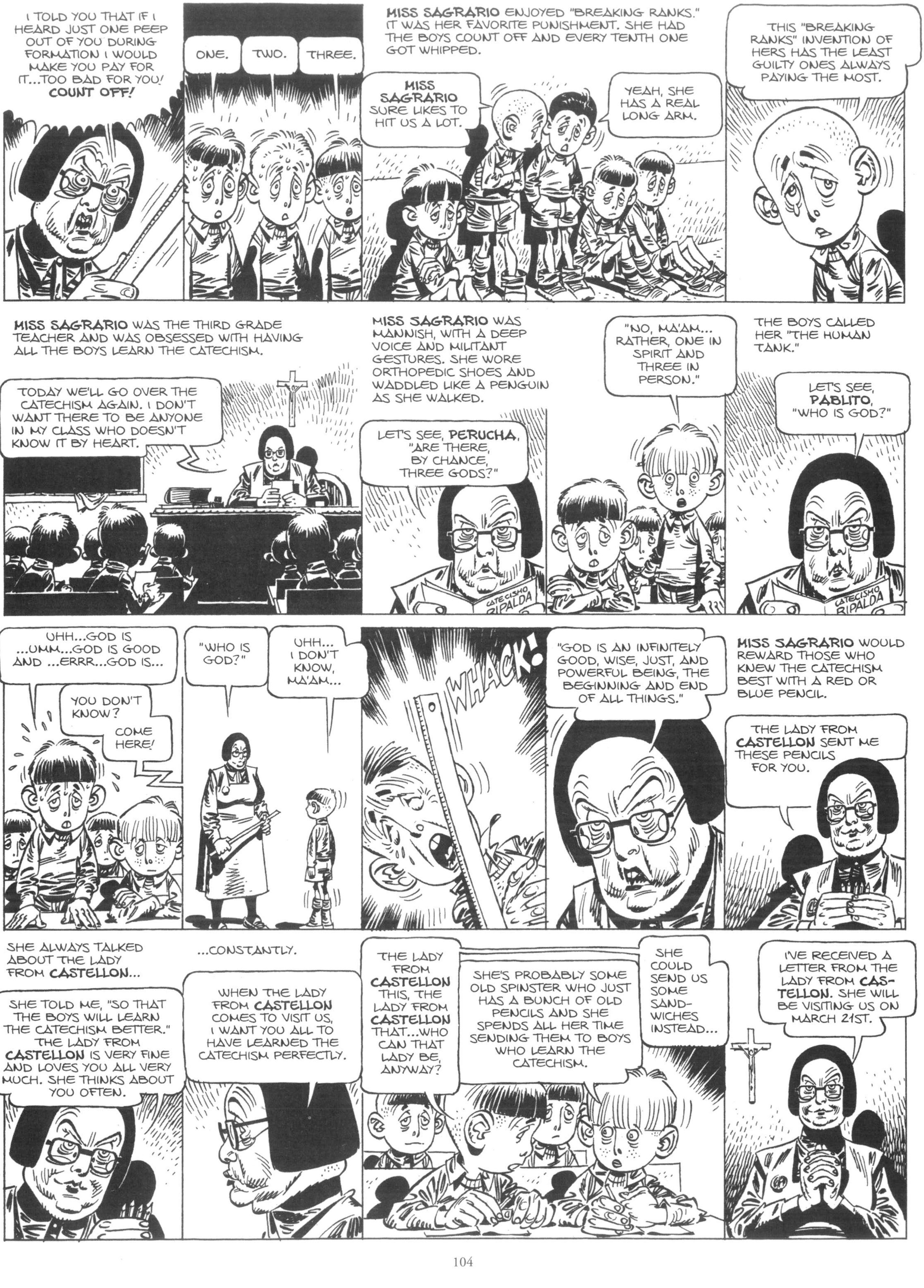

I TOLD YOU THAT IF I HEARD JUST ONE PEEP OUT OF YOU DURING FORMATION I WOULD MAKE YOU PAY FOR IT...TOO BAD FOR YOU! COUNT OFF!
ONE.
TWO.
THREE.
MISS SAGRARIO ENJOYED "BREAKING RANKS." IT WAS HER FAVORITE PUNISHMENT. SHE HAD THE BOYS COUNT OFF AND EVERY TENTH ONE GOT WHIPPED.
MISS SAGRARIO SURE LIKES TO HIT US A LOT.
YEAH, SHE HAS A REAL LONG ARM.
THIS "BREAKING RANKS" INVENTION OF HERS HAS THE LEAST GUILTY ONES ALWAYS PAYING THE MOST.
MISS SAGRARIO WAS THE THIRD GRADE TEACHER AND WAS OBSESSED WITH HAVING ALL THE BOYS LEARN THE CATECHISM.
TODAY WE'LL GO OVER THE CATECHISM AGAIN. I DON'T WANT THERE TO BE ANYONE IN MY CLASS WHO DOESN'T KNOW IT BY HEART.
MISS SAGRARIO WAS MANNISH, WITH A DEEP VOICE AND MILITANT GESTURES. SHE WORE ORTHOPEDIC SHOES AND WADDLED LIKE A PENGUIN AS SHE WALKED.
LET'S SEE, PERUCHA, "ARE THERE, BY CHANCE, THREE GODS?"
CATECISMO RIPALDA
"NO, MA'AM... RATHER, ONE IN SPIRIT AND THREE IN PERSON."
THE BOYS CALLED HER "THE HUMAN TANK."
LET'S SEE, PABLITO, "WHO IS GOD?"
CATECISMO RIPALDA
UHH...GOD IS ...UMM...GOD IS GOOD AND ...ERRR...GOD IS...
YOU DON'T KNOW?
COME HERE!
"WHO IS GOD?"
UHH... I DON'T KNOW, MA'AM...
WHACK!
"GOD IS AN INFINITELY GOOD, WISE, JUST, AND POWERFUL BEING, THE BEGINNING AND END OF ALL THINGS."
MISS SAGRARIO WOULD REWARD THOSE WHO KNEW THE CATECHISM BEST WITH A RED OR BLUE PENCIL.
THE LADY FROM CASTELLON SENT ME THESE PENCILS FOR YOU.
SHE ALWAYS TALKED ABOUT THE LADY FROM CASTELLON...
SHE TOLD ME, "SO THAT THE BOYS WILL LEARN THE CATECHISM BETTER." THE LADY FROM CASTELLON IS VERY FINE AND LOVES YOU ALL VERY MUCH. SHE THINKS ABOUT YOU OFTEN.
...CONSTANTLY.
WHEN THE LADY FROM CASTELLON COMES TO VISIT US, I WANT YOU ALL TO HAVE LEARNED THE CATECHISM PERFECTLY.
THE LADY FROM CASTELLON THIS, THE LADY FROM CASTELLON THAT...WHO CAN THAT LADY BE, ANYWAY?
SHE'S PROBABLY SOME OLD SPINSTER WHO JUST HAS A BUNCH OF OLD PENCILS AND SHE SPENDS ALL HER TIME SENDING THEM TO BOYS WHO LEARN THE CATECHISM.
SHE COULD SEND US SOME SAND-WICHES INSTEAD...
I'VE RECEIVED A LETTER FROM THE LADY FROM CAS-TELLON. SHE WILL BE VISITING US ON MARCH 21ST.

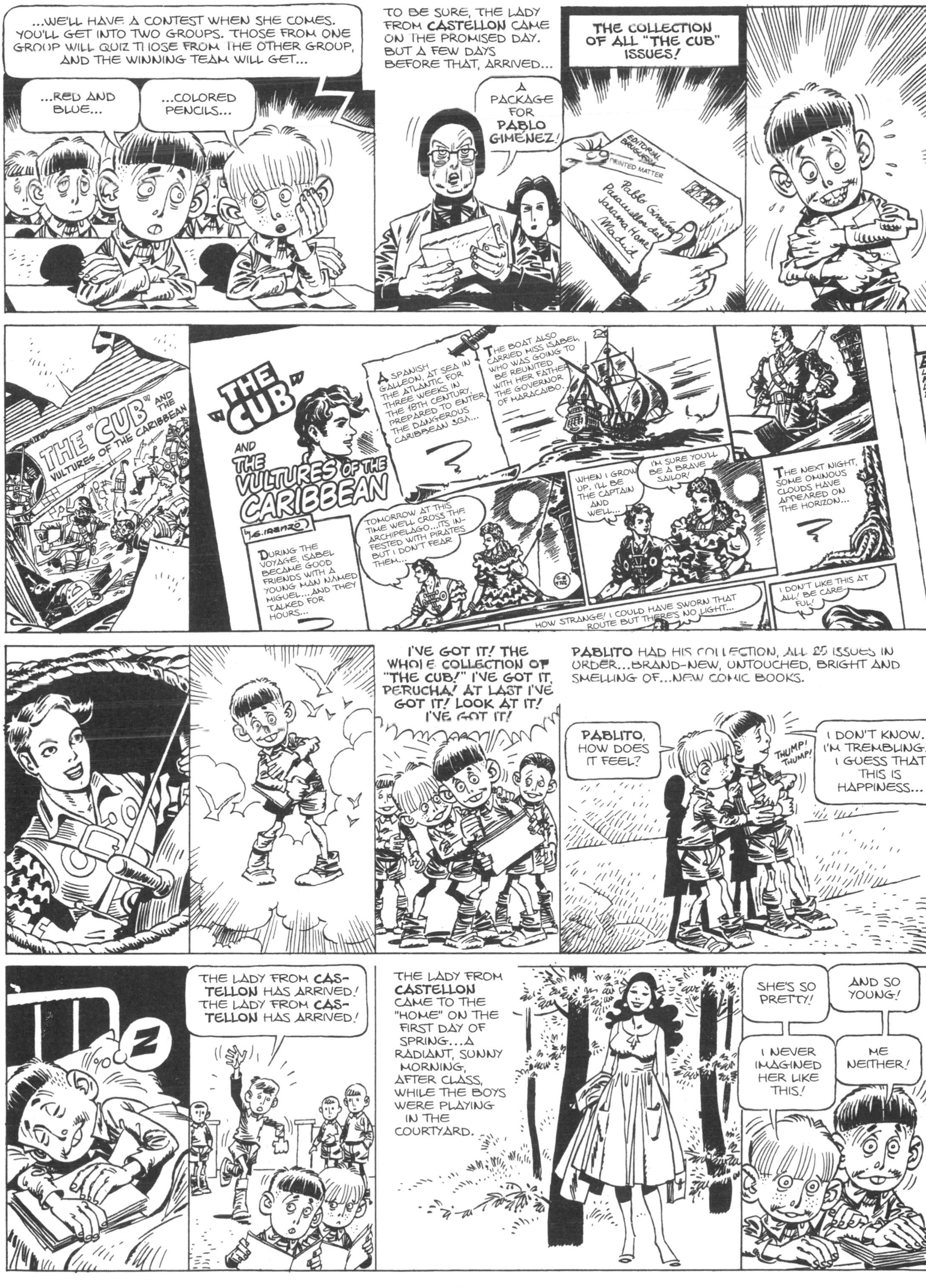
...WE'LL HAVE A CONTEST WHEN SHE COMES. YOU'LL GET INTO TWO GROUPS. THOSE FROM ONE GROUP WILL QUIZ THOSE FROM THE OTHER GROUP, AND THE WINNING TEAM WILL GET...
...RED AND BLUE...
...COLORED PENCILS...
TO BE SURE, THE LADY FROM CASTELLON CAME ON THE PROMISED DAY. BUT A FEW DAYS BEFORE THAT, ARRIVED...
A PACKAGE FOR PABLO GIMENEZ!
THE COLLECTION OF ALL "THE CUB" ISSUES!
EDITORIAL BRUGUERA
PRINTED MATTER
THE "CUB" AND THE VULTURES OF THE CARIBBEAN
"THE CUB"
AND THE VULTURES OF THE CARIBBEAN
by G. IRANZO
A SPANISH GALLEON, AT SEA IN THE ATLANTIC FOR THREE WEEKS IN THE 18TH CENTURY, PREPARED TO ENTER THE DANGEROUS CARIBBEAN SEA...
THE BOAT ALSO CARRIED MISS ISABEL, WHO WAS GOING TO BE REUNITED WITH HER FATHER, THE GOVERNOR OF MARACAIBO.
DURING THE VOYAGE, ISABEL BECAME GOOD FRIENDS WITH A YOUNG MAN NAMED MIGUEL...AND THEY TALKED FOR HOURS...
TOMORROW AT THIS TIME WE'LL CROSS THE ARCHIPELAGO...ITS INFESTED WITH PIRATES BUT I DON'T FEAR THEM...
WHEN I GROW UP, I'LL BE THE CAPTAIN AND WE'LL...
I'M SURE YOU'LL BE A BRAVE SAILOR!
THE NEXT NIGHT, SOME OMINOUS CLOUDS HAVE APPEARED ON THE HORIZON...
HOW STRANGE! I COULD HAVE SWORN THAT ROUTE BUT THERE'S NO LIGHT...
I DON'T LIKE THIS AT ALL! BE CAREFUL!
I'VE GOT IT! THE WHOLE COLLECTION OF "THE CUB!" I'VE GOT IT, PERUCHA! AT LAST I'VE GOT IT! LOOK AT IT! I'VE GOT IT!
PABLITO HAD HIS COLLECTION, ALL 25 ISSUES IN ORDER...BRAND-NEW, UNTOUCHED, BRIGHT AND SMELLING OF...NEW COMIC BOOKS.
PABLITO, HOW DOES IT FEEL?
THUMP! THUMP!
I DON'T KNOW... I'M TREMBLING... I GUESS THAT THIS IS HAPPINESS...
Z
THE LADY FROM CASTELLON HAS ARRIVED! THE LADY FROM CASTELLON HAS ARRIVED!
THE LADY FROM CASTELLON CAME TO THE "HOME" ON THE FIRST DAY OF SPRING...A RADIANT, SUNNY MORNING, AFTER CLASS, WHILE THE BOYS WERE PLAYING IN THE COURTYARD.
SHE'S SO PRETTY!
AND SO YOUNG!
I NEVER IMAGINED HER LIKE THIS!
ME NEITHER!

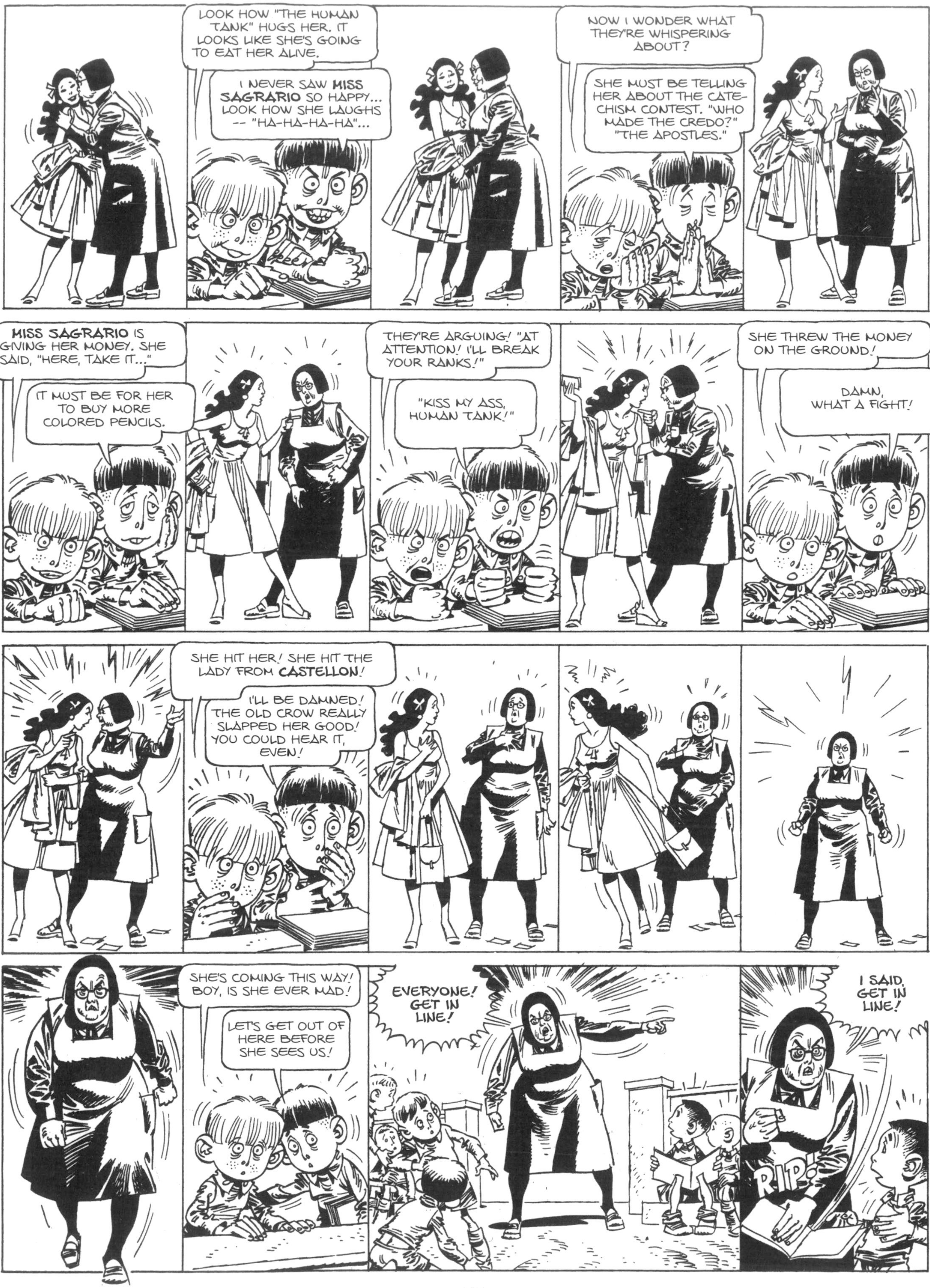
LOOK HOW "THE HUMAN TANK" HUGS HER. IT LOOKS LIKE SHE'S GOING TO EAT HER ALIVE.
I NEVER SAW MISS SAGRARIO SO HAPPY... LOOK HOW SHE LAUGHS -- "HA-HA-HA-HA"...
NOW I WONDER WHAT THEY'RE WHISPERING ABOUT?
SHE MUST BE TELLING HER ABOUT THE CATECHISM CONTEST. "WHO MADE THE CREDO?" "THE APOSTLES."
MISS SAGRARIO IS GIVING HER MONEY. SHE SAID, "HERE, TAKE IT..."
IT MUST BE FOR HER TO BUY MORE COLORED PENCILS.
THEY'RE ARGUING! "AT ATTENTION! I'LL BREAK YOUR RANKS!"
"KISS MY ASS, HUMAN TANK!"
SHE THREW THE MONEY ON THE GROUND!
DAMN, WHAT A FIGHT!
SHE HIT HER! SHE HIT THE LADY FROM CASTELLON!
I'LL BE DAMNED! THE OLD CROW REALLY SLAPPED HER GOOD! YOU COULD HEAR IT, EVEN!
SHE'S COMING THIS WAY! BOY, IS SHE EVER MAD!
LET'S GET OUT OF HERE BEFORE SHE SEES US!
EVERYONE! GET IN LINE!
I SAID, GET IN LINE!
RIP!

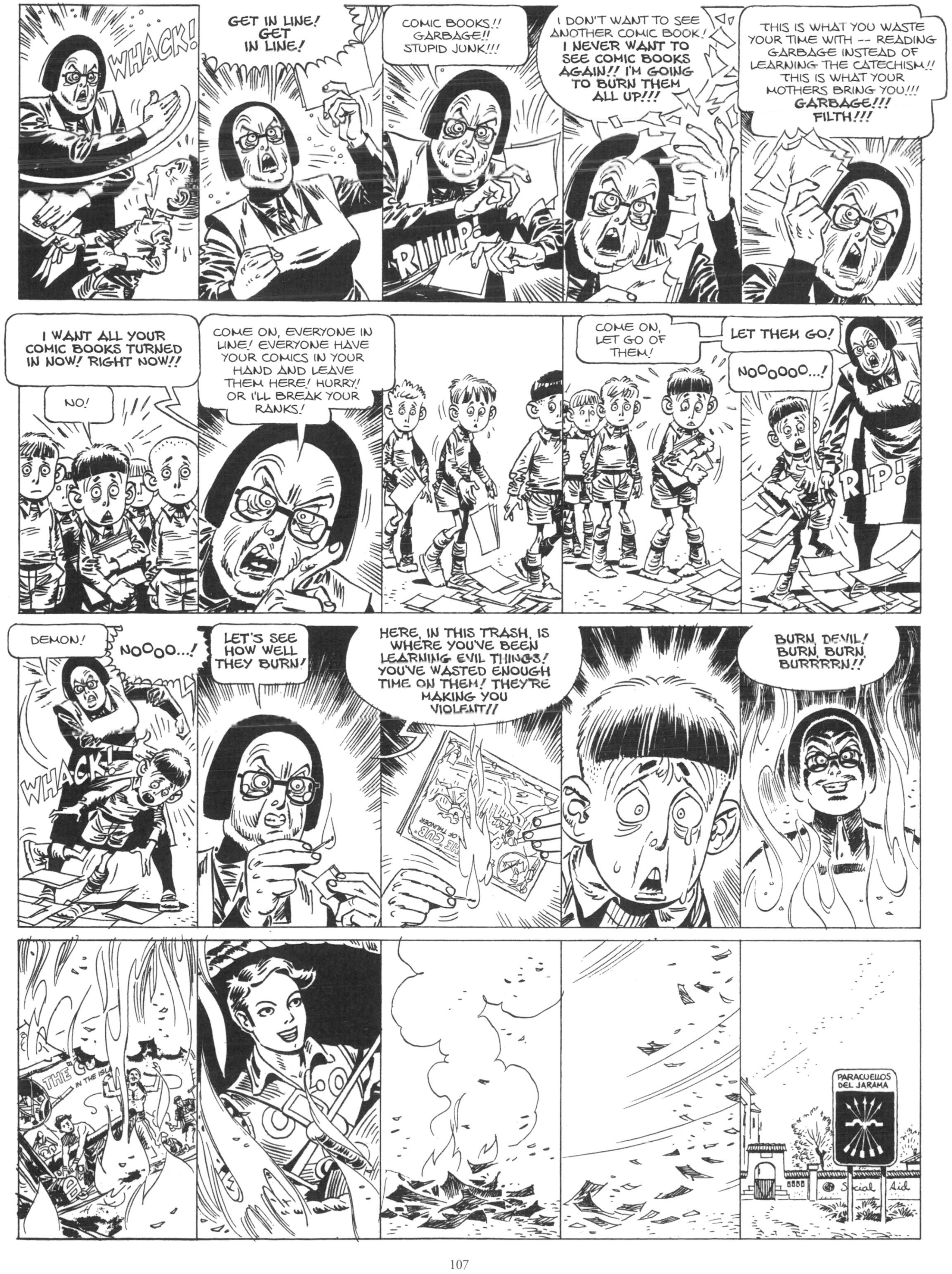

WHACK!
GET IN LINE! GET IN LINE!
COMIC BOOKS!! GARBAGE!! STUPID JUNK!!!
RIIIIP!
I DON'T WANT TO SEE ANOTHER COMIC BOOK! I NEVER WANT TO SEE COMIC BOOKS AGAIN!! I'M GOING TO BURN THEM ALL UP!!!
THIS IS WHAT YOU WASTE YOUR TIME WITH -- READING GARBAGE INSTEAD OF LEARNING THE CATECHISM!! THIS IS WHAT YOUR MOTHERS BRING YOU!!! GARBAGE!!! FILTH!!!
I WANT ALL YOUR COMIC BOOKS TURNED IN NOW! RIGHT NOW!!
NO!
COME ON, EVERYONE IN LINE! EVERYONE HAVE YOUR COMICS IN YOUR HAND AND LEAVE THEM HERE! HURRY! OR I'LL BREAK YOUR RANKS!
COME ON, LET GO OF THEM!
LET THEM GO!
NOOOOOO...!
RIP!
DEMON!
NOOOO...!
WHACK!
LET'S SEE HOW WELL THEY BURN!
HERE, IN THIS TRASH, IS WHERE YOU'VE BEEN LEARNING EVIL THINGS! YOU'VE WASTED ENOUGH TIME ON THEM! THEY'RE MAKING YOU VIOLENT!!
BURN, DEVIL! BURN, BURN, BURRRRN!!
PARACUELLOS DEL JARAMA
Social Aid

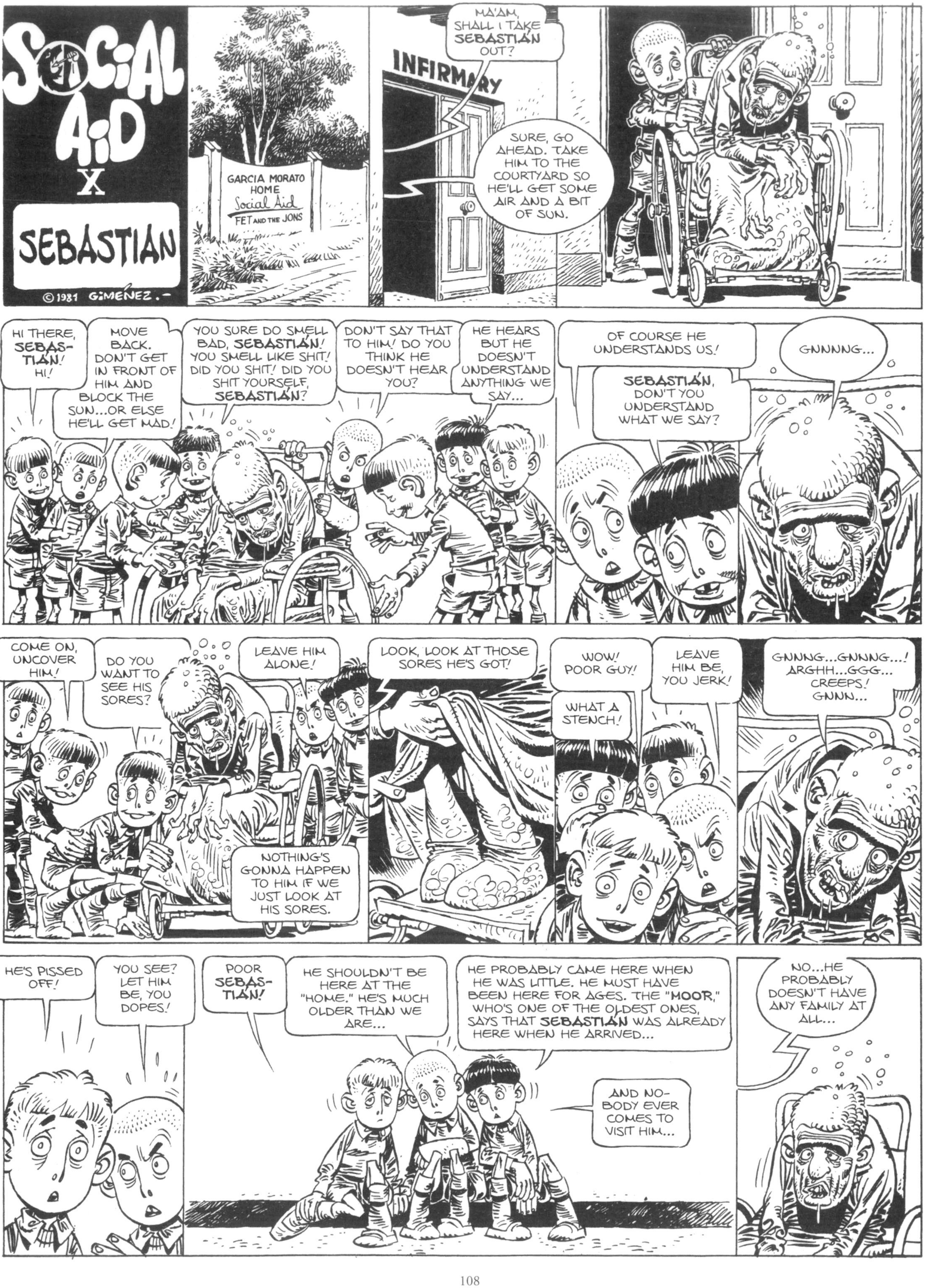
SOCIAL AID
X
SEBASTIAN
©1981 GIMÉNEZ.-
GARCIA MORATO HOME
Social Aid
FET AND THE JONS
INFIRMARY
MA'AM, SHALL I TAKE SEBASTIÁN OUT?
SURE, GO AHEAD. TAKE HIM TO THE COURTYARD SO HE'LL GET SOME AIR AND A BIT OF SUN.
HI THERE, SEBASTIÁN! HI!
MOVE BACK. DON'T GET IN FRONT OF HIM AND BLOCK THE SUN...OR ELSE HE'LL GET MAD!
YOU SURE DO SMELL BAD, SEBASTIÁN! YOU SMELL LIKE SHIT! DID YOU SHIT! DID YOU SHIT YOURSELF, SEBASTIÁN?
DON'T SAY THAT TO HIM! DO YOU THINK HE DOESN'T HEAR YOU?
HE HEARS BUT HE DOESN'T UNDERSTAND ANYTHING WE SAY...
OF COURSE HE UNDERSTANDS US!
SEBASTIÁN, DON'T YOU UNDERSTAND WHAT WE SAY?
GNNNNG...
COME ON, UNCOVER HIM!
DO YOU WANT TO SEE HIS SORES?
LEAVE HIM ALONE!
NOTHING'S GONNA HAPPEN TO HIM IF WE JUST LOOK AT HIS SORES.
LOOK, LOOK AT THOSE SORES HE'S GOT!
WOW! POOR GUY!
WHAT A STENCH!
LEAVE HIM BE, YOU JERK!
GNNNG...GNNNG...! ARGHH...GGG... CREEPS! GNNN...
HE'S PISSED OFF!
YOU SEE? LET HIM BE, YOU DOPES!
POOR SEBASTIÁN!
HE SHOULDN'T BE HERE AT THE "HOME." HE'S MUCH OLDER THAN WE ARE...
HE PROBABLY CAME HERE WHEN HE WAS LITTLE. HE MUST HAVE BEEN HERE FOR AGES. THE "MOOR," WHO'S ONE OF THE OLDEST ONES, SAYS THAT SEBASTIÁN WAS ALREADY HERE WHEN HE ARRIVED...
AND NOBODY EVER COMES TO VISIT HIM...
NO...HE PROBABLY DOESN'T HAVE ANY FAMILY AT ALL...

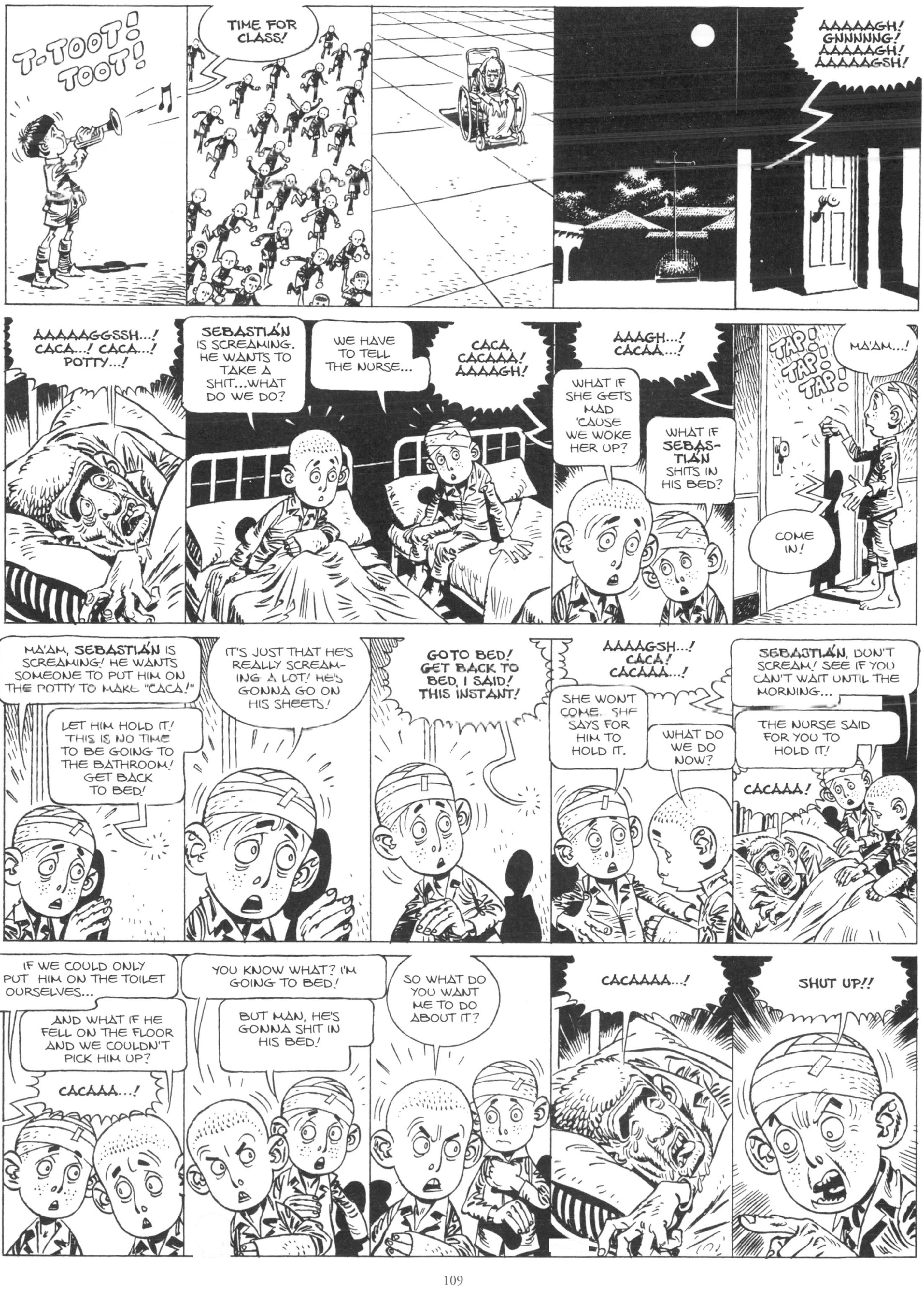
T-TOOT! TOOT!
TIME FOR CLASS!
AAAAAGH! GNNNNNG! AAAAAGH! AAAAAGSH!
AAAAAGGSSH...! CACA...! CACA...! POTTY...!
SEBASTIÁN IS SCREAMING. HE WANTS TO TAKE A SHIT...WHAT DO WE DO?
WE HAVE TO TELL THE NURSE...
CACA, CACAAA! AAAAGH!
AAAGH...! CACAA...!
WHAT IF SHE GETS MAD 'CAUSE WE WOKE HER UP?
WHAT IF SEBASTIÁN SHITS IN HIS BED?
TAP! TAP! TAP!
MA'AM...!
COME IN!
MA'AM, SEBASTIÁN IS SCREAMING! HE WANTS SOMEONE TO PUT HIM ON THE POTTY TO MAKE "CACA!"
LET HIM HOLD IT! THIS IS NO TIME TO BE GOING TO THE BATHROOM! GET BACK TO BED!
IT'S JUST THAT HE'S REALLY SCREAMING A LOT! HE'S GONNA GO ON HIS SHEETS!
GO TO BED! GET BACK TO BED, I SAID! THIS INSTANT!
AAAAGSH...! CACA! CACAAA...!
SHE WON'T COME. SHE SAYS FOR HIM TO HOLD IT.
WHAT DO WE DO NOW?
SEBASTIÁN, DON'T SCREAM! SEE IF YOU CAN'T WAIT UNTIL THE MORNING...
THE NURSE SAID FOR YOU TO HOLD IT!
CACAAA!
IF WE COULD ONLY PUT HIM ON THE TOILET OURSELVES...
AND WHAT IF HE FELL ON THE FLOOR AND WE COULDN'T PICK HIM UP?
CACAAA...!
YOU KNOW WHAT? I'M GOING TO BED!
BUT MAN, HE'S GONNA SHIT IN HIS BED!
SO WHAT DO YOU WANT ME TO DO ABOUT IT?
CACAAAA...!
SHUT UP!!

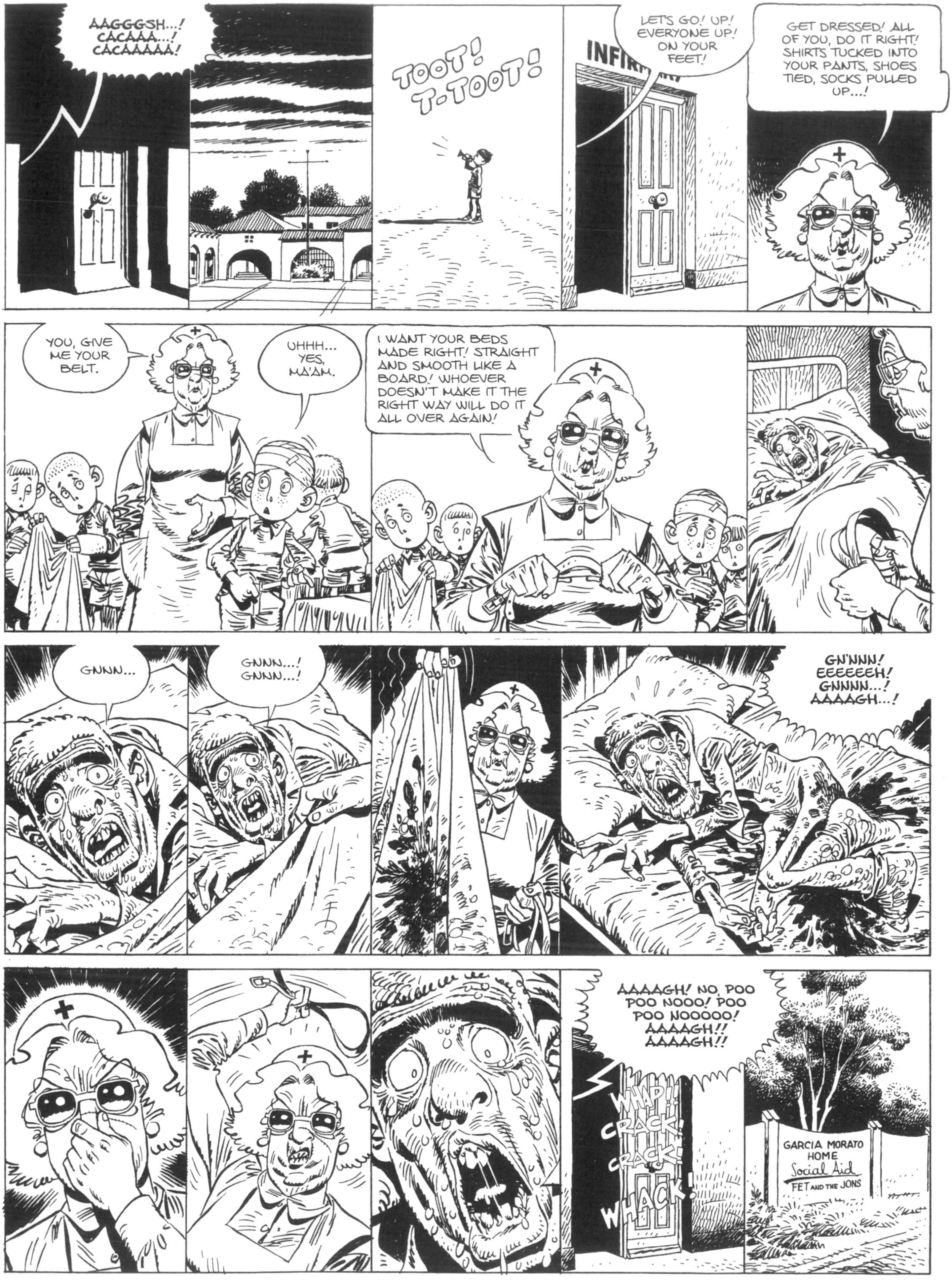
AAGGGSH...! CACAAA...! CACÁÁÁÁÁ!
TOOT! T-TOOT!
INFIRMARY
LET'S GO! UP! EVERYONE UP! ON YOUR FEET!
GET DRESSED! ALL OF YOU, DO IT RIGHT! SHIRTS TUCKED INTO YOUR PANTS, SHOES TIED, SOCKS PULLED UP...!
YOU, GIVE ME YOUR BELT.
UHHH... YES, MA'AM.
I WANT YOUR BEDS MADE RIGHT! STRAIGHT AND SMOOTH LIKE A BOARD! WHOEVER DOESN'T MAKE IT THE RIGHT WAY WILL DO IT ALL OVER AGAIN!
GNNN...
GNNN...! GNNN...!
GN'NNN! EEEEEEH! GNNNN...! AAAAGH...!
AAAAGH! NO, POO POO NOOO! POO POO NOOOOO! AAAAGH!! AAAAGH!!
WHAP!! CRACK! CRACK! WHACK!
GARCIA MORATO HOME
Social Aid
FET AND THE JONS

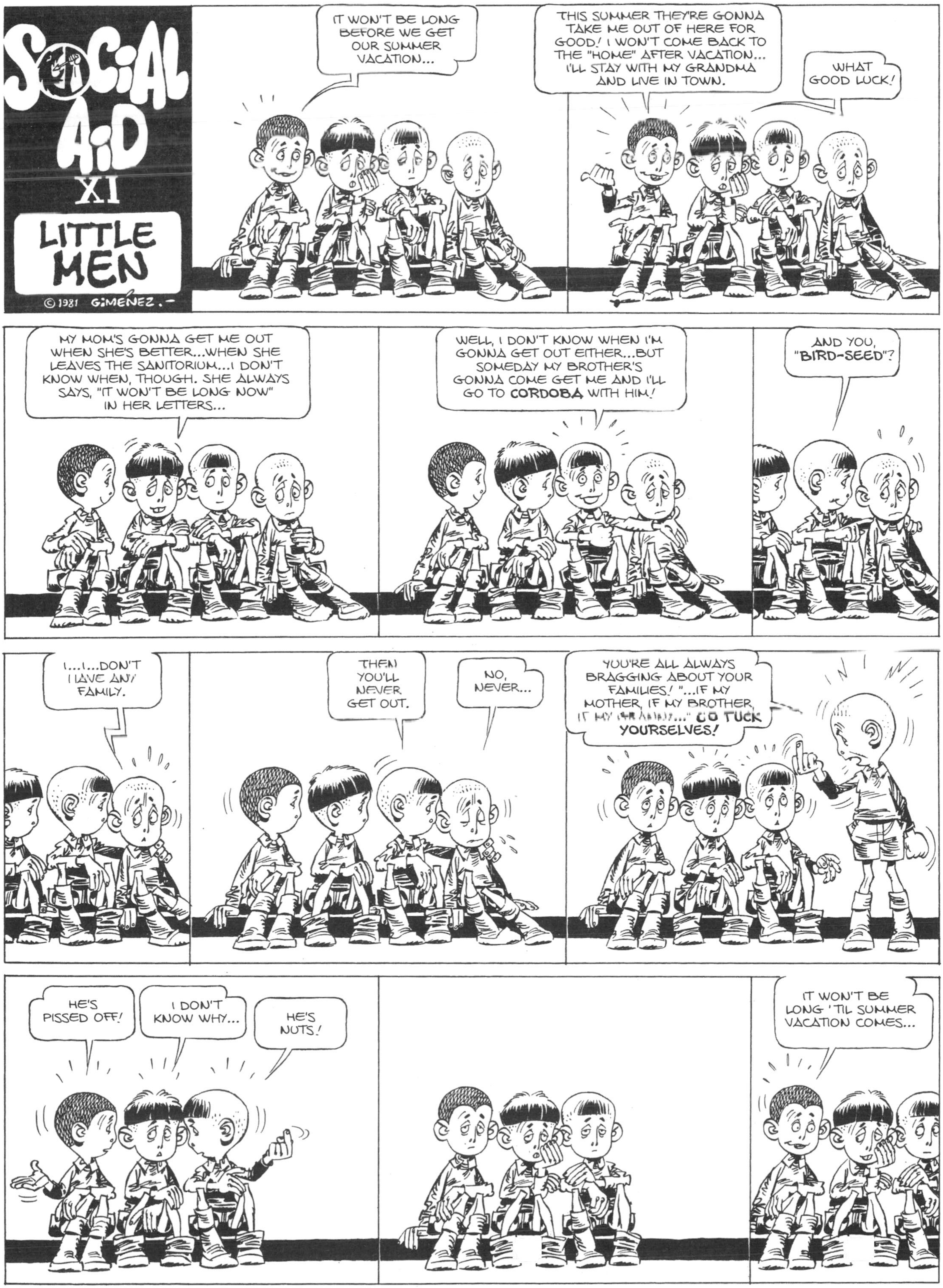
SOCIAL AID
XI
LITTLE MEN
©1981 GIMÉNEZ.-
IT WON'T BE LONG BEFORE WE GET OUR SUMMER VACATION...
THIS SUMMER THEY'RE GONNA TAKE ME OUT OF HERE FOR GOOD! I WON'T COME BACK TO THE "HOME" AFTER VACATION... I'LL STAY WITH MY GRANDMA AND LIVE IN TOWN.
WHAT GOOD LUCK!
MY MOM'S GONNA GET ME OUT WHEN SHE'S BETTER...WHEN SHE LEAVES THE SANITORIUM...I DON'T KNOW WHEN, THOUGH. SHE ALWAYS SAYS, "IT WON'T BE LONG NOW" IN HER LETTERS...
WELL, I DON'T KNOW WHEN I'M GONNA GET OUT EITHER...BUT SOMEDAY MY BROTHER'S GONNA COME GET ME AND I'LL GO TO CORDOBA WITH HIM!
AND YOU, "BIRD-SEED"?
I...I...DON'T HAVE ANY FAMILY.
THEN YOU'LL NEVER GET OUT.
NO, NEVER...
YOU'RE ALL ALWAYS BRAGGING ABOUT YOUR FAMILIES! "...IF MY MOTHER, IF MY BROTHER, ..." GO TUCK YOURSELVES!
HE'S PISSED OFF!
I DON'T KNOW WHY...
HE'S NUTS!
IT WON'T BE LONG 'TIL SUMMER VACATION COMES...

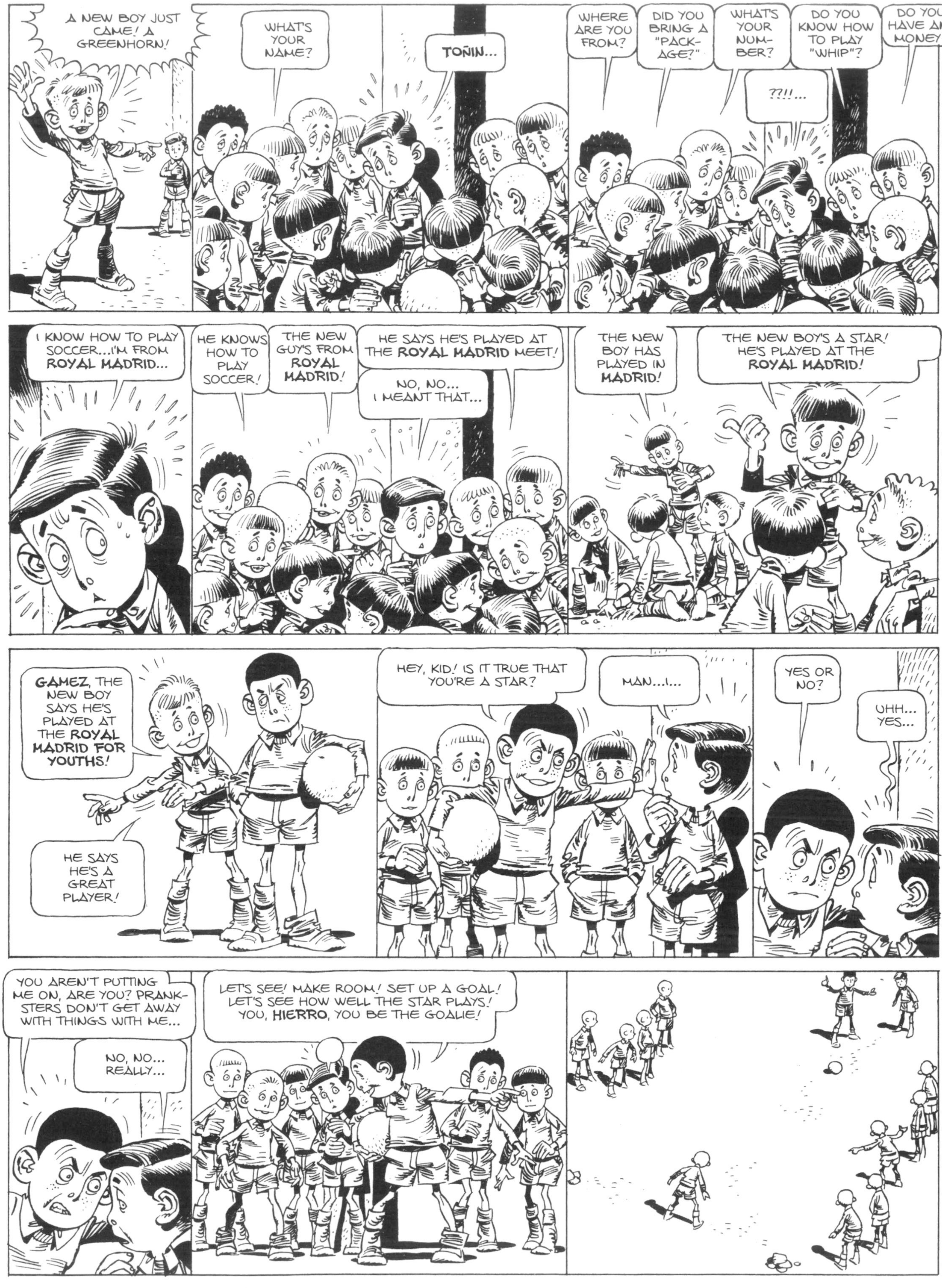
A NEW BOY JUST CAME! A GREENHORN!
WHAT'S YOUR NAME?
TOÑIN...
WHERE ARE YOU FROM?
DID YOU BRING A "PACK-AGE?"
WHAT'S YOUR NUM-BER?
DO YOU KNOW HOW TO PLAY "WHIP"?
DO YOU HAVE ANY MONEY?
??!!...
I KNOW HOW TO PLAY SOCCER...I'M FROM ROYAL MADRID...
HE KNOWS HOW TO PLAY SOCCER!
THE NEW GUY'S FROM ROYAL MADRID!
HE SAYS HE'S PLAYED AT THE ROYAL MADRID MEET!
NO, NO... I MEANT THAT...
THE NEW BOY HAS PLAYED IN MADRID!
THE NEW BOY'S A STAR! HE'S PLAYED AT THE ROYAL MADRID!
GAMEZ, THE NEW BOY SAYS HE'S PLAYED AT THE ROYAL MADRID FOR YOUTHS!
HE SAYS HE'S A GREAT PLAYER!
HEY, KID! IS IT TRUE THAT YOU'RE A STAR?
MAN...I...
YES OR NO?
UHH... YES...
YOU AREN'T PUTTING ME ON, ARE YOU? PRANK-STERS DON'T GET AWAY WITH THINGS WITH ME...
NO, NO... REALLY...
LET'S SEE! MAKE ROOM! SET UP A GOAL! LET'S SEE HOW WELL THE STAR PLAYS! YOU, HIERRO, YOU BE THE GOALIE!

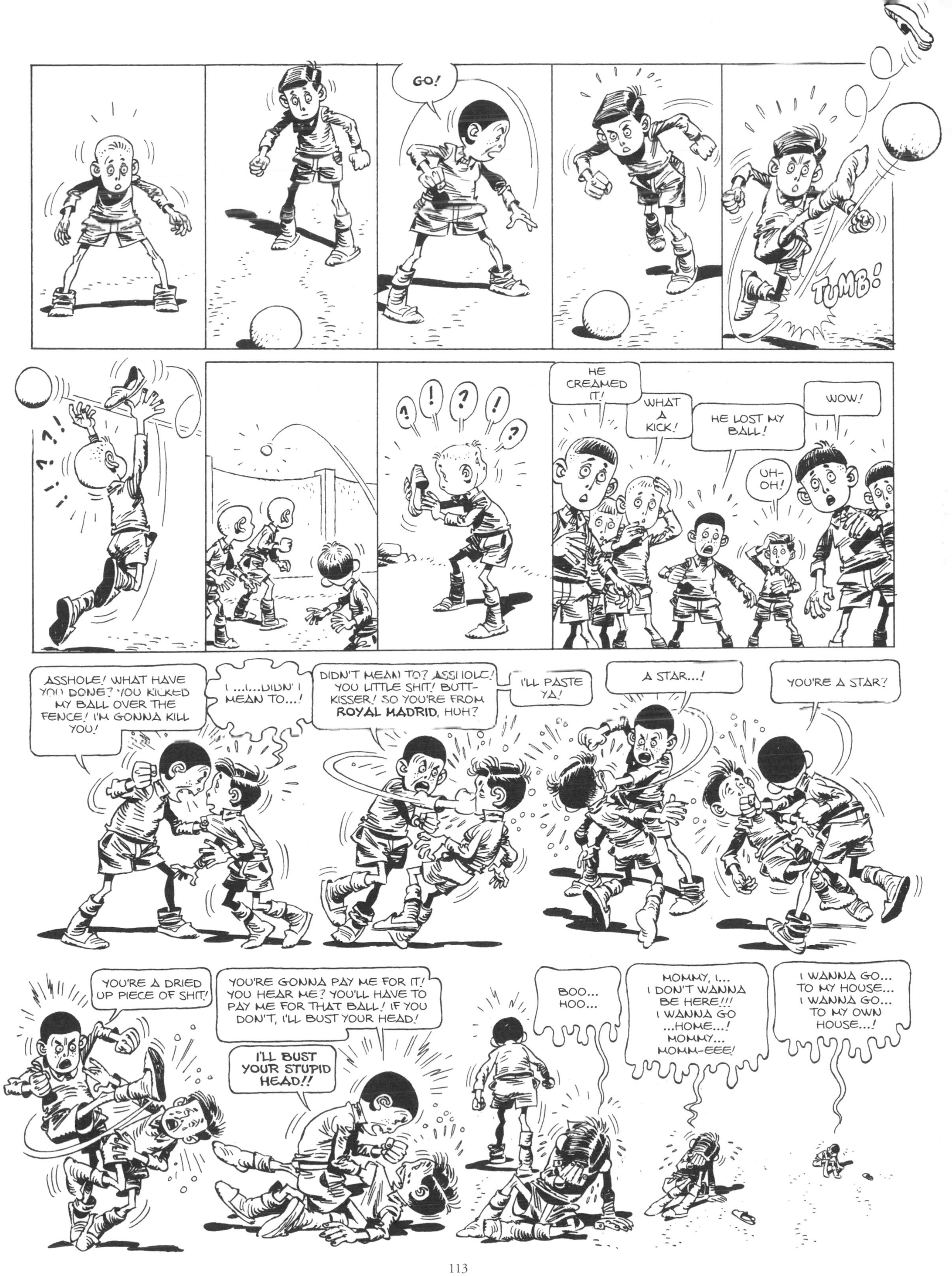

GO!
TUMB!
HE CREAMED IT!
WHAT A KICK!
HE LOST MY BALL!
UH-OH!
WOW!
ASSHOLE! WHAT HAVE YOU DONE? YOU KICKED MY BALL OVER THE FENCE! I'M GONNA KILL YOU!
I ...I...DIDN'T MEAN TO...!
DIDN'T MEAN TO? ASSHOLE! YOU LITTLE SHIT! BUTT-KISSER! SO YOU'RE FROM **ROYAL MADRID**, HUH?
I'LL PASTE YA!
A STAR...!
YOU'RE A STAR?
YOU'RE A DRIED UP PIECE OF SHIT!
YOU'RE GONNA PAY ME FOR IT! YOU HEAR ME? YOU'LL HAVE TO PAY ME FOR THAT BALL! IF YOU DON'T, I'LL BUST YOUR HEAD!
I'LL BUST YOUR STUPID HEAD!!
BOO... HOO...
MOMMY, I... I DON'T WANNA BE HERE!!! I WANNA GO ...HOME...! MOMMY... MOMM-EEE!
I WANNA GO... TO MY HOUSE... I WANNA GO... TO MY OWN HOUSE...!

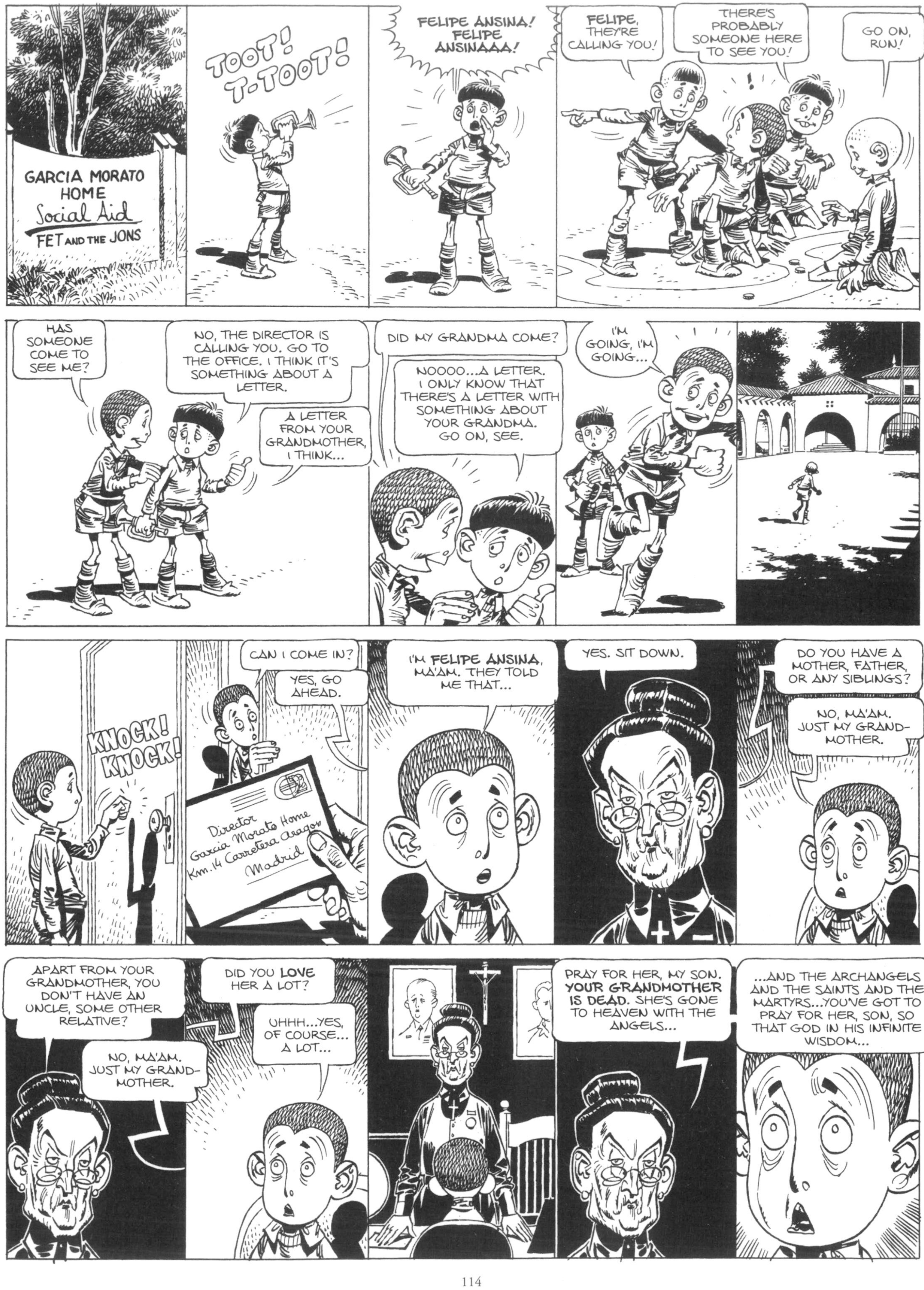
GARCIA MORATO HOME
Social Aid
FET AND THE JONS
TOOT! T-TOOT!
FELIPE ANSINA! FELIPE ANSINAAA!
FELIPE, THEY'RE CALLING YOU!
THERE'S PROBABLY SOMEONE HERE TO SEE YOU!
!
GO ON, RUN!
HAS SOMEONE COME TO SEE ME?
NO, THE DIRECTOR IS CALLING YOU. GO TO THE OFFICE. I THINK IT'S SOMETHING ABOUT A LETTER.
A LETTER FROM YOUR GRANDMOTHER, I THINK...
DID MY GRANDMA COME?
NOOOO...A LETTER. I ONLY KNOW THAT THERE'S A LETTER WITH SOMETHING ABOUT YOUR GRANDMA. GO ON, SEE.
I'M GOING, I'M GOING...
KNOCK! KNOCK!
CAN I COME IN?
YES, GO AHEAD.
Director Garcia Morato Home Carretera Aragon Km. 14 Madrid
I'M FELIPE ANSINA, MA'AM. THEY TOLD ME THAT...
YES. SIT DOWN.
DO YOU HAVE A MOTHER, FATHER, OR ANY SIBLINGS?
NO, MA'AM. JUST MY GRANDMOTHER.
APART FROM YOUR GRANDMOTHER, YOU DON'T HAVE AN UNCLE, SOME OTHER RELATIVE?
NO, MA'AM. JUST MY GRANDMOTHER.
DID YOU LOVE HER A LOT?
UHHH...YES, OF COURSE... A LOT...
PRAY FOR HER, MY SON. YOUR GRANDMOTHER IS DEAD. SHE'S GONE TO HEAVEN WITH THE ANGELS...
...AND THE ARCHANGELS AND THE SAINTS AND THE MARTYRS...YOU'VE GOT TO PRAY FOR HER, SON, SO THAT GOD IN HIS INFINITE WISDOM...

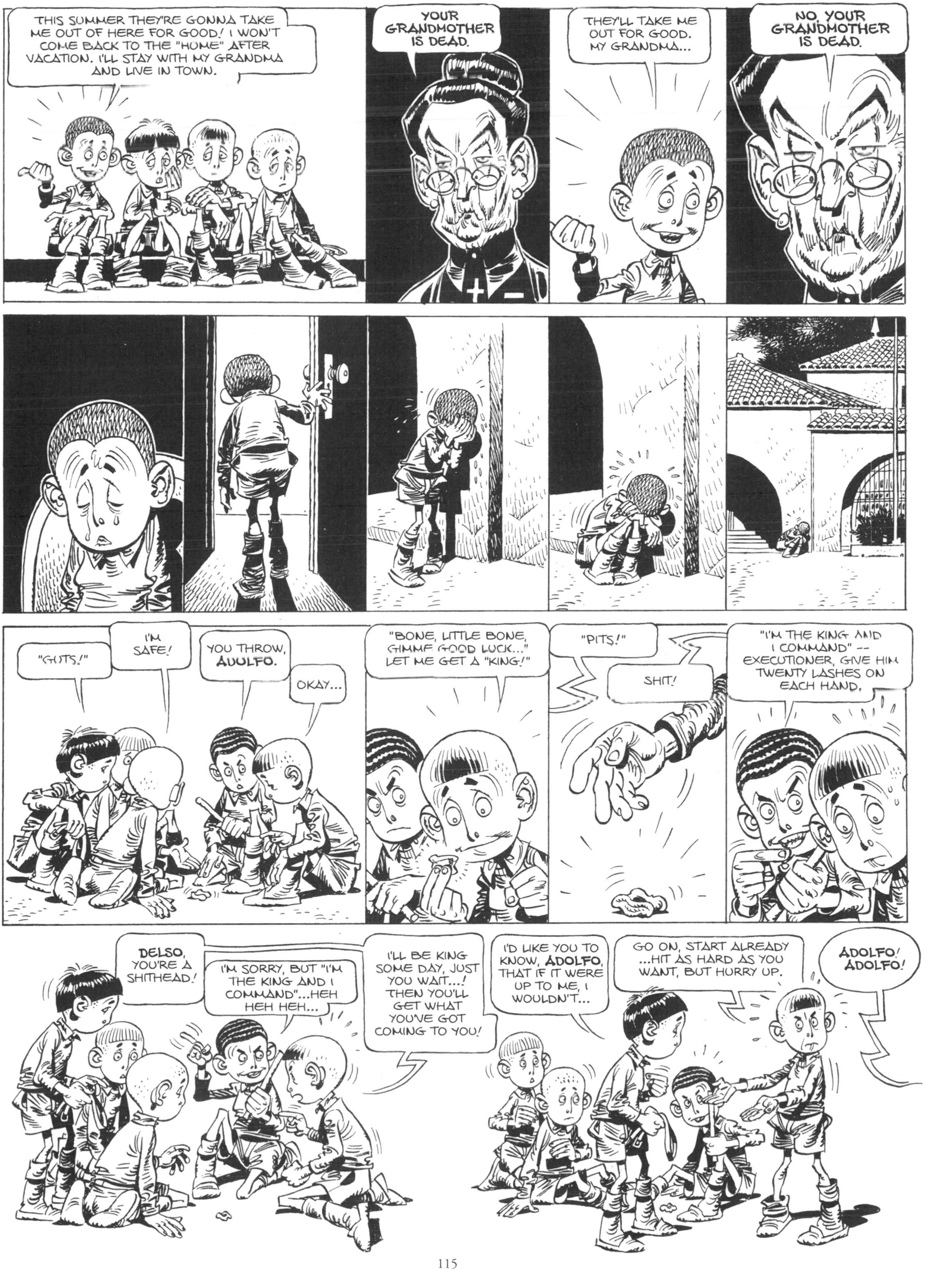
THIS SUMMER THEY'RE GONNA TAKE ME OUT OF HERE FOR GOOD! I WON'T COME BACK TO THE "HOME" AFTER VACATION. I'LL STAY WITH MY GRANDMA AND LIVE IN TOWN.
YOUR GRANDMOTHER IS DEAD.
THEY'LL TAKE ME OUT FOR GOOD. MY GRANDMA...
NO, YOUR GRANDMOTHER IS DEAD.
"GUTS!"
I'M SAFE!
YOU THROW, ADOLFO.
OKAY...
"BONE, LITTLE BONE, GIMME GOOD LUCK..." LET ME GET A "KING!"
"PITS!"
SHIT!
"I'M THE KING AND I COMMAND" -- EXECUTIONER, GIVE HIM TWENTY LASHES ON EACH HAND.
DELSO, YOU'RE A SHITHEAD!
I'M SORRY, BUT "I'M THE KING AND I COMMAND"...HEH HEH HEH...
I'LL BE KING SOME DAY, JUST YOU WAIT...! THEN YOU'LL GET WHAT YOU'VE GOT COMING TO YOU!
I'D LIKE YOU TO KNOW, ADOLFO, THAT IF IT WERE UP TO ME, I WOULDN'T...
GO ON, START ALREADY ...HIT AS HARD AS YOU WANT, BUT HURRY UP.
ADOLFO! ADOLFO!

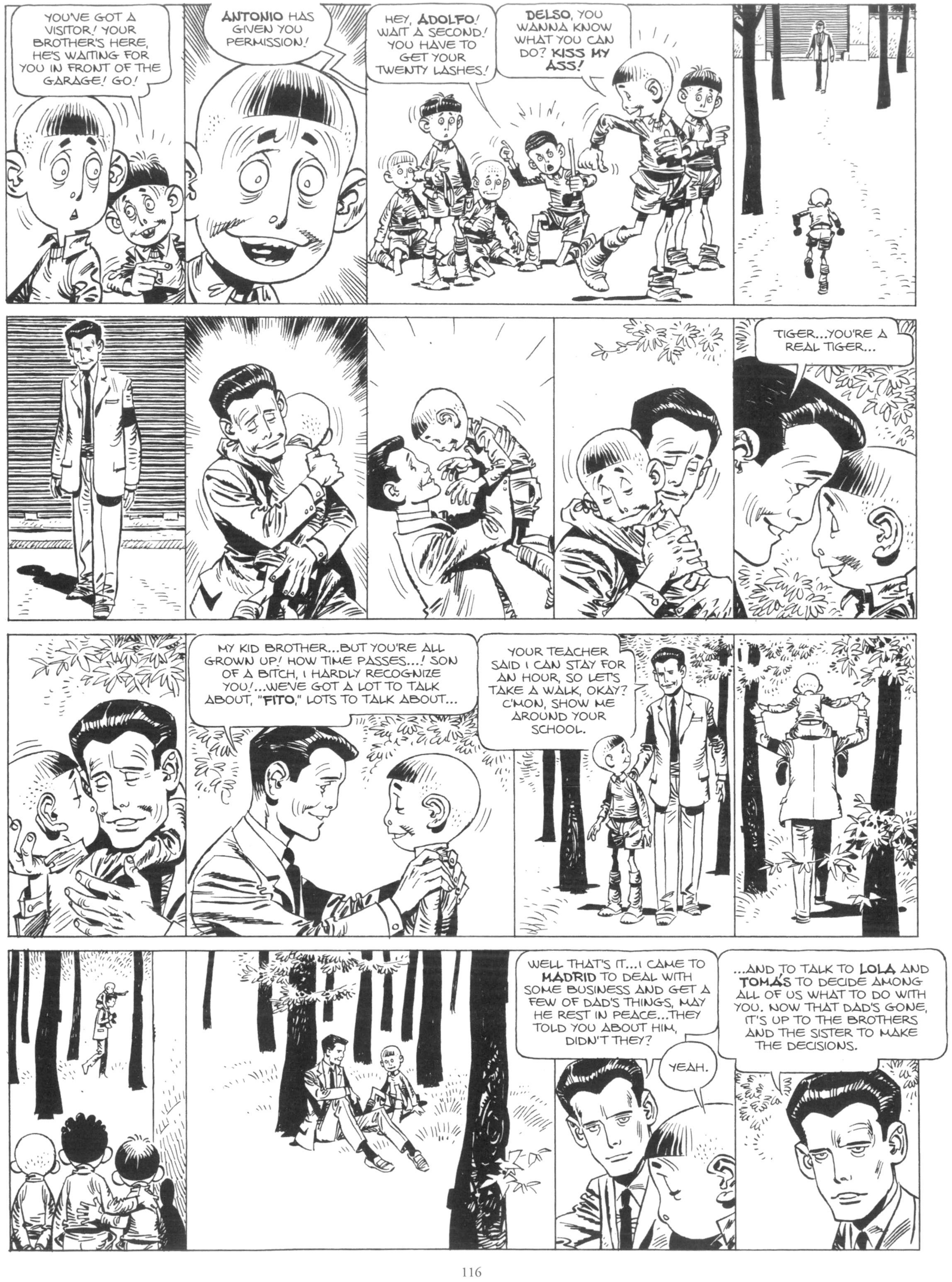

YOU'VE GOT A VISITOR! YOUR BROTHER'S HERE, HE'S WAITING FOR YOU IN FRONT OF THE GARAGE! GO!
ANTONIO HAS GIVEN YOU PERMISSION!
HEY, ADOLFO! WAIT A SECOND! YOU HAVE TO GET YOUR TWENTY LASHES!
DELSO, YOU WANNA KNOW WHAT YOU CAN DO? KISS MY ASS!
TIGER... YOU'RE A REAL TIGER...
MY KID BROTHER... BUT YOU'RE ALL GROWN UP! HOW TIME PASSES...! SON OF A BITCH, I HARDLY RECOGNIZE YOU!... WE'VE GOT A LOT TO TALK ABOUT, "FITO," LOTS TO TALK ABOUT...
YOUR TEACHER SAID I CAN STAY FOR AN HOUR, SO LET'S TAKE A WALK, OKAY? C'MON, SHOW ME AROUND YOUR SCHOOL.
WELL THAT'S IT... I CAME TO MADRID TO DEAL WITH SOME BUSINESS AND GET A FEW OF DAD'S THINGS, MAY HE REST IN PEACE... THEY TOLD YOU ABOUT HIM, DIDN'T THEY?
YEAH.
...AND TO TALK TO LOLA AND TOMÁS TO DECIDE AMONG ALL OF US WHAT TO DO WITH YOU. NOW THAT DAD'S GONE, IT'S UP TO THE BROTHERS AND THE SISTER TO MAKE THE DECISIONS.

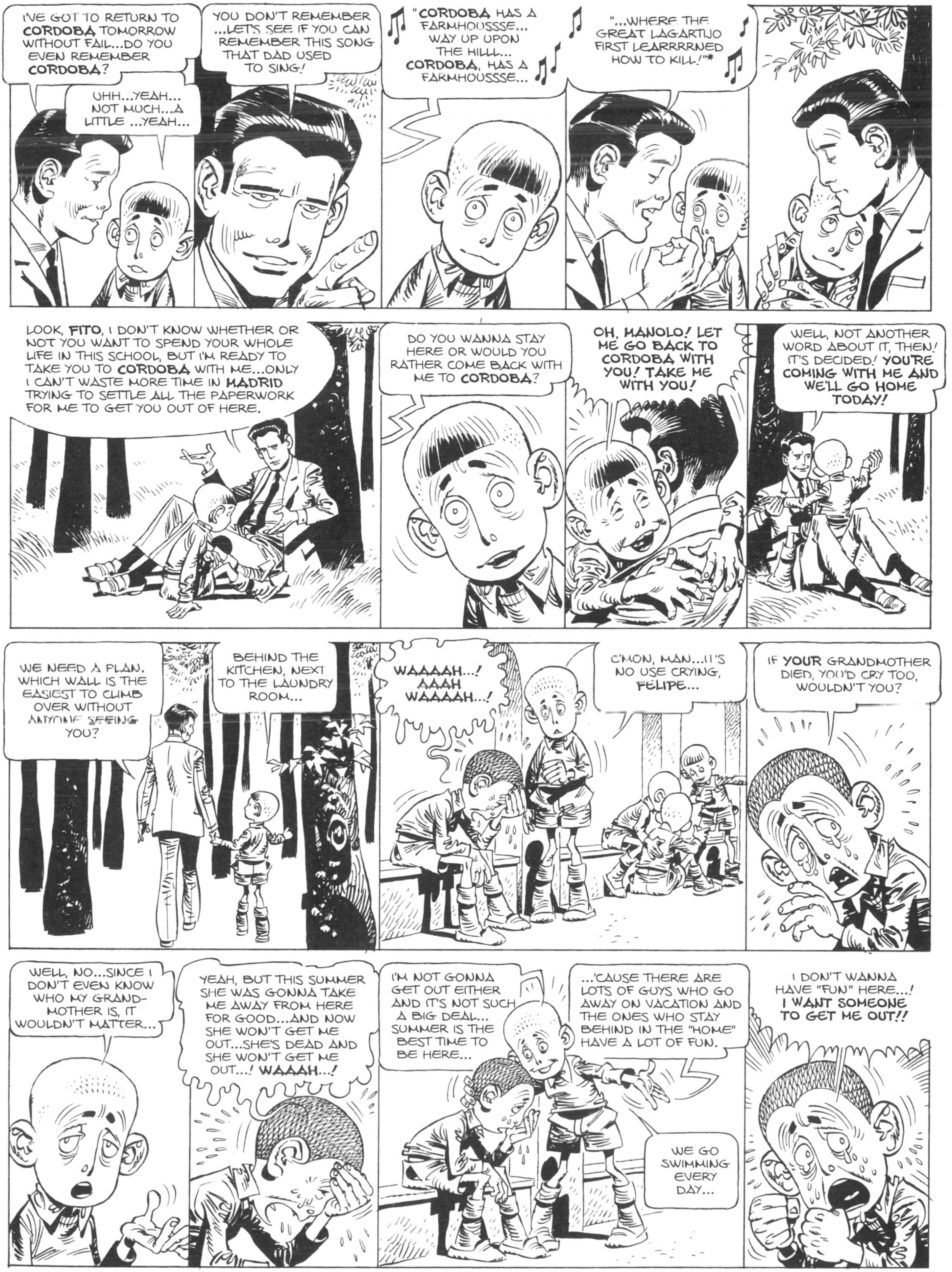

I'VE GOT TO RETURN TO CORDOBA TOMORROW WITHOUT FAIL...DO YOU EVEN REMEMBER CORDOBA?
UHH...YEAH... NOT MUCH...A LITTLE ...YEAH...
YOU DON'T REMEMBER ...LET'S SEE IF YOU CAN REMEMBER THIS SONG THAT DAD USED TO SING!
"CORDOBA HAS A FARMHOUSSSE... WAY UP UPON THE HILLL... CORDOBA, HAS A FARMHOUSSSE...
"...WHERE THE GREAT LAGARTIJO FIRST LEARRRRNED HOW TO KILL!"*
LOOK, FITO, I DON'T KNOW WHETHER OR NOT YOU WANT TO SPEND YOUR WHOLE LIFE IN THIS SCHOOL, BUT I'M READY TO TAKE YOU TO CORDOBA WITH ME...ONLY I CAN'T WASTE MORE TIME IN MADRID TRYING TO SETTLE ALL THE PAPERWORK FOR ME TO GET YOU OUT OF HERE.
DO YOU WANNA STAY HERE OR WOULD YOU RATHER COME BACK WITH ME TO CORDOBA?
OH, MANOLO! LET ME GO BACK TO CORDOBA WITH YOU! TAKE ME WITH YOU!
WELL, NOT ANOTHER WORD ABOUT IT, THEN! IT'S DECIDED! YOU'RE COMING WITH ME AND WE'LL GO HOME TODAY!
WE NEED A PLAN. WHICH WALL IS THE EASIEST TO CLIMB OVER WITHOUT ANYONE SEEING YOU?
BEHIND THE KITCHEN, NEXT TO THE LAUNDRY ROOM...
WAAAAH...! AAAH WAAAAH...!
C'MON, MAN...IT'S NO USE CRYING, FELIPE...
IF YOUR GRANDMOTHER DIED, YOU'D CRY TOO, WOULDN'T YOU?
WELL, NO...SINCE I DON'T EVEN KNOW WHO MY GRAND-MOTHER IS, IT WOULDN'T MATTER...
YEAH, BUT THIS SUMMER SHE WAS GONNA TAKE ME AWAY FROM HERE FOR GOOD...AND NOW SHE WON'T GET ME OUT...SHE'S DEAD AND SHE WON'T GET ME OUT...! WAAAH...!
I'M NOT GONNA GET OUT EITHER AND IT'S NOT SUCH A BIG DEAL... SUMMER IS THE BEST TIME TO BE HERE...
...'CAUSE THERE ARE LOTS OF GUYS WHO GO AWAY ON VACATION AND THE ONES WHO STAY BEHIND IN THE "HOME" HAVE A LOT OF FUN.
WE GO SWIMMING EVERY DAY...
I DON'T WANNA HAVE "FUN" HERE...! I WANT SOMEONE TO GET ME OUT!!

* LAGARTIJO WAS A FAMOUS BULLFIGHTER IN THE LATE 19TH CENTURY WHO HAILED FROM CORDOBA.

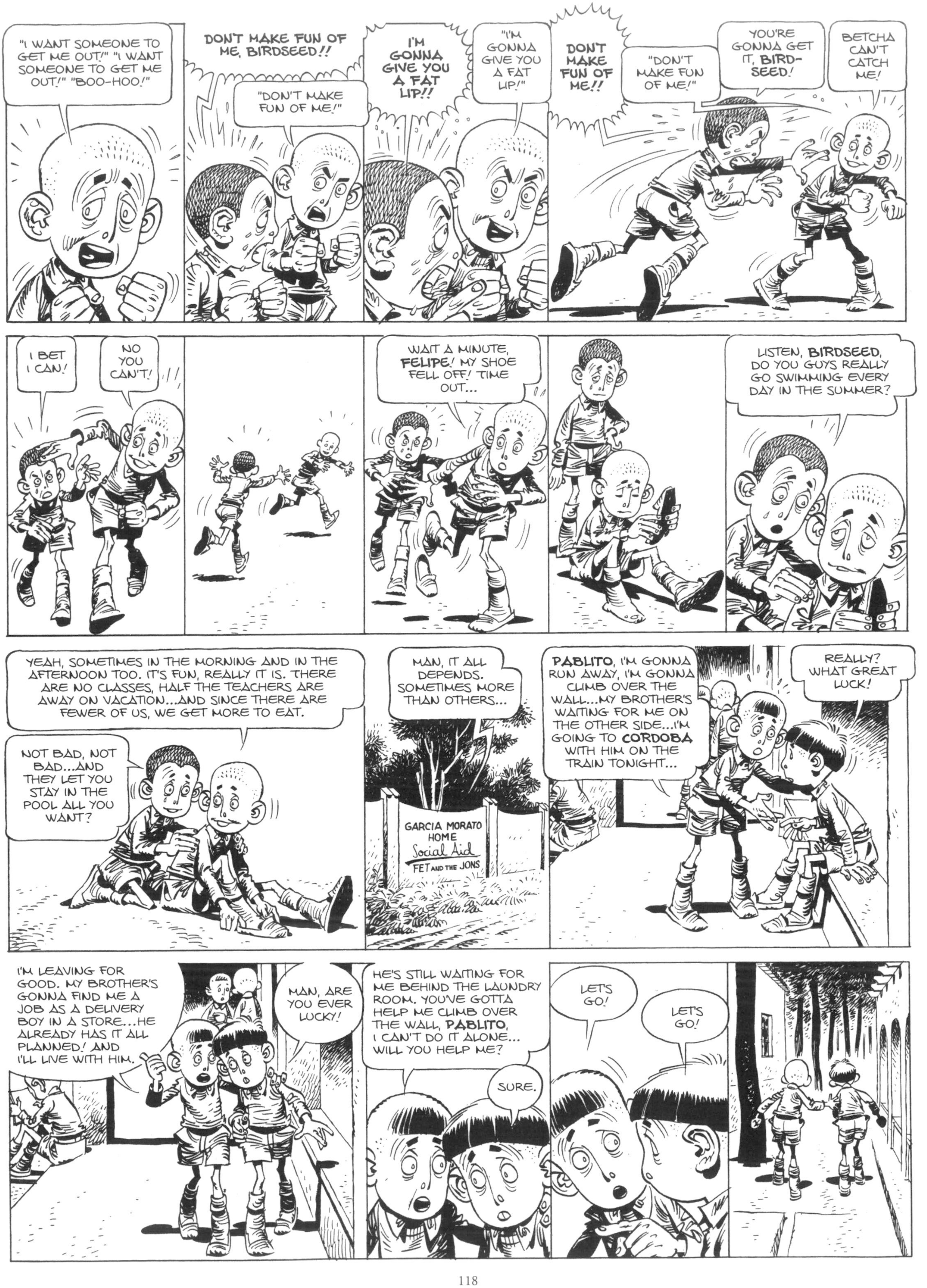
"I WANT SOMEONE TO GET ME OUT!" "I WANT SOMEONE TO GET ME OUT!" "BOO-HOO!"
DON'T MAKE FUN OF ME, BIRDSEED!!
"DON'T MAKE FUN OF ME!"
I'M GONNA GIVE YOU A FAT LIP!!
"I'M GONNA GIVE YOU A FAT LIP!"
DON'T MAKE FUN OF ME!!
"DON'T MAKE FUN OF ME!"
YOU'RE GONNA GET IT, BIRD-SEED!
BETCHA CAN'T CATCH ME!
I BET I CAN!
NO YOU CAN'T!
WAIT A MINUTE, FELIPE! MY SHOE FELL OFF! TIME OUT...
LISTEN, BIRDSEED, DO YOU GUYS REALLY GO SWIMMING EVERY DAY IN THE SUMMER?
YEAH, SOMETIMES IN THE MORNING AND IN THE AFTERNOON TOO. IT'S FUN, REALLY IT IS. THERE ARE NO CLASSES, HALF THE TEACHERS ARE AWAY ON VACATION...AND SINCE THERE ARE FEWER OF US, WE GET MORE TO EAT.
NOT BAD, NOT BAD...AND THEY LET YOU STAY IN THE POOL ALL YOU WANT?
MAN, IT ALL DEPENDS. SOMETIMES MORE THAN OTHERS...
GARCIA MORATO HOME
Social Aid
FET AND THE JONS
PABLITO, I'M GONNA RUN AWAY, I'M GONNA CLIMB OVER THE WALL...MY BROTHER'S WAITING FOR ME ON THE OTHER SIDE...I'M GOING TO CORDOBA WITH HIM ON THE TRAIN TONIGHT...
REALLY? WHAT GREAT LUCK!
I'M LEAVING FOR GOOD. MY BROTHER'S GONNA FIND ME A JOB AS A DELIVERY BOY IN A STORE...HE ALREADY HAS IT ALL PLANNED! AND I'LL LIVE WITH HIM.
MAN, ARE YOU EVER LUCKY!
HE'S STILL WAITING FOR ME BEHIND THE LAUNDRY ROOM. YOU'VE GOTTA HELP ME CLIMB OVER THE WALL, PABLITO, I CAN'T DO IT ALONE... WILL YOU HELP ME?
SURE.
LET'S GO!
LET'S GO!

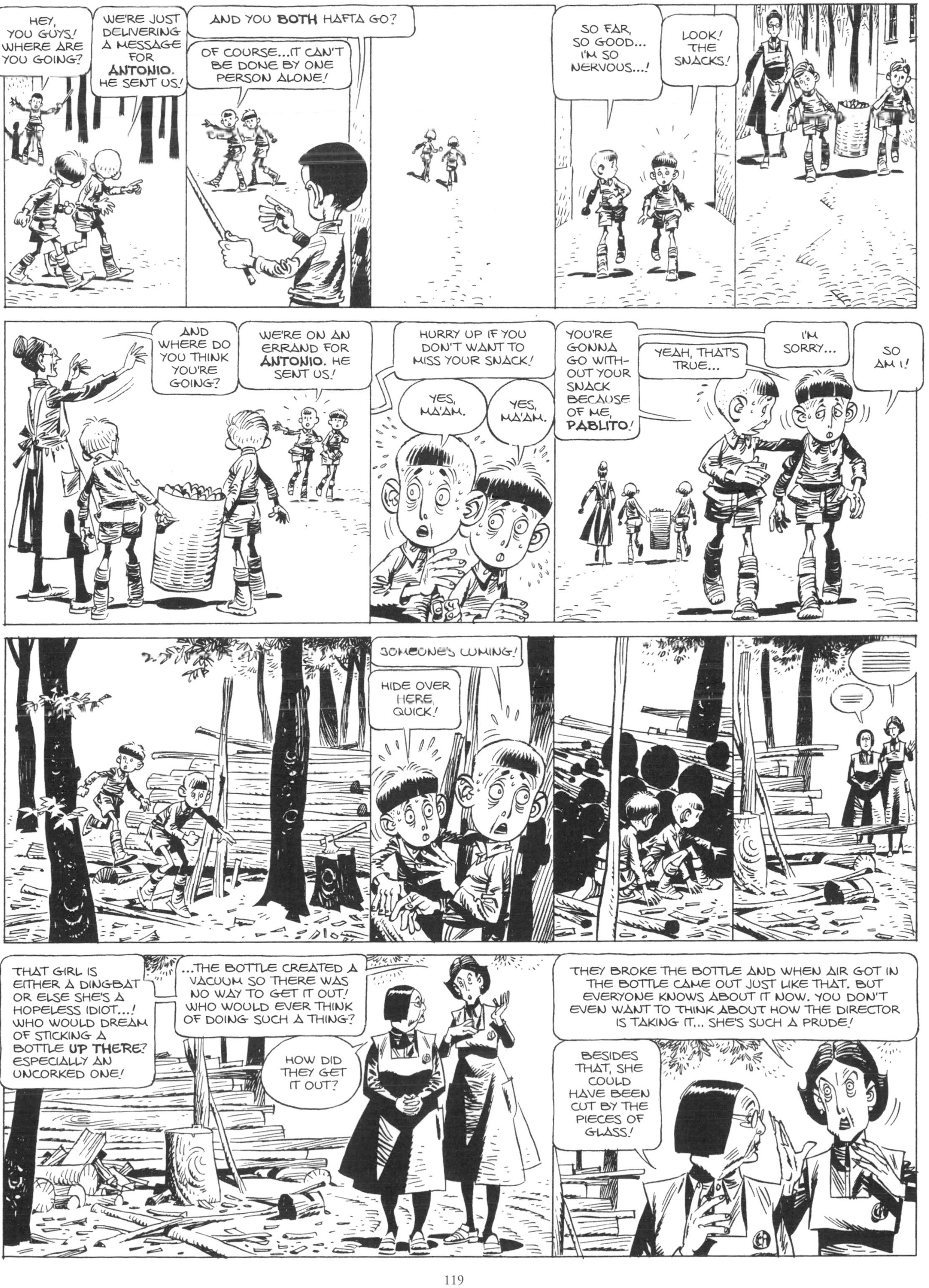
HEY, YOU GUYS! WHERE ARE YOU GOING?
WE'RE JUST DELIVERING A MESSAGE FOR ANTONIO. HE SENT US!
AND YOU BOTH HAFTA GO?
OF COURSE...IT CAN'T BE DONE BY ONE PERSON ALONE!
SO FAR, SO GOOD... I'M SO NERVOUS...!
LOOK! THE SNACKS!
AND WHERE DO YOU THINK YOU'RE GOING?
WE'RE ON AN ERRAND FOR ANTONIO. HE SENT US!
HURRY UP IF YOU DON'T WANT TO MISS YOUR SNACK!
YES, MA'AM.
YES, MA'AM.
YOU'RE GONNA GO WITHOUT YOUR SNACK BECAUSE OF ME, PABLITO!
YEAH, THAT'S TRUE...
I'M SORRY...
SO AM I!
SOMEONE'S COMING!
HIDE OVER HERE, QUICK!
THAT GIRL IS EITHER A DINGBAT OR ELSE SHE'S A HOPELESS IDIOT...! WHO WOULD DREAM OF STICKING A BOTTLE UP THERE? ESPECIALLY AN UNCORKED ONE!
...THE BOTTLE CREATED A VACUUM SO THERE WAS NO WAY TO GET IT OUT! WHO WOULD EVER THINK OF DOING SUCH A THING?
HOW DID THEY GET IT OUT?
THEY BROKE THE BOTTLE AND WHEN AIR GOT IN THE BOTTLE CAME OUT JUST LIKE THAT. BUT EVERYONE KNOWS ABOUT IT NOW. YOU DON'T EVEN WANT TO THINK ABOUT HOW THE DIRECTOR IS TAKING IT... SHE'S SUCH A PRUDE!
BESIDES THAT, SHE COULD HAVE BEEN CUT BY THE PIECES OF GLASS!

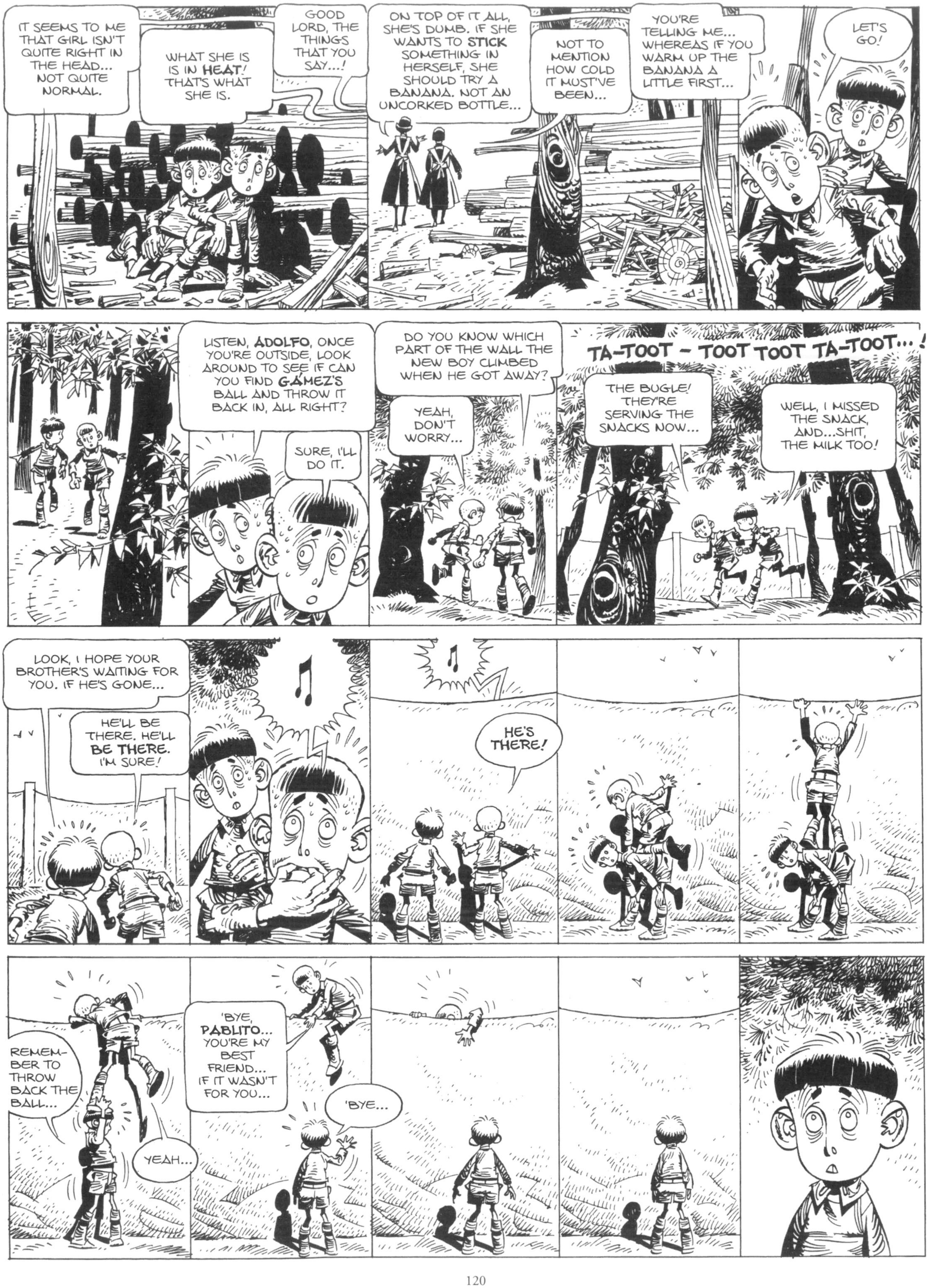

IT SEEMS TO ME THAT GIRL ISN'T QUITE RIGHT IN THE HEAD... NOT QUITE NORMAL.
WHAT SHE IS IS IN HEAT! THAT'S WHAT SHE IS.
GOOD LORD, THE THINGS THAT YOU SAY...!
ON TOP OF IT ALL, SHE'S DUMB. IF SHE WANTS TO STICK SOMETHING IN HERSELF, SHE SHOULD TRY A BANANA. NOT AN UNCORKED BOTTLE...
NOT TO MENTION HOW COLD IT MUST'VE BEEN...
YOU'RE TELLING ME... WHEREAS IF YOU WARM UP THE BANANA A LITTLE FIRST...
LET'S GO!
LISTEN, ADOLFO, ONCE YOU'RE OUTSIDE, LOOK AROUND TO SEE IF CAN YOU FIND GÁMEZ'S BALL AND THROW IT BACK IN, ALL RIGHT?
SURE, I'LL DO IT.
DO YOU KNOW WHICH PART OF THE WALL THE NEW BOY CLIMBED WHEN HE GOT AWAY?
YEAH, DON'T WORRY...
TA-TOOT - TOOT TOOT TA-TOOT...!
THE BUGLE! THEY'RE SERVING THE SNACKS NOW...
WELL, I MISSED THE SNACK, AND...SHIT, THE MILK TOO!
LOOK, I HOPE YOUR BROTHER'S WAITING FOR YOU. IF HE'S GONE...
HE'LL BE THERE. HE'LL BE THERE. I'M SURE!
HE'S THERE!
REMEMBER TO THROW BACK THE BALL...
YEAH...
'BYE, PABLITO... YOU'RE MY BEST FRIEND... IF IT WASN'T FOR YOU...
'BYE...

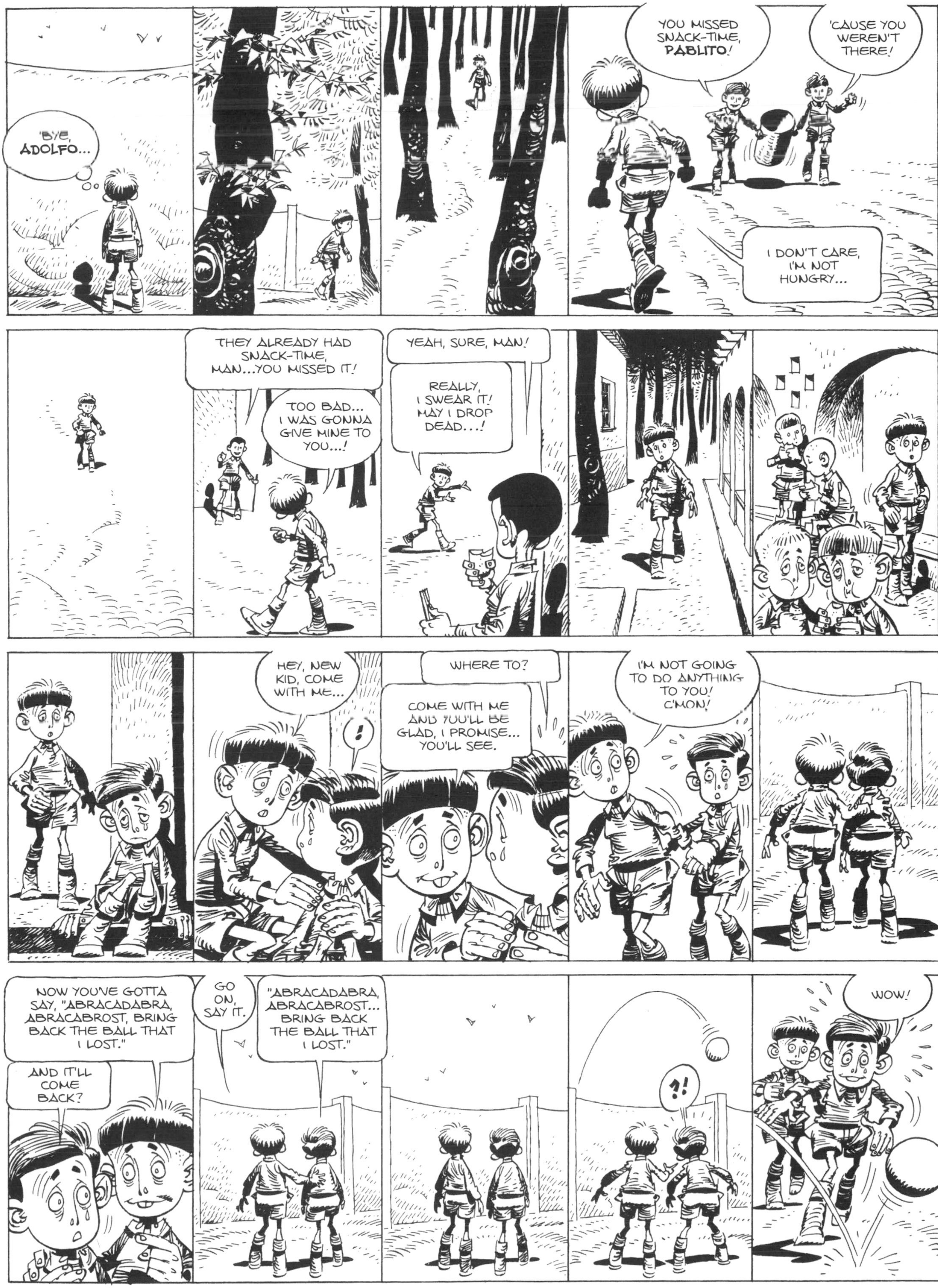
'BYE, ADOLFO...
YOU MISSED SNACK-TIME, PABLITO!
'CAUSE YOU WEREN'T THERE!
I DON'T CARE, I'M NOT HUNGRY...
THEY ALREADY HAD SNACK-TIME, MAN...YOU MISSED IT!
TOO BAD... I WAS GONNA GIVE MINE TO YOU...!
YEAH, SURE, MAN!
REALLY, I SWEAR IT! MAY I DROP DEAD...!
HEY, NEW KID, COME WITH ME...
!
WHERE TO?
COME WITH ME AND YOU'LL BE GLAD, I PROMISE... YOU'LL SEE.
I'M NOT GOING TO DO ANYTHING TO YOU! C'MON!
NOW YOU'VE GOTTA SAY, "ABRACADABRA, ABRACABROST, BRING BACK THE BALL THAT I LOST."
AND IT'LL COME BACK?
GO ON, SAY IT.
"ABRACADABRA, ABRACABROST... BRING BACK THE BALL THAT I LOST."
?!
WOW!

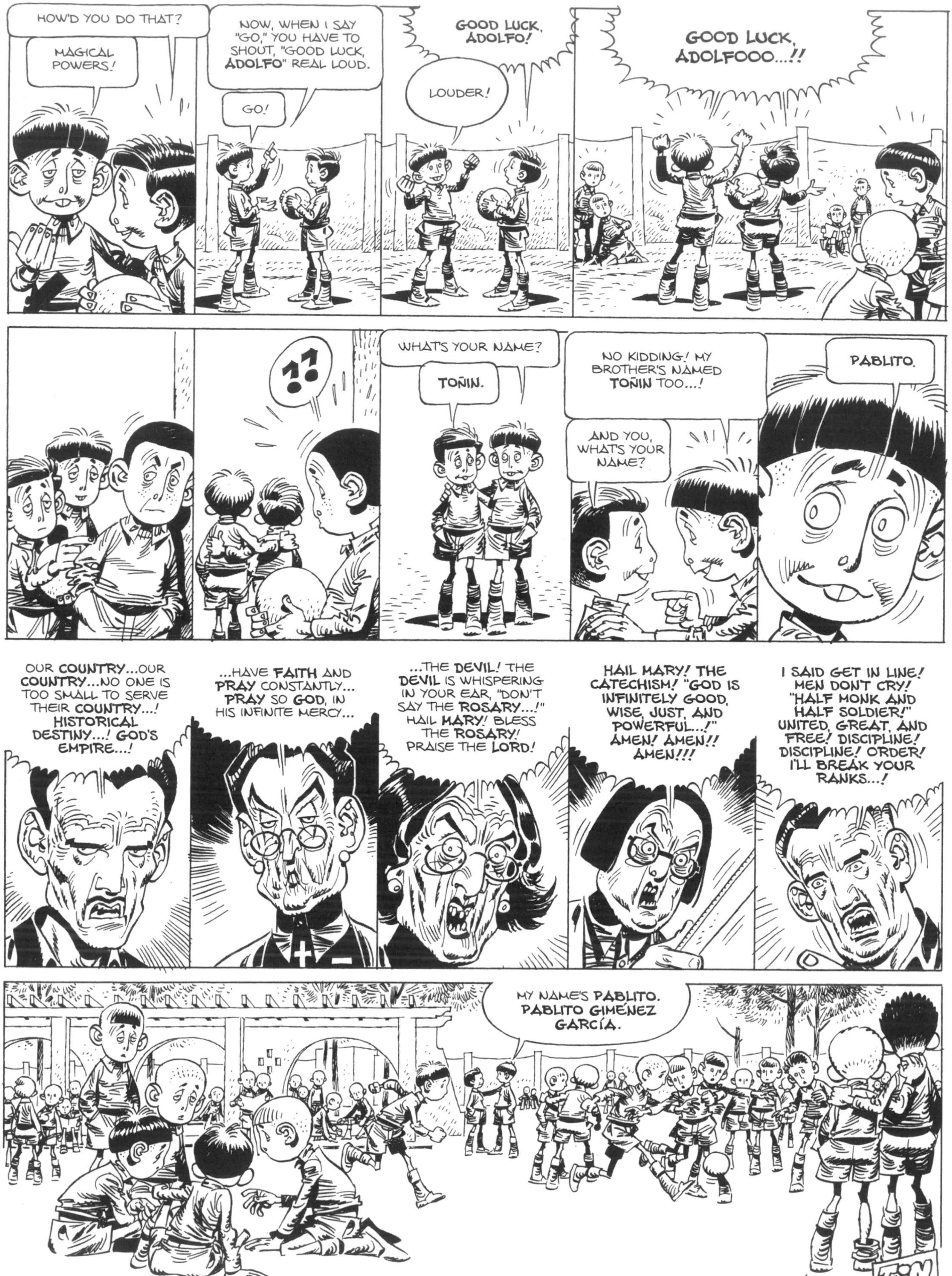
HOW'D YOU DO THAT?
MAGICAL POWERS!
NOW, WHEN I SAY "GO," YOU HAVE TO SHOUT, "GOOD LUCK, ADOLFO" REAL LOUD.
GO!
GOOD LUCK, ADOLFO!
LOUDER!
GOOD LUCK, ADOLFOOO...!!
??
WHAT'S YOUR NAME?
TOÑIN.
NO KIDDING! MY BROTHER'S NAMED TOÑIN TOO...!
AND YOU, WHAT'S YOUR NAME?
PABLITO.
OUR COUNTRY...OUR COUNTRY...NO ONE IS TOO SMALL TO SERVE THEIR COUNTRY...! HISTORICAL DESTINY...! GOD'S EMPIRE...!
...HAVE FAITH AND PRAY CONSTANTLY... PRAY SO GOD, IN HIS INFINITE MERCY...
...THE DEVIL! THE DEVIL IS WHISPERING IN YOUR EAR, "DON'T SAY THE ROSARY...!" HAIL MARY! BLESS THE ROSARY! PRAISE THE LORD!
HAIL MARY! THE CATECHISM! "GOD IS INFINITELY GOOD, WISE, JUST, AND POWERFUL...!" AMEN! AMEN!! AMEN!!!
I SAID GET IN LINE! MEN DON'T CRY! "HALF MONK AND HALF SOLDIER!" UNITED, GREAT, AND FREE! DISCIPLINE! DISCIPLINE! ORDER! I'LL BREAK YOUR RANKS...!
MY NAME'S PABLITO. PABLITO GIMÉNEZ GARCÍA.
© CARLOS GIMÉNEZ -81-
FIN

View of the church in which ten thousand
children had their first communion under
the auspices of Social Aid (1937).

BY Carmen Moreno-Nuño

AFTERWORD:

PARACUELLOS BY CARLOS GIMÉNEZ: CONFRONTING SPAIN'S ABSENT PAST

On October 21, 2007, the Chamber of Deputies in Spain approved the *Ley de Memoria Histórica* (Historic Memory Act). This legislation acknowledged and enlarged the rights of victims of Spain's Civil War (1936-1939), enabling the recovery of personal and family histories, in the process of recovering the dignity of the losers.

The Historic Memory Act was the culmination of a new social construct of memory that emerged in mid-1990s Spain, one that reflected the growing worldwide debate about human rights in wars and dictatorships, and that translated into an increased involvement by political parties, governments, and citizens (forming associations for the recovery of the lost memory and the opening of common graves). Spain's confrontation of its own traumatic past was meant to redress a historical injustice after thirty years of democracy following the death of the dictator, Francisco Franco. It rescued memory from a neutral ground and placed it into a cultural battlefield dominated by the political appropriation of its symbolic content.

Also in 2007 a Spanish publisher issued an omnibus of all six volumes of *Paracuellos*, Carlos Giménez's autobiographical series of stories about children who were reared in State and Church-run Social Aid "Homes" after the Civil War. Giménez published the first volume of *Paracuellos* in 1977 in the wake of Franco's death, anticipating the possibilities of a new political climate—never dreaming that anything like the Historic Memory Act lay three decades in the future. He released a second volume in 1982 and then four more from 1997 to 2003.

By rejecting the so-called Pact of Silence about the Civil War and the Franco repression that endured throughout the democratic period in Spain, *Paracuellos* places itself firmly within the spirit that promoted the drafting of the Historic Memory Act by recognizing and dignifying the victims of the war and the dictatorship.

During this period Carlos Giménez expanded his autobiography in comics, creating a trilogy that included *Barrio* (about his life after leaving the "Homes") and *Los Professionales* (stories of his career as a comics artist). *Paracuellos*, however, remains the masterpiece of his career. The novelist and critic Antonio Altarriba calls *Paracuellos* "one of the key comic-strip works in Spain" because of its narrative mastery, its skillful management of dramatic and expressive resources, and its firm political denunciation. Juan Marsé, the novelist and screenwriter, has observed that in *Paracuellos* Giménez "shows extraordinary artistic and documentary genius."

· · · · ·

In *Paracuellos* the protagonists are direct witnesses to history or members of the first generation after the trauma.

In his introduction to the *Paracuellos* omnibus Carlos Giménez points out, "In the first episodes…I used to give a date and place for each story, so as to confer a documentary appearance to the work…. Everything that is told in these six volumes, all the stories and anecdotes, are taken—I repeat—taken from real events. I haven't invented anything. Everything I have said really happened. My objective in writing these stories was to leave a true account of life as it was lived in the Social Aid 'Homes.'"

Beginning in *Paracuellos 2* the dates disappear, replaced in the majority of stories by the emblem of Social Aid, a fist clutching a dagger to fight a dragon that represents hunger, functioning as a powerful dramatic leitmotif.

Literature and art often echo the desire to acknowledge and understand the past as a lesson to the present and the future. *Paracuellos* follows that tradition as Giménez recovers, through art, a collective (rather than a broad historic) memory about Spain's Civil War, the postwar years, and the repression of the Franco regime. The cartoonist presents an idealist conception where literature becomes cathartic therapy, an exercise in moral justice, and a tool for repairing the fragmented community. Giménez also commits himself to an historic memory in which political discourse—his denunciation of the exercise of power shows how the "Homes" seek to establish popular conformity—comes loaded with a social content. Since the treatment of the underprivileged is a key element of the moral fiber of the State, the children in *Paracuellos* represent not only the vanquished, but also the great mass of the population placed outside the production process, and hence outside the social protection benefits of the new Spain, however paltry those benefits may have been.

The boys' collective memory, then, becomes part of historic memory of the country at large.

· · · · ·

While traditional asylum centers, such as orphanages and children's homes, based their admission criteria on condition of the children being alone, abandoned, or lacking resources, the Social Aid "Homes" added a special clause: "the moral conditions of the parents." As a result, the children in families that did not meet the moral expectations of the regime would be sent to the "Homes." Furthermore, Social Aid reserved the right to decide whether or not it would return the child to the family, which carried the threat of permanent loss of the minor.

In many ways the "Homes" reproduced the punishment aspect of the adult prison system. The Fascist *Falange* party and the Catholic Church were the main agents in charge of administering a violence which, in the "Homes," sought compliance with the regulations that systematically unfolded after the Civil War. Giménez denounces the physical abuse meted out to the children in a critical discourse on violence throughout all six books: malnourished bodies, faces and hands slapped and hit. Youngsters broken by physical punishments, their bare feet wounded, standing rigidly in line, alienated, their faces sweating with fear of the inevitable blows and punishment. As Foucault noted in *Discipline and Punish*, physical punishment as a public spectacle could be said to perform an exemplary role in the goal of maintaining the arbitrary and despotic power of the State, and of attaining a re-education of minds through the segregation of bodies.

Giménez stages his characters to emphasize the power relationship between the children and their keepers. The adult authority figures are often seen from below, in towering "up-shots," while the children are drawn in a downward perspective. The panel composition illustrates the prison-like uniformity of the "Homes," their contained spaces saturated with ceiling beams, bedposts, closed gates, and impassable walls [20, 32, 39, 32, 120]. The concise drawings of children separated from their families reflect a desolation underscored by the pan shots of a yard represented, in deep perspective, as an immense deserted field. The zooming in and out emphasizes the solitude of the child alone in the yard [25, 115]. Overall, the staging reveals the disparity between the official discourse and the reality within the "Homes" by contrasting the words with images that belie them: the image of a child crying while, in the word balloons, other children sing the praises of the regime [37], or the image of an ambulance carrying away a wounded child while in the balloon another song speaks of the happiness that reigns in the "Home" [97].

One never leaves the "Homes," as shown by the ample, landscaped last panels of the stories and by the recurrent depictions of the entrance gate in the opening and final panels. Indeed, the sense of imprisonment in the circular enclosure of a temporality from which there is no escape is highlighted by the confinement within the "Homes," whose everyday routine was strictly regulated by among other religious activities eight compulsory prayers per day, attendance at daily Mass, plus rosary on Sundays, holidays, and Lent…activities that defined the daily existence of the children, regulated their time, and set the tone for the routines in the rest of the day.

The helplessness of the children in *Paracuellos* against violence underscored by the tenderness of Giménez's pen line is coupled with the representation of the suffering family members who are forced to leave their children in the Social Aid "Homes." The mother's story is never told; it is almost always the men who carry the children to the "Homes" and this becomes a center of gravity on which the children of *Paracuellos* shed their tears.

Narrating the past is an ethical act and this ethical dimension is presented in *Paracuellos* around the problem of victimization. The events in *Paracuellos* repeatedly verge on victimization, dominated as they are by the representation of a ubiquitous and ruthless violence. Giménez, however, avoids falling into Manicheism by revealing that the children themselves and not only the keepers can produce that violence in a not-surprising process of assimilation of the cruelty that surrounds them.

• • • • •

Giménez employs various narrative strategies to deconstruct the enormous propaganda campaign associated with the work of the Social Aid program. They range from the use of different planes to the multiplication of narrative perspectives. The composition of his panels, the great recurrence of close-ups and even extreme close-ups, intensifies the feeling of anguish. It reduces the space between the characters and the reader to a bare minimum, while simultaneously reflecting the totalitarian way in which the winners impose their ideology: the grotesque faces of priests, nurses, teachers; keepers with taut grimaces, disgusted gestures, and menacing looks. On the medium-range shots, the zooms on the long, sharp fingernails of the housekeepers metonymically exemplify the aggression that prevailed in the "Homes." On numerous occasions, the word balloons weep larger tears than the children when they cry.

The cartoonist deliberately chose a rigid standardized grid for his layout, in contrast with the complexity of the topics he narrates. Most of the early stories are comprised of twenty panels per page, as opposed to the relatively standard four to six panels in many comic books. Giménez explained in a 1998 interview that the small panels allowed him to include more information in a more nuanced way. He abbreviated the dialogue for the same reason. He further explained that large panels lend themselves to detailed, beautiful drawing when, instead, he wanted to depict the ugliness of the schools in a minimalistic manner.

Giménez makes use of several narrative voices in *Paracuellos*—autobiographical first person, communal first person plural referring to the children interned in the "Homes," and omniscient third person, providing a narrator who passes judgment from an adult point of view. It is interesting to note that the cartoonist avoids the subjective first-person for his own character. In fact, the boy's name morphs from Carlines to Pablito Giménez, and although the narrator uses a more personal and inclusive "we" in the first volume, later books shift to the more distanced and objective third-person. These techniques

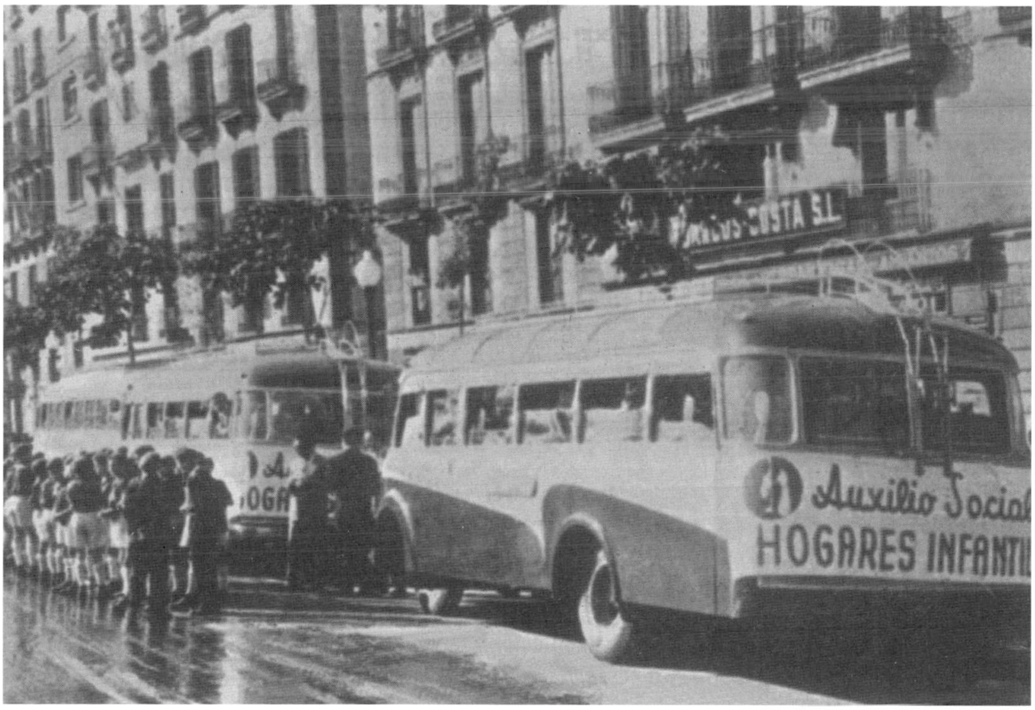
Auxilio Social
HOGARES INFANTI

add complexity to a testimonial function that is affirmed by the historical dates that appear in the title panel of each story in the first series.

• • • • •

Unlike most comic books, *Paracuellos* was printed in black and white, underscoring the historical past in which their stories take place. It is a key to Giménez's aesthetics and a possible technical constraint, and also the appropriate medium to evoke within the reader the very popular cinema of the Franco era where the protagonist is a child: the child as a propitiatory victim and as a privileged witness to a historical period. Thus historic memory appears as if it were an image faded by the passage of time.

Although the children of *Paracuellos* live in the marginalization of public welfare, *Paracuellos* does not fall into the hyperbolic kind of narrative that characterizes much of the literature dealing with trauma through devices such as metafictional reflection. While comic books play a part in the stories, they are a means of escape, a transgression, an action taken against suffering. The comic books the boys read—such as *El pequeño luchador* (*The Young Fighter*) [63], *El guerrero del antifaz* (*The Masked Warrior*) [63], *El cachorro* (*The Cub*) [71, 105], and *Jaimito* (*Jimmy*) [75, 77]—are adventure stories favored by the children over the "official magazines" whose mission was one of indoctrination of National-Catholicism during the first stages of the regime.

Comic books also have intrinsic value in the stories. Some boys steal comic books as punishment from a child who is the director's pet [42-43]; in later

The "blunder-busses" that Social Aid used to move children from one "Home" to another.

stories they use the comics as moral capital, and even win money prizes when their drawings receive awards and are published in famous comic books [77].

· · · · ·

Paracuellos stems from a sense of historic urgency to create a legacy of witnesses that recognizes the profound connection between the personal and the historical. The stories simultaneously reflect upon the violent destruction of childhood in the orphanages while speaking to history as an act of reconstruction—memory as a public process of reconstructing voices in which no voice must have the last word.

Paracuellos acknowledges the limits of fiction as a means of establishing historical truth, as well as the paradox that the comic strip inherently employs exaggeration as a basic method to convey meaning. Yet it answers the human need for coherence and sense, affirming the power of stories to restore and maintain individual, family, and group identity.

Moreover, *Paracuellos* brings forth a revisionist memory that proclaims the authority of the persecuted and the oppressed, giving biography a transformative power that enables people to encounter their own voice through the narration of communal history. In doing so, Carlos Giménez uses his mastery of the comic strip medium to create a new paradigm that establishes a dialogue between history and memory, and converts it into a demand for moral justice.

Carmen Moreno-Nuño is an associate professor in the Department of Hispanic Studies at the University of Kentucky specializing in the cultural representation of the historical memory of the Spanish Civil War and the postwar era in democratic Spain. She holds a BA in Philosophy from Universidad de Granada, Spain, and a PhD. from the University of Minnesota. This essay was adapted and expanded from one that first appeared in the Vanderbilt University e-Journal of Luso-Hispanic Studies.

Works Cited:

Altarriba, Antonio. "La historieta española de 1960 a 2000." *Historietas, cómics y tebeos españoles.* Ed. Viviane Alary. Toulouse: Presses Universitaires du Mirail, 2002. 76-120.

Casanova, Julián. "Después de tanta memoria…" *El País* 28-6-2008.

www.elpais.com/articuloCompleto/opinion/Despues/memoria/elpepiopi/20070920elpepiopi_12/Tes [28-6-2008].

Cenarro, Ángela. *La sonrisa de Falange: Auxilio Social en la guerra civil y en la posguerra.* Barcelona: Crítica, 2006.

Corrado, Danielle. "Carlos Giménez y el pacto autobiográfico." *Historietas, cómics y tebeos españoles.* Ed.Viviane Alary. Toulouse: Presses Universitaires du Mirail, 2002. 174-94.

Foucault, Michel. *Discipline and Punish: The Birth of the Prison.* New York: Pantheon Books, 1977.

Gubern, Roman. *El lenguaje de los cómics.* Barcelona: Ediciones Península, 1972.

Hutcheon, Linda. "The Pastime of Past Time: Fiction, History, Historiographic Metafiction." *Genre* 20.3-4 (1987): 285-305.

Lara, Antonio. "Los tebeos del franquismo." *Historietas, cómics y tebeos españoles.* Ed. Viviane Alary. Toulouse: Presses Universitaires du Mirail, 2002. 44-74.

Margalit, Avishai. *The Ethics of Memory.* Cambridge: Harvard UP, 2002.

McCloud, Scott. *Understanding Comics: The Invisible Art.* New York: HarperCollins Publishers, 1993.

Moreno-Nuño, Carmen. *Las huellas de la Guerra Civil: Mito y trauma en la narrativa de la España democrática.* Madrid: Ediciones Libertarias, 2006.

Resina, Joan Ramon and Ulrich Winter, eds. *Casa encantada: lugares de memoria en la España constitucional, 1978-2004.* Madrid: Iberoamericana, 2005.

Todorov, Tzvetan. "Los dilemas de la memoria (Un texto para Valientes): Ponencia en la Cátedra Julio Cortázar de la Universidad de Guadalajara, Méjico."

Trashorras, Antonio and Muñoz David. "Interview with Carlos Gimenez." Urich U.'s son, no. 9, March 1998.

http://www.caratula.net. [May 2008]

Whitlock, Gillian. "Autographics: The Seeing 'I' of the Comics." *Modern Fiction Studies* 52.4 (2006): 965-79.

BY Carlos Giménez

AFTERWORD:
FURTHER STORIES OF SOCIAL AID

There are so many more things left to tell about the Social Aid "Homes." There are so many people that we lived with there, there are so many anecdotes, so much that eight years of a boy's life retains, the facts engraved in the memory of those childhood years:

Still left to be told, for example, is what happened to Germán and to "Little Flea" when they went "crazy" after eating toadstools, and how Germán, in his madness, threw a pot of beans at the head-mistress's head and how later on, in the kitchen, they were crammed full of caster oil.

Still needing to be told is what happened on the day when we first arrived at the Paracuellos "Home." Our first day of school. How they let us play for hours on the soccer field, which was covered with a thick blanket of weeds almost a yard high. And how, when the teachers finally noticed, we had eaten all the weeds and the soccer field looked like a desert and where nothing ever grew again because we'd even eaten the roots, which tasted like creosote.

And the ones about the baggy pants that were given to Adolfo, which were so big that he looked like a sheik from *1,001 Arabian Nights*. And how a great-aunt of his, during one Christmas when they took him to spend the holidays outside the school, fixed his pants so painstakingly that he looked like a bull-fighter. And everyone laughed and called him "Matador! Matador! Matador!"

It also remains to be told what the long, mysterious subterranean passages that lay under the whole main building of the Garcia Morato "Home" were like and what they were for.

And the banquets that were served once a year in an enormous underground room there, and about those who comprised the general staff of Social Aid attending them, from the Women's Section and the National Delegation's Don Manuel Teña, including priests and Falangists and even about Perico Chicote, who fixed the cocktails. And how we boys who knew how to draw had to hand letter the menus, one by one.

Also remaining to be told is how a gang of us kids decided to write a magazine of our own. I remember that I did the cover. Adolfo, Felipe Díaz, and José Luis Muñoz were the artists; Yañez was the script-writer, and Antonio Sánchez was in charge of the humor page. It was going to be called *Tararí (Chuckles)* and we set up the publishing "house" in the toilets of the "package room." I remember how there was a photo of actress Ann Blyth in my toilet stall, and how, of course, I had no idea who she was.

Also remaining to be told is how they cut our hair and how mad the nurse got when she found head-lice on us and how she'd shave us bald with the clippers.

And how every night, at the General Mola "Home," we made the "promise" ("I promise to be good and obedient, to not speak in the dormitories," etc.) and then, the next morning when they told all those who had broken "the promise" to step forward, we "sinners" would voluntarily go to get our punishment. No one ever tried to get out of it since we all firmly believed what the teachers used to tell us: "You can fool me, but not God."

It also hasn't been told how Cándido swapped a ball that his mother had brought him for some apricot pits, how he smashed the pits with a stone and ate up the bitter "almonds" inside.

Or how they took us out of the dining hall halfway through a meal for having spoken aloud at the tables, and how Antonio, the instructor, slapped everyone as we came back in.

Or how this same Antonio used to brag about how strong he was, and how he would hit the first boy in line on the head and knock the entire row of boys to the ground. The same Antonio who made us sing songs like:

> *In a beloved "Home," where I live so happily,*
> *with lovely memories of the finest hours*
> *that I've had in my entire life...*

I could have told about how they punished us by denying us water and shutting off the faucets, and how "Pichi" climbed up on a toilet tank to drink the water inside and how the tank came loose and almost cracked open his skull, and how they had to rush him to the infirmary.

And how we'd eat any kind of garbage, refuse, rinds that we could find; how we made "gum" by chewing on candle wax, crepe soles, rubber balls, and tar. How we ate "Pelikanol" toothpaste, rubber erasers, and all kinds of weeds which we had perfectly classified: "horns," "cow teats," "buns," "Baby Jesus shoes," "bread and cheese," "sours," etc.

Or how none of the boys at the "Home" could tell time because there wasn't a single clock in the entire school.

Or how Father Rodríguez, the director of the Garcia Morato "Home," gave us double slaps, with both hands at the same time, one on each side of the face, which was good, according to him, because that way we didn't fall down.

Or how Antonio, the Phalanx instructor, had us in formation for a whole afternoon, doing knee-bends and marching in place with our arms outstretched, yelling "Long Live Spain!" because we hadn't said goodbye the right way to the National Social Aid delegate who came by the "Home" one day...

Or how Máximo got a cyst on his lung from eating the food for Cardenas, the director's dog, and how they took him to the infirmary and we never saw him again.

Or how Cardenas would get furious whenever the boys started a fight and how he'd bark and bark until the terrified boys stopped hitting each other.

Or how Dionisio Polo bit Cardenas one day, and how Cardenas, a wolf-like dog that looked like he meant business, never bit a single boy.

Or how we did exercises in the middle of the Castilian winter, on a ground white with frost and ice, our hands and feet breaking out in chilblains.

Or how Cándido would come back to the "Home" after vacation with his mother, trying not to cry so that she wouldn't feel worse than she already did, praying for the trolley to derail, praying for the train to derail, and making desperate attempts to not be like most of the boys who were dragged back to the "Home" kicking and screaming and making the relatives who brought them cry too. And how Cándido, when night came and he went to bed, covered his head with the blanket so that no one would see him as he cried and cried until he fell asleep. And his weeping would last an entire week.

In short, there are many, many things about the Social Aid "Homes" that haven't been told yet. Most of them are bad, but there are a few good things.

Like how good and affectionate were Miss Justi, Miss Sole, Miss Paula, and Miss Amalia, who I keep fond memories of. They were all girls from the town of Paracuellos, young girls who weren't from the *Falange* or from the Women's Section or from any other institution. They were girls who did their job with good cheer and affection, girls who saw us more as little brothers than "the men of tomorrow." We eagerly waited for those days when they came to be our wardens because those days were always much happier. Miss Sole was very pretty and we composed a song especially for her, modeled on an old one we knew:

> *Sole, Sole, Sole, Sole*
> *How I love your name, Soledad,*
> *Sole, Sole, Sole, Sole,*
> *You're the prettiest one at the "Home!"*

—Carlos Giménez, 1981

Carlos Giménez was born in Madrid in 1941. His first series in comics was *Drake & Drake*, followed by the popular *Gringo*, *Delta 99*, and *Dani Futuro*. It was with the publication of his powerful and moving tales of childhood in Franco's Spain—*Paracuellos* in 1977 and *Paracuellos 2* in 1982— that Giménez made the transition from craftsman to artist. His other non-fiction works include the trilogy *Spain United, Great, and Free* (a chronicle of the political transition after Franco's death), *Barrio* (tales of his teenaged years after leaving the orphanage), and *The Professionals* (his much lauded inside story of the Spanish comics world in the 1960s).